THE SEATTLE BUNGALOW

JANET ORE

UNIVERSITY OF WASHINGTON PRESS   SEATTLE & LONDON

THE SEATTLE BUNGALOW

PEOPLE AND HOUSES

1900—1940

University of Washington Press

P.O. Box 50096, Seattle, WA 98145, U.S.A.

www.washington.edu/uwpress

Library of Congress Cataloging-in-Publication Data

Ore, Janet.

The Seattle bungalow : people and houses, 1900-1940 / Janet Ore.

p. cm.

Includes bibliographical references and index.

ISBN 0-295-98627-1

1. Bungalows—Washington (State)—Seattle.   2. Architecture—
Washington (State)—Seattle—20th century.   3. Architecture—
Social aspects—Washington (State)—Seattle.   4. Seattle
(Wash.)—Social life and customs.   I. Title.

NA7571.O74 2006

728'.3730977977209041—dc22   2006002429

Cover photo: The Stapp family's home in the Wallingford neigh-
borhood of Seattle, circa 1928. Stan Stapp, private collection.
Title page illustrations by Jud Yoho, from *The Bungalow Craftsman*
(Seattle: 1913). © 1913 by Jud Yoho.
Decorative chapter openings from *Bungalow Magazine* 2 (1913).

For Mark and Alexandra

CONTENTS

PREFACE ix

ACKNOWLEDGMENTS xv

1 BLUEPRINTS FOR "THE SEATTLE BUNGALOW" 1

2 IDEALIZING THE SEATTLE BUNGALOW 18

3 BUILDING THE SEATTLE BUNGALOW 52

4 SELLING THE SEATTLE BUNGALOW 73

5 LIVING IN THE SEATTLE BUNGALOW 96

6 LEGACY OF THE SEATTLE BUNGALOW 124

APPENDIX 131

NOTES 139

BIBLIOGRAPHY 175

INDEX 193

PREFACE

In the past twenty years, Americans have become fascinated with bungalows, particularly those with Craftsman detailing. Histories of bungalows abound, ranging from glossy coffee-table books to scholarly global analyses. Recognized in historic districts complete with walking tours, bungalows are now objects of intense interest and desire. Promoted by a glossy magazine devoted exclusively to this "style," a new appreciation for them has sparked a full-fledged bungalow revival in architecture as well. Present-day home buyers who want their own up-to-date bungalow can obtain original floor plans or purchase such dwellings in contemporary neobungalow residential developments. The nostalgia for these seemingly simple but cozy homes has made bungalows valuable commodities and status markers. Increasingly, only the most affluent can afford authentic Craftsman bungalows and furnishings.

The irony is that the vast majority of such dwellings began as modest housing for the lower middle class, the families of those workers in the skilled trades and in clerical and sales occupations making the transition from an older entrepreneurial economy to the twentieth-century consumer economy. This book interprets bungalows from their perspective. Bungalows are cultural artifacts not just of those who originally conceived them but also of the people who most directly produced and used them.

My interest in bungalows began in the mid-1980s with my work as a local historic preservation officer in the mining town of Butte, Montana. On the hill and down on the flats, I encountered blocks of small, historic dwellings where all kinds of Butte residents lived. But when I tried to identify the houses, I found that existing architectural histories and guidebooks only minimally explained what I was seeing. Most books assumed that the vernacular landscape reflected watered-down, high-style, architect-derived designs and ignored commonplace structures. My preservation work contributed to my sense that I must look elsewhere for explanations. I found that architects had little interest in Butte's inexpensive housing. Yet every day I talked with home owners, contractors, and small-business people passionately committed to maintaining their houses.

I realized that to understand vernacular dwellings—bungalows in particular—I needed to view them as more than architecture. These structures served as homes for families, at once emotional symbols, economic assets, and sites of everyday life. My goal became to connect the people who used and constructed the built environment with the bungalows that resulted from their efforts. I needed to recover the decisions that produced bungalows, of both the people who shaped their design and those who had only the ability to make individual consumer choices. By bringing together all of these different influences on modest bungalows, I could show a new side of these houses' creation.

Determining the mindset of articulate, idealistic architectural reformers proved relatively easy, as they left behind both copious records of their visions and their domiciles. The Special Collections and Manuscripts Division at the University of Washington and the Seattle Public Library's art department contained numerous architectural plan books, manuscript collections, journals, and photographs of early twentieth-century architectural design. Early on, I came across the extraordinary community of Beaux Arts Village. There, I discovered the utopian ambitions for Craftsman architecture so eloquently articulated by the professional middle class.

But I remained committed to explaining the lives of less affluent, ordinary people, particularly those in the lower middle class. The world view of Beaux Arts Village's professional middle class did not necessarily transfer to the thoughts and practices of the clerks and foremen who inhabited Seattle's many nondescript bungalows. I wished to illuminate how they actually lived, not just the architectural ideals espoused in published sources. This approach necessarily limited my research options. For instance, I hoped to discover interior photographs of average homes. However, informal shots of nonelite interiors proved exceedingly rare, and I could not assume that everyone lived as depicted in the beautiful photographs shown in easily available magazines or plan books. I had to rely on other methods to analyze the use of space by people who did not usually record their lives or who left almost no record in public repositories.

For this, I turned to both social history and vernacular architectural history methodologies. Determined to highlight the agency of the nonelite, social history's goal dovetailed perfectly with my desire to place ordinary people squarely at the heart of my study. Discovering vernacular architectural studies was a turning point for me. Both a subject of inquiry and a method of analysis, this field focuses on everyday landscapes as artifacts of past societies and cultures. Bungalows themselves could provide evidence of cultural meanings. My intent, however, remained to emphasize people in structures, not just the structures themselves. Both disciplines emphasize a case-study approach, examining closely a locality and its primary sources.

With an overwhelming abundance of early twentieth-century housing, Seattle proved ideal for such scrutiny. But so vast a pre–World War II landscape required me to further narrow my study areas. With the help of Kate Krafft, a historian then in Seattle's Department of Community Development, I chose to concentrate on four neighborhoods, thick with modest bungalows, just north of Lake Union and the Lake Washington Ship Canal: Ballard, Fremont, Green Lake, and Wallingford. In each, I delineated forty- to sixty-block sample areas that contained five unifying features: a south-to-north growth pattern consistent with Seattle's expansion as a whole, a streetcar line, a school, a park or playground, and direct access to a local business district. To study the houses that existed before World War II (and not just the houses standing there today), I utilized a remarkable resource, the original tax assessor's records compiled by the Works Progress Administration in 1937. Located in the Washington State Puget Sound Regional Archives then in Burien and now in Bellevue, Washington, individual cards provided astonishingly detailed information about every King County house and its alterations. At least one photograph and sometimes a floor plan accompanied each address. As I looked at every structure for the sample areas, I entered the physical description of every fifth house (20 percent of the sample area) into a database. In the end, I had a collection of architectural information on over 800 houses in Seattle's north end.

As useful as this database of physical features was, it still left vague the relationship between houses and their inhabitants. To find the people behind the architectural choices, I turned to the manuscript census and oral histories. When I added 1920 census information to the addresses in my database, I finally could connect families to dwellings. Now I knew who had made decisions concerning specific houses in the north end. Yet my database could not explain just how families used or conceptualized their domestic spaces. Homes carried far more emotional weight and economic importance than such material could reveal. I needed the recollections of people who had grown up in Seattle's north end bungalows. When interviewees opened their memories to me, they gave insights into the inner workings of domestic life unobtainable in any other fashion. Their memories gave voice and life to the story of how average families interacted with their homes.

As often happens in research, it was happenstance that acquainted me with Stan Stapp, whose family figures prominently in the book. I discovered a five-part series of newspaper columns he wrote for *The North Seattle Press* in 1987 that gave me exactly the sort of material I sought: stories of how his family had used its 1919 bungalow as both a home and a work place. In numerous interviews, Mr. Stapp not only detailed his family's story but opened his father's remarkably well-archived papers to show me his father's letters, newspaper articles, and artwork. Some of the furniture Orrill Stapp hand built in the Arts and Crafts period of his life still graced Stan's home. More than any other research for this book, this encounter with Stan Stapp, and vicariously with Orrill Stapp, evoked feelings of life in a bungalow before World War II.

The photograph albums Mr. Stapp so generously shared with me gave a poignant visual accounting of that interior life. Here were the informal pictures that I sought of a nonelite family using its bungalow spaces. Thanks to Mr. Stapp, *The Seattle Bungalow* features some of these images. However, due to the high cost of reproducing photographs that all presses now face, I was unable to include all of the floor plans, neighborhood landscapes, maps, and advertising graphics that I would have liked. Ultimately, I chose to focus the illustrations on the homes of families I specifically discuss in the book.

The vividness of the stories and photographs, particularly those of the Stapp family, impelled me toward narrative history. Stories animate the physical object, imparting a warmth and intimacy that reflect the deeply personal meanings that people invest in their homes. Equally important, storytelling can reach a broad audience, as the success of Laurel Thatcher Ulrich's *A Midwife's Tale* and more recently Kevin Boyle's *Arc of Justice* have shown. I have tried to let the individual stories shine through my analysis and to keep my narrative uncluttered with references that fit more appropriately in the footnotes.

The Seattle Bungalow thus falls into overlapping historiographies. It is part of contemporary architectural history, an interdisciplinary approach that scrutinizes for cultural meanings specific parts of the vernacular built environment. For social historians, this book will further explain how average Americans organized daily life. For architectural historians, it will highlight the importance of consumerism in influencing design. For students of popular culture, it joins a growing literature that sees cultural change as emanating from the mass of people who occupied the lower reaches of the nation's socio-economic order. Lastly, this study seeks to bring the techniques of narrative history to an analysis of the built environment, to tell stories about people and their homes that illuminate the early twentieth-century world.

With this book, I intend to add yet another face to our understanding of bungalows. When we revel in the bungalow's appeal, I hope we see more than architectural ideology and simplistic nostalgia. These artistic yet homey dwellings represent real people coping with the realities of everyday life in the early twentieth century. No one group or class can claim sole credit for the bungalow's creation. In this act of genesis, ordinary people played a vital role

ACKNOWLEDGMENTS

IT IS NOT BY SERENDIPITY that I chose to study the homes and families of ordinary people. A product of one such happy and loving family, I grew up in old houses that seemed under constant modification by my artistic mother and jack-of-all-trades father. I learned early on to appreciate the home as a source of nurturing and as a symbol of artisanal independence. It is to my parents, Florence Ore and the late Wesley Ore, that I owe the first and most long-standing debt for this book. Like my parents, my brothers August and Stephen Ore have kept me rooted with a strong sense of place. I am deeply grateful that I have brothers who are my dearest friends. Their wives, Anne and Margaret, are models of patience and generosity. My sister, Margaret Ore, has shown me how families can change over time, and I am very pleased that she is part of mine. Though not alive to read this, my sister Susan and brothers David and, especially, Spencer remained in my heart as I wrote about family. My late cousin Elaine Schmid opened her Seattle home to me during my research and gave endless emotional support. Seattle won't be the same for me without her. My family became immeasurably larger when I married, and this extended family also succored me during the long years of writing. My mother-in-law, Phyllis Fiege, cheerfully weathered the process of this book, serving me fresh salmon and hospitality on my many research trips conducted out of her home in Woodinville, Washington. To her and to my sister-in-law, Gale Fiege, I give my sincere appreciation for their gift of family. To all my family, I extend a grateful thank you for your love and your insights about home.

My professors in the University of Utah's History Department helped me fashion a dissertation centered on my questions about early twentieth-century popular domestic architecture. My project crossed several disciplinary boundaries, so I relied on a variety of historians. I wish to thank my dissertation committee members, each of whom lent me their valuable expertise. Paul E. Johnson inspired me with his sparkling prose and intimate, funny, and often sad stories. Peggy Pascoe was a consummate role model; she gave unflagging moral support, incredibly thoughtful critiques, and patient encouragement. Thomas Carter opened up the field of vernacular architecture to me, and Katherine Grier introduced me to material culture studies; they made the study of these subfields intensely exciting. Ever gracious, Peter Goss extended to me his vast knowledge of architectural history and suburbanization. Ronald Smelser, Jim Lehning, and Ed Davies helped me with the subtleties of the historical discipline and with understanding the twentieth century. Though never officially my adviser, Richard White became my greatest guide through the pitfalls of publication and academic life. For that and his loyalty, warmth, and generosity, I am intensely grateful.

Financial support proved critical in undertaking my research. My thanks to the University of Utah, which awarded me a Steffensen Cannon Scholarship and a Graduate Research Fellowship, and the University of Utah Humanities Center, which provided me with the James and Carol Macfarlane Graduate Fellowship. Colorado State University's College of Liberal Arts and History Department assisted with the acquisition and enhancement of the book's photographs. I am especially appreciative of these funds, as they ensured cleaner versions of the original tax assessor photographs, the only known historic images of many of these houses.

Portions of this book have appeared elsewhere. *Pacific Northwest Quarterly* granted me permission to reprint parts of chapter 2, and University of Tennessee Press allowed me to include material in chapter 4 it had published earlier. I thank them for their willingness to extend me this courtesy.

In Seattle, numerous individuals and institutions greatly aided my project. Most particularly, I am appreciative of the professionals at the Washington State Puget Sound Regional Archives, without whom I could not have acquired such invaluable data. Mike Saunders allowed me special entrance into the archives, where Philippa Stairs cheerfully lugged hundreds of tax-assessment books from the nether regions of an old elementary school for me to use. Mike and Phil exemplify the best in archival assistance. Kate Krafft kindly acquainted me with city neighborhoods and architectural research sources. Her assistance was crucial in determining the trajectory of my research, and I am deeply grateful to her. Jo Ann Fenton in the Seattle Public Library's art department, and Scott Cline, Seattle City archivist, assisted me with finding historic journals and city records. Beaux Arts Villagers Tandy Ford, Helen Lewis, and Marnie Ross generously allowed me to dig into the rich visual sources and records that documented the community's Arts and Crafts origins. My thanks to staffs at the Special Collections and Manuscripts Division at the University of Washington for the years of patiently retrieving materials for me.

Listening to people's stories was the most enjoyable and rewarding part of researching this book. I am immensely grateful to these Seattleites, who warmly offered a stranger a glimpse into their pasts: Ray and Kathi Abendroth, John and Jane Boitano, Betty Bostrom, Ruth Fall, Ruth Hughbanks, Harry Jacobsen, Charlotte Lenz, Hugh Miracle, Anne Marie Steiner, John and Marian Wallace, and Eileen Wolgamott. My deepest thanks go to the late Stan Stapp for his incredible generosity. The richness and humanity of the Stapps' story has made my book a stronger, more compelling history.

As I transformed the dissertation into a book, other academics helped me focus my argument. I wish to thank John Findlay, Marsha Weisiger, Kingston Heath, Chris Wilson, Matt Klingle, and other participants in the Vernacular Architecture Forum and the Western History Association who provided both critiques and camaraderie. Working across disciplines and fields often means working in isolation, and so I especially appreciate their assistance and understanding. The extensive and thoughtful critiques of six anonymous reviewers greatly improved my work. Though I cannot thank them in person, I wish to convey my sincere appreciation for their time and effort.

I am immensely grateful for the professionalism and creativity of the people at the University of Washington Press, who made this a much more beautiful book than I ever imagined. My deepest thanks go to Julidta Tarver, who guided my project through the publishing process with an uncommon graciousness and consideration. Both Kerrie Maynes, who expertly copyedited my manuscript, and Ashley Saleeba, who developed the book's striking design, took special efforts to ensure a handsome publication.

My home is now in Colorado, and here friends have supported me during the seemingly endless revisions. I must first thank my colleagues in the Colorado State University History Department and university community. Most importantly, Ruth Alexander showed extraordinary faith in my work. I owe much to her courage, her sense of justice, and her scholarly example. Greg Smoak used levity and wine to mitigate the most difficult parts of the revision process. Jared Orsi, Ann Little, Kelly Long, Doug Yarrington, Bruce Ronda, and Chris Nelson either reviewed my writing or offered support during the worst moments. Along with these exceptional colleagues, I wish to thank the students in my various undergraduate and graduate classes who widened my thinking with their perceptive analyses. Outside of the university, local preservationists have continually expressed interest in my progress. I especially thank Karen McWilliams for her loyalty and her exceptional listening skills. Marcia De Moss at Digigraphics handled the copying of my historic photos with patience and professionalism, for which I am most grateful.

Beyond Colorado, a network of friends and mentors shaped my development as a historian. Then at the Utah State Historic Preservation Office and now at the Oregon State Historic Preservation Office, Roger Roper was an important sounding board for my early ideas about vernacular architecture. At Carroll College, Bob Swartout taught my first history seminar and set me on my career path. He directed me to Washington State University, where I was most fortunate to work with Leroy Ashby. Both of these scholars have high standards for research and writing, which I hope I have lived up to. They have become friends as well as mentors. I give them all profound thanks.

For me, in the end, everything returns to family. During the course of my book revisions, my daughter, Alexandra Fiege Ore, has grown from a newborn into an articulate fourth-grader. Though she might think she has had to compete with the book, in reality she will always be at the center of my heart. I save my most passionate gratitude for my husband and colleague, Mark Fiege, who has labored with me on every part of this book. For over two decades, he has built with me an enduring home that rests on a foundation of a shared personal and intellectual commitment. In his scholarship and his person, Mark combines compassion and imagination, which allows him to explore the full range of humanity; he is my greatest inspiration. This book is for him and for Alexandra. It is our love that makes our house a home.

THE SEATTLE BUNGALOW

BLUEPRINTS FOR
"THE SEATTLE BUNGALOW"

ON THE CORNER OF Woodlawn Avenue and North Forty-second Street in Seattle's Wallingford neighborhood stands a lovely, graceful house (fig. 1.1). Its large, sweeping roofs and simple shape convey a sense of shelter and serenity. Even though it exists within a community of tightly packed residences, the house's abundance of wood siding and full-length front porch suggest an intimacy with nature. The details are simple and geometric, but the very lack of elaborate decoration creates an appeal that still stirs an early twenty-first-century viewer. Completed in 1919, this dwelling has all the elements of a typical Craftsman bungalow. From the early 1900s to the eve of the Great Depression, builders in the United States erected hundreds of thousands of such houses, many perhaps exact replicas of this one.

The family that owned this commonplace house for forty-eight years was, too, an ordinary family, neither rich nor poor, neither a part of Seattle's elite nor of its working class. Orrill Stapp (fig. 1.2) typified many Seattle residents of the early twentieth century. He had migrated to the city from the rural areas and small towns of Iowa and Nebraska in Seattle's prosperous times after the 1897 Klondike gold rush. With a young wife and a growing family, Stapp settled

1.1 *Finished in 1919, the Stapp family's home at 4203 Woodlawn in the Wallingford neighborhood of Seattle typifies a common Craftsman bungalow, circa 1928. Photo: Stan Stapp, private collection.*

into a series of small houses in Seattle's new suburbs, first in south Seattle and then in the north end. A self-trained musician and graduate of the eighth grade, Stapp supported his family by giving music lessons. In 1922, when the Stapps moved into 4203 Woodlawn Avenue in the Wallingford area, their neighbors were much like them: white native-born clerks, salespeople, skilled workers, and small entrepreneurs. They all carried on their workaday lives in houses like the Stapps', making personal decisions about their homes that juggled the competing pressures of a modern economy.[1]

The Stapps were just one average family in an ordinary bungalow that stood in the suburban landscape of a western American city. Yet in their very ordinariness, their home and family represented the nation's transformation out of a Victorian mindset that occurred in the early twentieth century—a metamorphosis in which people like Orrill Stapp played a vital role. Nowhere was the change more evident than in popular domestic architecture. The residential environment of the early twentieth-century looked startlingly different from its nineteenth-century precursor. Tall and complex in shape, with complicated roof lines, Victorian houses reveled in textures, colors, and ornamentation.

Next to them, early twentieth-century homes seemed to hunker on the earth in unobtrusive, horizontal, rectangular shapes. In contrast to Victorian dwellings' fanciful decoration, bungalows seemed cozy, warm, and inviting. Most significantly, bungalows featured a revamped interior. For practical and ideological reasons, Victorians had separated and closed off rooms from one another. The bungalow plan, however, began the twentieth-century practice of opening spaces to allow the integration of public and private, indoor and outdoor. Bungalows also formed the vanguard of twentieth-century domestic minimalism that emphasized simplicity, a conscious paring down of complex shapes and decorations. Straight, uninterrupted lines; right angles; and low, overarching roofs presented a spare, trim contrast to the intricacies and curvaceousness of Victorian dwellings. These two qualities—open interiors and minimalism—characterized popular housing through most of the twentieth century, regardless of what exterior style cloaked the structure. Homes like 4203 Woodlawn, therefore, materialized as the first modern houses and set a precedent for the rest of the century.[2]

1.2 A musician, Orrill Stapp appears dressed for a performance, around 1906. Photo: Stan Stapp, private collection.

Who fashioned this pathbreaking house type? Architects and affluent reformers who redefined the idea of home usually receive the accolades for creating the visually appealing new dwellings of the early twentieth century. Their lofty aesthetic conceptions, so goes this interpretation, then trickled down to the realm of popular architecture. Beginning in about 1900 in the Chicago suburbs, Frank Lloyd Wright gained national attention for his Prairie-style houses. Many scholars consider these imaginative high-style residences, with their horizontal lines, stripped appearance, and fluid interior spaces as the ideological wellspring for the bungalow and as the first great breakthrough in twentieth-century domestic architecture. At the same time, in Pasadena, California, the brothers Charles S. Greene and Henry M. Greene constructed their "ultimate bungalows," sprawling Asian-inspired residences that featured exposed handcrafted wood joinery, terraces for outdoor living, and extensive landscaping. Along with Wright and the Greenes, magazines and plan book purveyors—most notably Gustav Stickley's *Craftsman Magazine*—disseminated the bungalow idea.[3]

Socially conscious professionals in the Progressive Era, too, questioned

Victorian values, and called for a radical rethinking of the city and the home, and so contributed to the creation of bungalows. Not only architects but home economists, public health officials, and urban reformers advocated an efficient, hygienic, and functional single-family dwelling that would foster democratic families and an improved society. Furthermore, a new middle and upper-middle class conceived a modern suburban ideal and manifested its principles in planned, exclusive suburbs. These Americans, claims historian Mary Corbin Sies, actively shaped the planning and values of all suburban developments regardless of class or race. The elite created a new suburban architecture and landscape.[4]

But did commonplace bungalows like 4203 Woodlawn reflect only upper-class ideas and models for living? If we place the distinctive bungalow form within the context of a new economic environment, we can see how modest-income families influenced the physical form of early twentieth-century houses through their growing power as customers. Although historians argue about when a consumer economy and society came to maturity in the United States, clearly by the mid-nineteenth century, upper-middle-class and many middle-class Americans were beginning to enjoy the comfort and goods emanating from industrial capitalism. By 1900, the economy entered a new consumer phase. The ability to mass-produce prodigious quantities of goods impelled companies to broaden their consumer base as widely as possible to distribute and sell on an equivalent mass scale. This meant reaching further and further into society, to groups previously unable to make unnecessary or expensive purchases. To develop these markets, advertising became a crucial component in encouraging consumption, and businesses created elaborate merchandising strategies to lure new customers. Concurrently, a major shift in consumer credit occurred. By 1915, new methods and sources of credit democratized the ability and willingness to acquire more goods. The most important consumer item the average family could acquire was a house.[5]

With ordinary people's expanded ability to purchase a dwelling, a lucrative market in small houses flourished. However, Americans never considered residences to be like automobiles or radios, modern products churned out by monopolistic companies for the eager buying public. Homes came laden with older values and traditions that reinforced the primacy of individually constructed, single-family homes and precluded their complete mass production. Small builders and sellers who handled only a few structures at a time quickly exploited this tremendous opportunity. They understood people's desire for domestic spaces they could control and manipulate, and they reoriented their products to the demands of these new home buyers. As customers, moderate-income people who wanted affordable, technologically advanced, conveniently located dwellings became a powerful force in determining what features modern homes would have. Thus, the residential neighborhoods of the early twentieth century embodied just as much these people's newfound ability to buy as they did the elite's dominant suburban ideal.

From this perspective, architectural change did not occur in one direction only. To see this, we must shift our gaze beyond architectural ideology and planned suburbs to the vast early twentieth-century neighborhoods of the sort that contained 4203 Woodlawn. Architects rarely ventured into such places. There, modest entrepreneurs sought to profit from the housing boom. Small builders erected simple, unexceptional houses that ambitious real-estate promoters sold to an aspiring lower middle-class. Home owners modified their dwellings, using them flexibly to fit changing economic and personal circumstances. The decisions and actions of these people helped shape early twentieth-century popular housing.[6]

To trace the origins of twentieth-century popular architecture, we must look at where it first emerged: in the new cities of the western United States. In the twentieth century, this region pioneered a particular urban form that came to define urban and suburban development. In their early settlement, western cities retained a common eastern model. When Americans migrated beyond the Mississippi River in the mid-nineteenth-century, they took their ideas of urban settlement with them. As a result, nineteenth-century cities such as San Francisco, Denver, and Portland acquired urban characteristics associated with established eastern metropolises: a definable urban identity; a central business district containing high-style commercial buildings; and an urban infrastructure of lighted, paved streets, fashionable residential neighborhoods, and street rail and communication networks. But in the twentieth century, western cities no longer conformed to a dense eastern shape. By the beginning of World War II, the region had created a new urban prototype that cities all over the United States would emulate. Instead of crowding close to their points of origin, western cities spread into their surrounding areas, creating a pattern of dispersed, low-density, suburban development. Although the West's unrestricted geography fostered suburban growth, the timing of western urbanization proved more important. In the late nineteenth and early twentieth centuries, just when the region experienced a population boom, technological advances provided opportunities for the physical decentralization of cities. Even before growth occurred, shrewd promoters constructed increasingly sophisticated systems of mass transportation—first horsecars and cable cars, then electrified streetcars and trolleys. Most important, automobiles scattered new neighborhoods well beyond the original urban center. These developments refashioned cities into an expansive pattern with distinct zones defined by function and class.[7]

A distinctive new house type, the bungalow, accompanied this western suburban layout. A particular form and floor plan defined the bungalow, not an exterior fashionable style. Rectangular in shape, with only one or one-and-a-half stories, and topped with a broad, sweeping hip or gable roof, the bungalow house type included an open floor plan for free-flowing access between its living and dining room. It eliminated the highly formal parlors that dominated Victorian dwellings. Sheltering the entrance, a front porch produced the only transitional space between the bungalow's inner life and its surrounding environment. Beginning with the bungalow form, the open plan permeated all levels of suburban housing, from the smallest homes for workers to the most expensive high-style architecture of the elite. On the exterior, bungalows manifested a variety of styles: Craftsman, Prairie, Colonial, Tudor, and Asian, to name the most common. But whatever the architectural embellishments, the low, rectangular-shaped form appeared along the rapidly proliferating streetcar lines in North American cities, defining twentieth-century suburbanization and establishing the basic popular house plan for the entire century.[8]

Because Americans identified bungalows with their point of origin in southern California, they often called them "California bungalows." A convergence of factors promoted this association of place and structure. According to bungalow historians Clay Lancaster and Anthony King, the origins of the bungalow lay in colonial India. There, the British appropriated for official housing the banggolo, a vernacular, rectangular-shaped Indian structure with a dominant hip roof and wraparound veranda adapted to the hot climate.[9] By the mid-nineteenth century, colonial agents had transferred the type to Britain, where it became a recreational dwelling for a burgeoning middle class. Though not widespread by the 1880s, the bungalow caught the attention of British and then American architects who, King and Lancaster argue, diffused the dwelling to Americans as a whole. Californians, more than any other people, seized on the bungalow's possibilities. Although most Americans still considered it a summer home, the bungalow became permanent housing in California, where a mild climate seemed compatible with a growing popular desire for an informal lifestyle close to nature. Simple and easy to erect, the bungalow solved the immediate need for affordable dwellings during the region's early twentieth-century population boom. Californians transformed uncomplicated structures previously identified with rustic vacation homes into year-round residences that filled the flourishing suburbs. At the center of the "bungalow craze," according to most architectural historians, was Los Angeles (and Pasadena). Timing for this city's growth was fortuitous. As the bungalow gained favor, Los Angeles burst with new residents, becoming the United States' fourth-largest metropolitan area by 1930. The sheer size and wealth of the city guaranteed the popularity of bungalow architecture. Economic and cultural currents carried the house type north to the booming cities of Portland, Seattle, and Vancouver. New types of mass media—plan books, magazines, and architectural journals—disseminated the

California bungalow to midwestern and eastern suburbs, and to rural America, until it became a truly national house type.[10]

After about 1905, bungalows like the Stapps' sprang up everywhere in the vast, relatively unplanned western American suburbs where ordinary people lived. In Salt Lake City, Phoenix, Denver, Vancouver, and, of course, Los Angeles, builders raised tens of thousands of these small, unobtrusive houses between 1905 and 1930, imposing a bungalow uniformity on the urban scene. Developers platted new additions along street grids and streetcar lines, tying these new neighborhoods to central business districts. Home owners bought the lots, and small contractors erected single-family dwellings for them. The residential skyline lowered, becoming a horizon of spreading, shallow-pitched hip and gable roofs punctuated occasionally by a two-story, cube-shaped house called the "four-square," which often embodied features of its bungalow cousin. House shapes along the streets became more rectangular, interrupted only by cantilevered breakfast nooks. Colors mellowed into warm browns and greens, soft grays and ivorys. Exposed rafter ends under the extended roof eaves and large porches marked dwellings as originating in the 1910s. Regional variations did occur. Southwesterners used stucco and elements of Spanish Colonial architecture. Asian-inspired bungalows appeared frequently in Pacific-Rim cities such as Los Angeles, Seattle, and Vancouver. Salt Lake City featured many brick bungalows influenced by Frank Lloyd Wright's Prairie architecture. By the mid-1920s, period-revival architectural fashions dominated new construction. Though stripped of the big porch, these new styles continued the bungalow's one-story, rectangular plan with a central living room, and nestled seamlessly within the low, expansive neighborhoods of bungalows throughout the west.[11]

Seattle was one of these western metropolises, crowded with bungalows and period-revival cottages. A city of the twentieth century, it expanded most rapidly after 1897 to become, by 1920, the Pacific Northwest's leader in population, economic strength, and influence.[12] Seattle's growth typified the West's suburban developments. Like other mid-nineteenth-century western settlements, Seattle began as a small community of wooden structures clustered around its primary transportation and industrial hub, Elliott Bay on Puget Sound. With gridded streets running parallel to the shoreline, it resembled a New England prototype. Until 1880, the town grew slowly and changed little, with only a gradual residential expansion to the east and north of the central business district. But with branch line access to Tacoma's transcontinental railroad terminus in the 1880s and then Seattle's own transcontinental railroad, the Great Northern, in 1893, Seattle metamorphosed into a regional urban center. The census leaped from 3,533 residents in 1880 to 42,837 in 1890, then to 80,671 in 1900. Among older wood-frame structures, brick-and-iron-fronted commercial buildings with Second Empire, Italianate, Queen Anne, and Gothic details arose in Seattle's core. When a fire in 1889 wiped out 116 acres of the central business district and environs, the city lost much of its early Victorian appearance. Architects and entrepreneurs built even taller masonry or terra-cotta-clad steel-frame buildings further north of the original business center. Throughout the early twentieth century, excavation and removal of the hills north of the commercial district drew retail activity in that direction and diminished more of the city's older Victorian presence. By the late 1920s, Seattle had a modern urban core, with skyscrapers, bustling department stores, palatial theaters, and large office buildings that lay ten blocks to the north of the deteriorating original nineteenth-century business district.[13]

While the city's center modernized, so too did its residential neighborhoods. Between 1900 and 1910, they developed the expansive layout characteristic of modern western cities. Stimulated by the Great Northern Railroad's arrival in 1893 and the Klondike Gold Rush four years later, Seattle's flourishing economy attracted tens of thousands of new residents. Its population almost tripled between 1900 and 1910, from 80,671 to 237,194. A "centrifugal movement," as sociologist Calvin Schmid called it, radiated new Seattleites away from downtown along a rapidly expanding transportation system. Cable cars had replaced horse-drawn vehicles by the 1880s, and after 1889, when streetcars electrified, lines stretched east and north of downtown. By 1920, after a series of corporate consolidations culminated in municipal ownership in 1919, streetcar lines proliferated throughout the suburban region, uniting distant neighborhoods with the city center. Tracks often preceded neighborhood development. An early example of this was the Madison Street Cable Railway. Beginning in 1890, this line ran from downtown through "virgin timberland" to Madison Park on the Lake Washington shore. There, the company created a "typical trolley park" with pavilions, baseball diamond, picnic grounds, boat house, racetrack, and swimming beaches.[14] Where the streetcar went, residential development soon followed, first along the line itself, then spreading out from the tracks. Houses mushroomed everywhere. A survey conducted in 1940 found that 83.4 percent of Seattle's dwelling units at that time had originated between 1900 and 1929. The suburbanites then clamored for annexation to the city so that they could draw on its water supply. Seattle obliged, adding ten areas to city jurisdiction by 1910, doubling its size and establishing the boundaries it would retain until the post-World War II era. Clearly, by 1920, Seattle exemplified the pattern of suburbanization characteristic of twentieth-century western American cities (see map).[15]

Most of this rapid expansion took place in Seattle's north end. Geography and transportation networks encouraged growth north of Lake Union and Salmon Bay. In the 1870s and early 1880s, settlers began acquiring tracts of land north of the lake and west toward Shilshole Bay on Puget Sound. There, before the 1880s, a few people farmed or logged the forested hills, but remained isolated

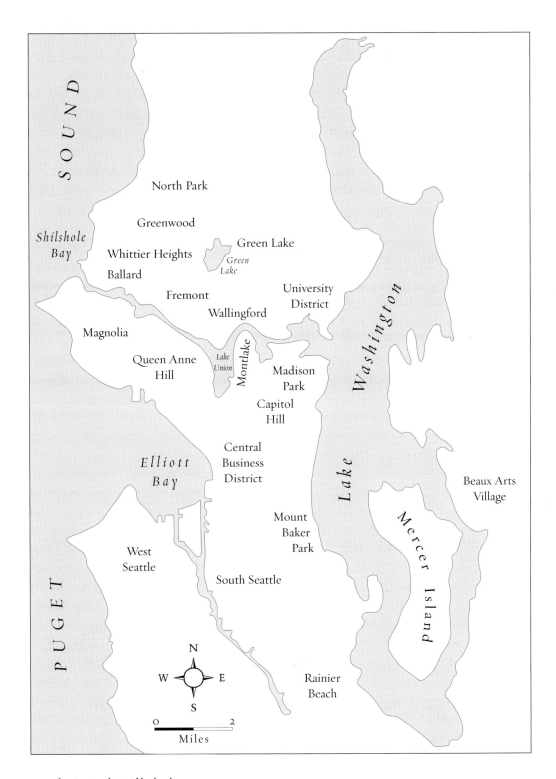

SOUND

Shilshole
Bay

North Park

Greenwood

Green Lake
Green Lake

Whittier Heights

Ballard

University
District

Fremont

Wallingford

Magnolia

Lake Union

Montlake

Queen Anne
Hill

Madison
Park

Capitol
Hill

Washington

Elliott Bay

Central
Business
District

Lake

Beaux Arts
Village

Mount
Baker
Park

Mercer Island

West
Seattle

South Seattle

PUGET

N

W   E

S

Rainier
Beach

0   2
Miles

Map Showing Seattle Neighborhoods

from the growing city. Nodes of settlement grew around sawmilling operations in Ballard (on Salmon Bay), near Green Lake, at Fremont (northwest of Lake Union), and at Latona (to the northeast). During Seattle's 1880s boom, developers in these areas stood ready to exploit opportunities in the north end. In 1887, the arrival of the Seattle, Lake Shore, and Eastern Railroad, which ran north from downtown Seattle to Ballard then east to Lake Washington, set off a flurry of building. In 1887 and 1888, entrepreneurs platted Green Lake, Fremont, Ballard, and Latona (later part of the Wallingford neighborhood) and lured industries to them. Shingle and sawmills, factories, iron works, and other manufacturing operations appeared along the waterfronts and rail lines of Ballard, Fremont, and Wallingford. In 1890, Guy Phinney built a streetcar line from Fremont to Green Lake and constructed a rudimentary park, thus sparking residential development in the area. Electric trolley lines that connected the communities to Seattle and to each other enabled even more construction. In 1891, Seattle annexed Fremont, Green Lake, and Latona, and, in 1907, Ballard became part of the metropolis. The 1893 depression temporarily slowed building, but with the return of prosperity generated by the Klondike Gold Rush, more home seekers rushed to the flourishing city. In 1894, the University of Washington moved from downtown Seattle to a site northeast of Lake Union. The 1909 Alaska-Yukon-Pacific Exposition held on its campus brought still more people to north-end neighborhoods. In the first two decades of the twentieth century, a construction boom in the north end coincided with the bungalow fad that had captured Americans' imaginations.[16]

Multistory apartment buildings rarely interrupted Seattle's neighborhoods. Typical of western cities, and presaging later twentieth-century growth, Seattle featured a landscape of single-family homes. The tenements common to eastern cities did exist, but stood close to the waterfront or near industrial areas. By 1940, Seattle's neighborhoods contained more than 90 percent single-family houses. Wood-framed, with five or six rooms, they dominated the districts that ringed a few islands of larger, high-style mansions such as Queen Anne Hill, Capitol Hill, Mount Baker Park, and Montlake. Following the streetcar lines into undeveloped tracts, small houses gradually changed in appearance from the late nineteenth century into the twentieth. The dwellings that early Seattleites erected in the 1880s, "pioneer" period homes, as historian John Owen labels them, replicated farmhouses throughout the United States: rectangular, two-story, relatively unornamented structures with a "temple" or gabled facade. When Seattle's first residential expansion began in the late 1880s, builders lowered the heights of common houses, and one- or one-and-a-half-story dwellings became popular. Irregular or ell-shaped, these so-called Queen Anne cottages featured front porches and embellishments such as turned porch posts, elaborate spindle- or scrollwork decorations, and fish-scale shingles in the front gable. After 1900, carpenters erected still simpler houses, with either a rectangular, gable-fronted form or a square, hipped box shape (fig. 1.3). Subtle classical details, such as cylindrical porch columns, often adorned them. With their single-hip or gable roofs, basic rectangular configurations, and front porches, these cottages immediately presaged bungalows. When building boomed between 1907 and 1915, bungalows became Seattle's dominant house type (fig. 1.4). In these years, builders favored Craftsman stylistic details such as rock porch piers and dark stained-wood siding that seemed especially appropriate to the lush, green environment. Until the early 1920s, Seattle contractors constructed almost no other kind of single-family dwelling.[17]

Paved arterial streets and increased automobile use contributed to even greater suburban growth in the 1920s, and exteriors shifted to period-revival styles. Tudor Revival (fig. 1.5) and Colonial Revival houses (fig. 1.6) filled the gaps in existing neighborhoods and appeared in large numbers on the expanding residential edge. In sheer numbers alone, more houses went up in the 1920s than in any other decade, forming the preponderance of small houses constructed between 1900 and 1930. They continued the bungalow precedent of utilizing a pared-down floor plan. On the exterior, they featured historic revival details: clipped gables, multipaned windows, shutters, steep gables, faux half-timbering, and stucco. By World War II, these two types of houses, bungalows and their successors, revival cottages, filled Seattle's northern-most neighborhoods. Here and there, the rather stark, unornamented houses of the late 1930s and early 1940s appeared in places such as Whittier Heights north of Ballard (fig. 1.7). After the war, a few ranch-style houses dotted previously vacant lots. These blended well with existing houses. Invariably low and unobtrusive, they were the direct descendants of neighboring bungalows.[18]

The small homes that sheltered Seattle's middling families existed within a larger landscape of social differentiation. Like twentieth-century cities throughout the United States, Seattle divided into zones of class and ethnicity. Unskilled, transient European American workers and minorities such as Chinese, Japanese, and African Americans settled in multi-family structures close to downtown and the port. Middle-class professionals, business owners, and their families congregated in neighborhoods of single-family residences adjacent to the University of Washington and along the Lake Washington shore. White-collar workers, skilled craftsmen, and their families, many of them immigrants from Canada, Scandinavia, and Northern Europe, took up residence in the fast-growing bungalow neighborhoods. Geography reinforced class distinctions. On Seattle's ridgetops the wealthy built their mansions, later abandoning the city entirely for distant, exclusive suburbs. Small houses covered the side hills and filled the lower-middle-class and working-class areas in the valleys, where factories clustered on waterfronts.[19]

1.3 *Sometimes called a worker's cottage, this house at 303 East Fifty-sixth Street has a basically square shape and hip roof, 1937. Photo: Puget Sound Regional Archives*

1.4 *Constructed between 1915 and 1917, the Williams family house at 2833 West Seventy-first Street in Ballard is a good example of a side-gable Craftsman bungalow, 1937. Photo: Puget Sound Regional Archives.*

1.5 *Built in 1931 by C. F. Hughbanks in Ballard, 6214 Thirty-seventh Street Northwest has Tudor Revival style characteristics, 1937. Photo: Puget Sound Regional Archives.*

1.6 *The Lange family occupied a 1925 Colonial Revival bungalow at 1205 North Forty-sixth Street, 1937. Photo: Puget Sound Regional Archives.*

1.7 *New Housing Inc. erected these duplexes in 1943 and 1945 on the 2600 block of West Fifty-sixth and West Fifty-seventh streets in Ballard, 1945. Photo: Puget Sound Regional Archives.*

By 1930, Seattle looked modern, with spreading suburbs of single-family dwellings surrounding an urban core. A modernizing economy supported it. As historian Earl Pomeroy noted, Seattle was "the product of the twentieth century, of the automobile, the airplane, the assembly line, the advertising agency"—all defining characteristics of the modern age.[20] Though founded in the 1850s, Seattle grew as a major West Coast metropolis only after the 1890s, during what some historians call the Second Industrial Revolution.[21] It rapidly established a commercial economy tied to the city's hinterlands, to Asia, and, after the 1897 Klondike Gold Rush, to Alaska. By 1916, it had become one of the leading ports on the Pacific Coast. The consequent population boom ensured that construction, especially housing, dominated the city's small manufacturing sector before World War I. An industrial economic base came with the outbreak of war and the expansion of military shipbuilding and its associated ventures. In 1918, nineteen shipyards employed some 35,000 of the port's roughly 50,000 industrial workers. The federal government also secured Seattle's future by awarding contracts to William Boeing's fledgling aircraft company, begun in 1916. By 1928, Boeing Airplane Company moved to first place among the city's manufacturing plants, employing about 900 workers. Thoroughly modern, Seattle's twentieth-century economy rested on international trade, large-scale industrial manufacturing, and widespread consumption.[22]

A western, modern, suburbanized city filled with bungalows, Seattle is an outstanding place to examine the ways that nonelite people contributed to the twentieth-century's prototypical popular domestic architecture. In fact, it may be an even better choice than Los Angeles, the purported epicenter of modern suburban form and architecture. At a critical time, between 1880 and 1910, Seattle actually grew faster than Los Angeles, increasing by 6,600 percent to Los Angeles's 2,700 percent. Seattle was never as large or as influential as the City of Angels, but it experienced its most formative stage just as bungalow construction expanded through the far west. It established its essential layout by 1910, after a flurry of annexations, and retained this outline until the 1960s. Today, its early twentieth-century appearance remains remarkably intact. Los Angeles, however, entered its biggest population surge somewhat later; between 1910 and 1940, its population increased five times. Los Angeles's landscape therefore reflects this later building phase. Squeezed between Puget Sound, Lake Union, and Lake Washington, Seattle's hilly terrain fostered distinctive neighborhoods with strong community identities that even today stand out in the larger urban context. Within these areas, thousands of relatively unchanged early twentieth-century homes still line the streets. Here, in Seattle's landscape of bungalows, we can uncover the circumstances of ordinary men, women, and families and their houses.[23]

One of these Seattle homes belonged to Orrill Stapp and his family. This handsome but unobtrusive house tells a story, in microcosm, of how average families like the Stapps participated in the making of modern homes and modern urban landscapes. Here the influences from a design elite met the practical needs of Americans adjusting to an expanding consumer economy. The bungalow emerged from the dynamic exchange between designer and user, builder and technology, and desired ideals and practical circumstances.

In design, 4203 Woodlawn and the thousands of houses like it were what they seemed: progressive houses. With its wide, sheltering roof and simple brackets extending over a prominent porch, Stapp's house expressed the principles of Craftsman architecture that arose from the broader Arts and Crafts movement of the early twentieth century. Inside, its open plan and advanced domestic technology—electricity, central heat, and plumbing—revealed the influence of domestic reform movements. It physically embodied a model home advanced by architects, home economists, and popular magazine editors. Idealists contributed this archetype to modern popular architecture.[24]

Yet in the design of Stapp's bungalow, consumer demands confronted ideological aims. Financial realities forced small builders to pare down their buildings. Although housing contractors supervised carpenter crews who followed time-honored building traditions, customers like Orrill Stapp needed the newest household technologies. During a period of inflation, the cost to produce such dwellings rose significantly. To meet the demand for modern homes, contractors simplified and cheapened the house's physical shape to compensate for the expensive infrastructure of electricity, central heating, and plumbing. Some well-capitalized companies began to employ economies of scale in house building, beginning the trend toward building entire tracts of speculative housing. But for the most part, small builders dominated bungalow construction. Their work culture and economic decisions helped to produce the bungalow house type that customers demanded.

The builders of bungalows like 4203 Woodlawn responded to the needs of a new group of consumers: families with moderate means—salespeople, clerks, skilled workers, and small businesspeople like Orrill Stapp previously ignored by the building industry. Energetic, diversified salespeople eagerly working to unite builder and consumer created a new housing market. They viewed bungalows not as progressive homes meant to reform society but as commodities for purchase. Operating in many aspects of building and selling, they capitalized on the desire for home ownership and innovated new financing techniques for middling families to buy homes. Although the professionalizing sectors of building—big real estate firms, corporate contracting companies, and college-educated architects—tried to quash the activities of the entrepreneurial, small-house salespeople, their efforts never totally succeeded. Through their salesmanship, small-time housing dealers reached a mass audience of modest-income families, ensuring that bungalows defined the new suburbs.

As home owners, Seattleites acquired homes laden with idealistic symbolism and domestic expectations. But the architectural precepts undergirding their houses did not prevent them from manipulating their spaces when circumstances challenged their economic well-being. Upon moving into his Craftsman bungalow in 1922, Orrill Stapp faced economic realities that forced him to modify his house, to use his home as a tool. Stapp and others like him blurred the categories embedded in his house's design. The site of newspaper publishing for forty-eight years, the Stapp home not only remained a residence for seven people but evolved into a place of employment, of economic production, and of consumer relations. This Craftsman bungalow became an agent in producing and furthering a new consumer society and economy. It still looked like a home, but its occupants reconceptualized its domestic meanings and readjusted its spaces. The fluidity of interior bungalow plans made such flexibility possible. The needs of ordinary people in a modern economy thus encouraged the creation of a house form, the bungalow, with an elasticity of use that defied architectural intent.

Though perhaps an extreme example, the Stapps exemplified many Americans who modified their houses to meet their changing situations. However, much their homes might have looked like those the professional reformers advocated, the same domestic ideology did not always apply. Ordinary people adopted a flexible understanding of home. They embraced the advantages of the new consumer economy with little ambivalence, and they used their houses as a means to do so. Highly valued, home ownership gave Orrill Stapp and other Seattleites in the north end the personal and cultural independence to mold their domesticity to their own ends.

The story of the Stapps and their Craftsman bungalow is but one small illustration of how middling Americans met the realities of a transforming economy and society by manipulating their built environment. In doing so, they helped create a particular house form that served as a prototype for popular architecture during the rest of the century. Through the study of real people making decisions in an actual place, we can see that architectural change in the suburban landscape emerged from a reciprocal exchange between society's elite and nonelite. This perspective forces us to modify the usual understanding that the nation's outspoken architects and professionals singlehandedly reinvigorated domestic architecture. Although overlaid with idealistic intentions, serene Craftsman bungalows at 4203 Woodlawn and elsewhere thus serve as artifacts of the labor that constructed and sold them and the families who used and modified them. Through such efforts, ordinary people not only shaped twentieth-century domestic architecture but helped create modern culture as well.

IDEALIZING THE
SEATTLE BUNGALOW

BUNGALOWS LIKE ORRILL STAPP'S appeared in a period of
cultural reorientation, at a time when many Americans challenged the rigid,
hierarchical value system of the nineteenth century. Early twentieth-century
idealists imagined a new and better society that rested on a home and family
refashioned both physically and conceptually. The Arts and Crafts movement
stimulated one of the most important reform efforts in this era. Above all, it
sought to recreate a meaningful life through fulfilling work, and thus directed
its attention to rethinking domesticity and domestic architecture. Its impulse
toward reform and critique of Victorianism appealed to men and women bent
on casting out the old and ushering in the new. One of these was Orrill Stapp.
Stapp espoused modern social ideals. He rejected his transient, midwestern,
conventionally religious past and adopted his own unique mystical beliefs
quite apart from mainstream Christianity. Critical of contemporary society, he
sympathized with the socialist analysis of competitive capitalism. An admirer
of Elbert Hubbard and his Arts and Crafts community, Roycroft, Stapp even
printed a small journal, *The Triton,* that imitated Hubbard's artfully produced
publication of social critique, *The Philistine.* Little wonder, then, that in 1908

2.1 Orrill Stapp's 1908 Craftsman home at 10143 Sixty-sixth Avenue South in Rainier Beach, a southern Seattle suburb, 1937. Photo: Puget Sound Regional Archives.

Stapp constructed a house (fig. 2.1) in Seattle's distant southern suburb, Rainier Beach, on the western shore of beautiful Lake Washington, that expressed his Arts and Crafts beliefs and embodied all of his idealism, all of his critique of industrial capitalism.[1]

To Stapp, the six-room house was not simply a dwelling. Rather, it reflected the Arts and Crafts philosophy of personal fulfillment through a simple life close to nature. Apparently planning and building at least part of it himself, Stapp carefully fit the structure to the sloped lot. By placing a daylight basement below the house's downhill end and installing dormers in the roof, he kept the dwelling low and tucked under one primary gable roof. Exposed rafter ends under the roof's extended eaves accentuated an ambience of sheltered refuge. A belt molding delineated the first floor from the two-room half-story on top, highlighting the horizontal profile. Dark stained cedar siding and shingles camouflaged the exterior against its shrubby location. The house's interior complemented its outward goal of fitting in with its natural site. The large open living room featured a massive cobblestone fireplace and stained beamed ceiling. To properly appoint such a house, Stapp labored over hand-built furniture: an oak desk, bookcases, and a trestle table. His own hammered metal lamp adorned the entrance. A product of Stapp's own heart and hand, this house articulated overtly the ideals of the Arts and Crafts movement.[2]

Orrill Stapp was one of many idealists in the early twentieth-century. He left posterity his house, his personal papers, and a few copies of *The Triton*, but little else. His Rainier Beach home gives us a glimpse of what the Arts and Crafts ideal meant to ordinary people, but probing more deeply into the thought behind Arts and Crafts creation requires a richer trove of written records and architecture.

The small community of Beaux Arts Village, Seattle's most prominent expression of Arts and Crafts idealism, provides such opportunity. There, across Lake Washington from Rainier Beach, we can carefully examine the intersection of the ideal and the real in homes like Stapp's because its founders both constructed buildings and published their intentions. Beaux Arts Village residents were not the elite of Seattle but members of a growing professional middle class. Though unusual in their commitment to carrying out a utopian venture, Beaux Arts Villagers demonstrated the ambivalence with which many of their class viewed the emerging modern world.

At the same time that Stapp so lovingly constructed his home, a group of Seattle artists planned a Chautauqua-like school and art colony set among the towering fir trees on Lake Washington's eastern shore. Eventually, over twenty houses consciously designed to follow the Arts and Crafts ideology formed a small, close-knit community. Models of reform architecture, these houses embodied contradictions that expressed the equivocation with which Arts and Crafts adherents viewed contemporary society. While their architecture critiqued the industrial, urban world, it also embraced factory technology and design. Although their rhetoric masked this juxtaposition of values, Arts and Crafts followers came to accept the world that emerged from the Second Industrial Revolution by living in houses that symbolically bridged the past and the present. The conflicted reform ideology espoused by Arts and Crafts advocates crucially influenced the design of popular architecture. In the twentieth century, pre-industrial-looking decoration concealed increasingly technologically advanced houses.

That houses expressing Arts and Crafts principles should embody such contradictory values is appropriate, for they appeared at a pivotal moment in U.S. history. In the late nineteenth century, the nation underwent a metamorphosis, largely stimulated by major structural innovations in industrial capitalism, called the Second Industrial Revolution. By 1930, technologically advanced, rationally-organized, bureaucratic corporations dominated the U.S. economy. This economic reorientation heralded major changes in the lives and work of both white-collar and blue-collar Americans. It followed quite logically that an institution as potent as the home would reflect the transforming world in which it was embedded.[3]

As Arts and Crafts disciples, Beaux Arts Villagers participated in a middle-class critique of the Second Industrial Revolution. In its English inception under William Morris, the Arts and Crafts movement emerged in the mid-nineteenth century as a rejection of both industrial goods and industrial labor relations. Along with other upper-class designers, artists, and reformers, Morris deplored the radical changes wrought by industrialization. Factory production had fundamentally altered the nature of work, divorcing the thought from the process, reducing labor to mind-numbing repetitive motions. Removing the fulfilling aspects of creation from work deskilled and degraded workers, reducing them to impoverished, dispirited husks. The results of their labor reflected the laborers' own degradation—artificial, overly ornamented, uniform, and ugly. Morris and his followers called for the restoration of handicraft that reintegrated design and process. By creating handmade objects of beauty, art would return to craft production, and a sense of fulfillment and joy would return to work. Ultimately, art could reform industrial society by improving the lives of the working class. Morris's rejection of industrialization led him "toward a revolutionary socialism" (as historian Eileen Boris terms it) that advocated recovering a society and economy based on cooperative communities of self-sustaining handicraft production. Manifesting his beliefs, Morris established a series of collaborative workshops intended to revive traditional craft skills and, optimistically, to create an economic alternative to industrial capitalism.[4]

Unable to stem the advance of increasing industrialization, Morris most profoundly affected design, becoming the central figure in the late-nineteenth-century Arts and Crafts movement. Morris and his adherents did not push a particular style. Instead, they emphasized the process of creation along certain broad principles. Following the ideas previously articulated by John Ruskin, they called for design that was honest and free of artificial decoration. They believed that any ornamentation that did occur should be rooted in nature and appropriate to the natural material from which the object sprang. Craftspeople completed unique creations by hand, from start to finish. Truly beautiful articles were simple, useful. A new aesthetic flowered under Morris's leadership. The goal of recreating a simple, fulfilling life and functional, beautiful products made Arts and Crafts advocates particularly concerned with domestic environments. British architects began to apply Arts and Crafts ideology to dwellings. Drawing on vernacular or medieval materials and architectural forms, they advocated functional structures that blended with the natural and built landscape and that eschewed dishonest revivalist styles.[5]

By the 1890s, the Arts and Crafts impulse had spread to the United States, paralleling the nation's rise to global industrial dominance. The movement's criticisms resonated especially with middle-class Americans worried about the unrestrained power of large corporations, the poverty of the urban working class, the spread of class conflict, and the loss of a sense of community. This new class entered into a period of activist reform that attempted to resolve the problems of corporate capitalism. Some believed that injecting art into craft production could solve part of society's greater problems. As Eileen Boris says, "Arts and crafts came to stand for the universalizing of art and the ennobling of labor, the merging of beauty and utility so as to regenerate the handicrafts, humanize the fine arts, and free workman and consumer from the tyranny of mass production."[6] This is so utopian a vision, one historian has likened it to a religious revival. After 1895, Arts and Crafts chapters began to meet and establish workshops across the United States. The earliest of these centered in California, where the San Francisco Guild of Arts and Crafts held the first organized exhibition on bookmaking in 1895–96. Other strong Arts and Crafts centers quickly followed in Boston and Chicago, and by 1904 as many as 2,000 groups may have existed throughout the United States. The design ideology of Morris, rather than his socialism, particularly attracted Americans. Arts and Crafts adherents eagerly adopted his principles of authenticity, honesty, simplicity, and naturalness, and an outpouring flowed forth—pottery, textiles, hammered metal pieces, jewelry, handmade books, and furniture with smooth shapes, earthy colors, medieval motifs, and elements abstracted from nature. In general, Americans reacted less strongly than the English to the primacy of handwork. Some thought that artists could retain aesthetic principles while employing machine production. However, according to Boris, most Americans held to the superiority of handicrafts. Unlike the English, American Arts and Crafts followers emphasized aesthetics far more than economic relations, believing that society would undergo a spiritual and social rejuvenation by making beautiful things.[7]

As in England, domestic architecture in the United States provided a natural medium for the application of Arts and Crafts ideology. Inspired by the movement, architects began to reject Victorian eclecticism and classicism and to search for an appropriate architecture rooted in the American vernacular environment. In Chicago after 1901, Frank Lloyd Wright and his disciples most famously reinterpreted Arts and Crafts ideals in Prairie school houses. In California, Henry and Charles Greene joined Morris's design principles with Asian-influenced building techniques to create the so-called ultimate bungalow. But without Gustav Stickley, Arts and Crafts-inspired architecture might have remained limited to the wealthy patrons of these few architects. Enamored with English Arts and Crafts and caught in the era's progressive impulse, Stickley turned from furniture design to recreating the home. In 1901, he began publishing *The Craftsman,* a magazine that not only disseminated the movement's ideals but also promoted his idea of a Craftsman house: simple homes for democratic families, situated close to nature and uniting art and life. Under Stickley's profound influence, the domestic architecture created using Arts and Crafts principles became known as Craftsman architecture. Eventually blending the popular bungalow form with Arts and Crafts design, *The*

Craftsman and other popular magazines like *House Beautiful* spread a new Craftsman architecture to the growing middle class of America.[8]

Seattle joined the devotion to Arts and Crafts early on. In the late 1890s, Finn Haakon Frolich, a Norwegian sculptor, founded Seattle's Arts and Craft chapter, the Beaux Arts Society (or Society of Beaux Arts). The name apparently derived from Paris' prestigious École des Beaux-Arts, where Frolich had studied under the famous American sculptor Augustus St. Gaudens. The society centered on the design school, the Beaux Arts Workshop, that Frolich created soon after his arrival in Seattle in 1898. Frolich's school probably operated on the École des Beaux-Arts' model of student participation in an atelier, or studio, supervised by a design professor. By the early twentieth century, the Frolich academy offered "instruction in all branches of artistic endeavor" with ten instructors of "marked ability" teaching "Modeling, Painting, Illustrating, Cartooning, Architecture, Wood-carving, [and] Metal-work."[9] Frolich's school for art fulfilled the Arts and Crafts emphasis on education. If art was to restore society, people—especially children—needed instruction in traditional crafts. Students would learn the joy and dignity of honest work while imbibing Arts and Crafts design principles.[10]

Like most American Arts and Crafts advocates, Beaux Arts Society members emphasized aesthetics, at best only weakly embracing the socialism of William Morris. While glorifying the craftsman, the group sought more to reform artistic taste and encourage personal self-development than to replace industrial capitalism. "Our Aim," a promotional brochure proclaimed, is "to awaken our people of the West to the great beauties and grandeur of our wonderful country and assist in developing their finer senses into perceiving, enjoying and appreciating that which nature has given us." The society hoped "to make an artist of the artisan," watering down Morris's ideal to produce only "a good workman and thereby a useful member of Society." Indeed, the workshop put forth an explicitly capitalistic argument to show the importance of the handicraft revival. "Aesthetic training is one of the most important agents in our industrial welfare," an early brochure contended. Because American production lacked "those finer forms of manufactured articles wherein the skill and the taste of the artisan have served to multiply many times over the value of the raw material employed," Americans were obligated to import foreign goods. If skilled craftsmen were "trained to higher artistic skill," the United States could save "ENORMOUS SUMS WHICH NOW FLOW TO FOREIGN MARKETS."[11]

This conservatism reflected the constituency of the Beaux Arts Society. Mostly middle-class professionals and well-to-do people created the group and formed its membership. Promotional material emphasized that successful, "practical straightforward businessmen" controlled the school. Indeed, commercial artists Alfred T. Renfro and Frank Calvert were instrumental in establishing both the club and school. Originally from Alabama, Renfro gained notoriety for his political caricatures while working for various Seattle newspapers. Raised in Seattle, Calvert studied commercial art while attending the National Academy of Design in New York City. Upon his return to Seattle, he joined the art staff of the *Seattle Times*. Similarly, the workshop's students were not independent artisans living off their talents and remaining outside the capitalist economy. Indeed, the group opened membership to all those who held "a love for the finer things," and included "a large number of wealthy and enthusiastic residents."[12]

With such well-heeled backing, Frolich soon envisioned a much more grandiose future for the Beaux Arts Society: its own full-fledged academy. In 1908, Frolich, Renfro, and Calvert incorporated the Western Academy of Beaux Arts (WABA) with the purpose of building a school for the fine arts, "such as painting, engraving, sculpture and architecture." Apparently Frolich saw his venture becoming America's West Coast equivalent of the École des Beaux Arts. But, unlike the French institute, Frolich imagined WABA as "a greater school of Arts and Crafts, such as was founded in the '70s by Burne-Jones, William Morris, Rossetti and the other Pre-Raphaelites." In true American Arts and Crafts fashion, the society's founders formed a business arm, the former Beaux Arts Workshop, and sought funding from "certain Western financiers."[13]

Had the Beaux Arts Society fulfilled its dream of opening an academy, it would have remained virtually indistinguishable from the nation's hundreds of design schools and vocational training programs inspired by the Arts and Crafts movement. But in 1909, circumstances transformed the group's purpose: rather than merely opening a school, the group would form a true community. Forced to move from its downtown location, the society decided it needed "a community of Artists and Craftsmen and other kindred tastes where the surroundings shall be in harmony with their work." As Seattle metamorphosed from a small town into a major West Coast city, uprooted souls of like mind would congregate together, apart from the degraded, teeming, artistically insensitive masses, and so revitalize society through their example. Only a "natural" site—wooded, undeveloped, and far removed from the city's smoky squalor—would do for such an artistic commune. To this end, Calvert obtained a $16,500 mortgage on fifty acres of dense cedar and fir across Lake Washington from Seattle. The Beaux Arts Society thus distanced itself from the increasingly heterogeneous city and sought to create a sense of belonging among kindred spirits.[14]

Undoubtedly, the Beaux Arts Society's communitarian impulse drew inspiration from both the English Arts and Crafts precedent and the American history of utopian ventures. For instance, as a socialist, William Morris intended his workshops to operate as cooperative fellowships of equal workers. Creating the Guild of Handicraft in 1888, Morris's colleague C. R. Ashbee brought together journeymen from London and relocated them to the country. In a close, integrated community, these workers were to find artistic fulfillment within a harmonious, pastoral setting. Because he traveled widely in the United States and established important connections between the English and American movements, Ashbee transmitted his ideas to American adherents. The Arts and Crafts idea of creating removed, self-contained communities of craftsmen dovetailed with a well-established American predilection for utopian communities. Across the nation, charismatic visionaries such as Elbert Hubbard in Roycroft and Will Price in Rose Valley, and lesser-known leaders like Frank Calvert, set up colonies of artists.[15]

The desire for community, however, warred with deeply held principles of individualism and private property, a tension that permeated Arts and Crafts communal ventures. From the outset, these competing pressures appeared in Beaux Arts Village, undergirding the village layout. Calvert clearly envisioned a community centered on an artistic purpose (fig. 2.2). At the village heart, he reserved ten acres for the academy workshop grounds and called it Atelier Square. Shaped like the five-sided outline of a gabled house, the "square" conformed to the venture's bungalow logo. There Calvert planned to establish the school buildings, a club house of "unique design, . . . [where] all the entertainments of the Society will be held," summer camp buildings for students, and recreational grounds for tennis and outdoor bowling. Calvert thoughtfully kept the 1,100-foot strip of breathtakingly beautiful waterfront as "the Commons," for use by all Beaux Arts residents. The Commons and all of

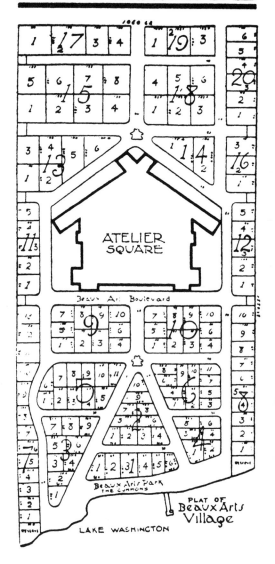

2.2 This map of Beaux Arts Village from a circa 1908–9 promotional brochure demonstrates its founders' vision of creating an Arts and Crafts community. University of Washington, Special Collections.

the rather narrow streets he deeded to the WABA. Later, he transferred all twenty blocks surrounding Atelier Square to the academy as well. But Calvert and the Beaux Arts Society still had to satisfy a large mortgage. They surveyed and platted lots ranging in size from about 60 x 100 feet to 100 x 125 feet and sold them to

2.3 *Alfred Renfro's 1913 Craftsman house in Beaux Arts Village, nestled into the wooded site. Photo:* Bungalow Magazine, *Seattle Public Library.*

prospective home builders. These lots faced a grid system of streets around Atelier Square. Calling them "all natural roadways," an early promotional brochure implied that the streets fit into the landscape, when in actuality their rational division allowed easy and efficient sale as subdivision lots. Atelier Square, the focal point for the entire venture, however, remained in Calvert's personal possession rather than as communal property.[16]

Calvert's conflict with the desire for community within a capitalistic economy was typical of Arts and Crafts communities that sprang up in the United States between 1900 and 1915. Although loosely following William Morris's English example, such communitarianism as Elbert Hubbard's Roycroft blended an antimodern rhetoric with a practical adaptation to capitalism. Instead of providing a clear alternative to industrial capitalism, as Morris originally envisioned, Arts and Crafts communities like Beaux Arts Village provided a way for middle-class Americans to both critique and accommodate early twentieth-century corporate capitalism.[17]

This tension between the rejection and acceptance of industrialization and its values was nowhere more apparent than in the twenty dwellings erected at Beaux Arts Village between 1909 and 1919. Set in a verdant forest near Lake Washington's crystalline waters, the houses expressed Craftsman styling, meant to convey the Arts and Crafts ideology of Gustav Stickley.[18] Overtly, their architectural symbolism harkened back to a simpler, pre-industrial time, before machines and factories had degraded the quality and beauty of homes. Yet, as we shall see, industrial values permeated the structures' designs.

One house in Beaux Arts Village (fig. 2.3), especially, stood as the ideal Craftsman home, articulating outwardly the anti-industrial concepts of the Arts and Crafts movement. Alfred Renfro began building the house in 1909, to manifest the Arts and Crafts fundamentals he had imbibed as an early participant in Frolich's atelier. In fact, he hoped to recreate physically the society's logo (fig. 2.4), which the group described

2.4 *The Beaux Arts Village logo reinforced the centrality of home building to Arts and Crafts communities. Appropriate homes were to replicate the rusticity and naturalness of the logo. University of Washington, Special Collections.*

as "the Beaux Arts cottage, a true arts and crafts bungalow, partly constructed of logs. It is a refinement of the pioneer cabin of the West, and emblematic of the 'home.'"[19] For Arts and Craftsmen, log cabins represented a truly American folk form, democratic, simple, and hand-built. Stickley featured them regularly in *The Craftsman* and built his own log clubhouse on Craftsman Farms in Parsippany, New Jersey. Following Stickley's lead, Renfro was eager to undertake the close personal involvement required in Craftsman architectural ideology. In 1913 he wrote, "Even before the purchase price was paid and the water plant put in, I began constructing the house." Renfro saw himself as an artist and craftsman finding joy in his house building by uniting his own labor with thoughtful design.[20]

True Craftsman homes like Renfro's expressed a conscious symbolism that separated them from all that seemed industrial and therefore artificial. This invariably meant that such houses should be "simple," "honest," and "natural," terms that reformers used repeatedly to distinguish Craftsman dwellings from seemingly mass-produced, complicated Victorian structures. In shape, Renfro's house was a simple rectangle with few interior divisions. Its construction was, as he termed it, "simple, substantial, honest." A rustic naturalness made Craftsman homes genuine and authentic. "In every detail," Stickley asserted, "the Craftsman house is an harmonious unit with its environment." "Harmony between

2.5 *Alfred Renfro's Beaux Arts Village house as it appeared in 1913. The large, open porch helped merge the family and nature, and provided a transitional space into the home, August 1913. Photo: Bungalow Magazine, Seattle Public Library.*

the house and its surroundings," a Craftsman mantra, meant a rural, camp-like appearance, as advocates never considered that the "environment" might be urban.[21] Renfro and his wife specifically selected Beaux Arts Village because "its beauty and primitiveness appealed to us." During construction, he allowed the removal of trees only directly within the foundation boundaries. He ultimately chose frame, not log, construction, but still "wanted a house made of timbers. It must be rough appearing material to fit the location, but the lumber itself must be the very best." Workers applied boards of rough fir to the exterior, later applying battens over the joints after the lumber had shrunk. Rather than painting the siding, they allowed the wood to weather before staining it a "rich, natured brown" with a mixture of creosote and oil.[22]

The ubiquitous Craftsman porch (fig. 2.5) manifested the overriding need to connect with "Nature," the antithesis of the industrial city.[23] Renfro's porch stretched full-length across the house, under a ponderous gable roof. It gave the family a sense of privacy and seclusion from the larger community, while allowing users to enjoy the outdoors. This direct contact with nature was a necessity for the Renfros. "The birds, squirrels and chipmunks are all welcome inside the house or outside," Renfro said in 1913.

We feed them and they can help themselves to anything we have. They were here first. They come into the house, and build their nests around it, and we are all friends. We have tried to live on peaceful terms with Nature, as her guests and disciples, rather than masters or innovators. We try hard not to molest her plans in any way, or mar her work by cutting down, digging up, or attempting to re-create artificially after our own ideas. The trees, shrubs and ferns grow just about as she placed them, and we only help as servants. Our motto, "Sine Cera," has been used out of doors as well as in the construction of the house.[24]

In a changing world fraught with turmoil, Renfro built for permanence. "We wanted stability," he said. "We had lived in enough flimsy houses."[25] His massive-looking house reflected this. Solid fourteen-inch-square posts supported the broad gable roof over the porch. When asked "Why the heavy construction?" he explained it in terms of aesthetics and protection from nature:

If one of the towering firs, which surround and guard us from the wind and rain of winter, should be swept over in defeat while battling with the elements, and fall crashing on our little home, then the heavy timbers would do their part in breaking the fall. Besides, we like the look and feel of heavy, massive timbers, and believe it has a good influence on the children.[26]

But Renfro sought protection from more than nature's hostile force. His house established a bulwark against the perceived instability and restlessness of an increasingly mobile society. As Stickley advocated, Craftsman houses created places "to last for generations, beautiful enough, comfortable enough and strong enough for grandchildren to inherit with delight and profit, homes such as our pioneer forefathers built, such as the English yeomen built."[27]

The reference to English farmers was deliberate and significant. Outwardly, Beaux Arts houses like Renfro's signaled their owners' desires to return to the supposed simplicity and unity of a premodern past. But that past looked decidedly Northern European. For instance, Renfro mortised together the verge boards of his gable ends so that the ends protruded "Norske fashioned" (fig. 2.4). This became a prominent physical feature of the Beaux Arts Society's emblem.[28] Renfro's neighbors constructed even more explicitly Northern European or Anglo-Saxon houses. Frank Calvert's 1912 "Swiss Chalet" (fig. 2.6) featured crossed verge boards, a second story, a balcony entrance, and stained siding, laid "in log house fashion with butts projecting beyond the corners."[29] In 1911, James Ditty used a pointedly English style (fig. 2.7). Rather than stained wood siding, Ditty sheathed his lower story in brick veneer and cobblestones and his upper story in light-colored stucco and false half-timbering, resulting in

2.6 *Frank Calvert's 1912 Swiss chalet-like bungalow in Beaux Arts Village closely approximated the Beaux Arts Village logo, July 1913. Photo:* Bungalow Magazine, *Seattle Public Library.*

a Tudor-styled bungalow. The visual message of these exteriors affirmed clearly that the only past worth returning to was Anglo-Saxon. And that past now belonged to the most modern people in society, the professional middle class. This group architecturally reasserted its cultural dominance in the face of massive southern and central European immigration, peoples from truly premodern societies.[30]

Such a concertedly Northern European heritage formed the basis for what Craftsman advocates saw as a new, truly American style of architecture that Stickley wrote should reflect "our character as a people." A substantial part of this "character" was "good citizenship" that only Craftsman homes could impart to children. As Renfro inferred, his substantial Craftsman house crucially shaped his children's character. Through such a good home, he would foster American democrats, "true citizens," in Stickley's words. Rental housing such as Renfro and his wife had lived in earlier could not "fulfill the function of a home," as it threatened the upbringing of children, who would become "criminals and perverts" without homes. Only single-family, middle-class Craftsman houses conveyed democracy. Forced to live in rented tenement rooms, families

2.7 *Using Tudor detailing, James Ditty erected this Beaux Arts Village bungalow in 1911. Through such styling, Ditty metaphorically linked himself with a romanticized Anglo-Saxon, premodern past, 1939. Photo: Puget Sound Regional Archives.*

of immigrants, workers, and the poor could never cultivate the "home instinct" and thus never become truly democratic. Nor could the wealthy, who lived in "silly, sham palaces," caught up in spiritless, meaningless luxury.[31]

Craftsmen such as Renfro and Stickley reinvented their houses to nurture families that would produce such American democrats. Their goals of "honesty," "naturalness," "simplicity," and "harmony" referred both to the architecture and the new family ideal. Renfro's house plan (fig. 2.8) featured all necessary rooms grouped on the first floor. A large, unpartitioned living room that took up the full front of the house dominated the layout. Renfro gave "a great deal of attention" to the living room, as he agreed with Stickley that here "the business of home life may be carried on freely and with pleasure." The living room openly and "honestly" contained the various functions of the family, including the man's leisurely activities, family recreation, children's play, and even visually incorporated dining, as the family ate at one end of the cedar-paneled living room. Such a centralized, flexible space ensured family togetherness and thus social stability.[32]

Renfro prided himself on his family's informality, as reflected in his house. No formal parlor reserved only for visitors sequestered callers. Instead, the spacious living room (fig. 2.9) immediately pulled them into the bosom of the family, where they received the warmth and friendliness of a true home environment.

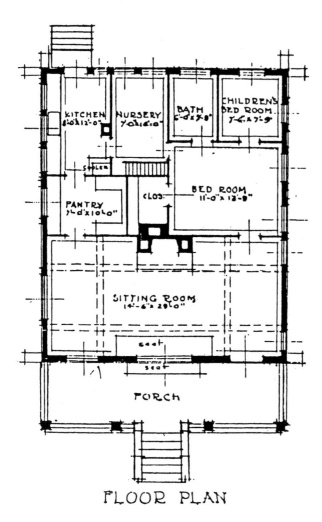

KITCHEN
8'-0"x12'-0"

NURSERY
7'-0"x16'-0"

BATH
5'-0"x7'-8"

CHILDRENS
BED ROOM
7'-6"x7'-9"

SHELVES

PANTRY
7'-6"x10'-0"

CLOS.

BED ROOM
11'-0"x13'-9"

SITTING ROOM
14'-6"x29'-0"

SEAT

SEAT

PORCH

FLOOR PLAN

2.8 First-floor plan of the Alfred Renfro house. The living room, opening seamlessly into the dining area, dominated the main floor of bungalows like Renfro's. Craftsman architectural advocates believed such integrated internal spaces allowed for harmonious family life, August 1913. Bungalow Magazine, Seattle Public Library.

The dining area, especially, radiated hospitality and "good cheer" because of its association with offering repast to guests. Of course, only like-minded members of the middle class received such openness. The large porch still served as a transitional public/private space, a place for evaluating strangers before allowing them into the house. Service people entered at the rear.[33]

Placing service and personal functions in the back of Craftsman houses continued a Victorian pattern. Yet the public/private line blurred in Craftsmans such as Renfro's. Renfro deleted the usual central interior hallway and attached the master bedroom to the living room. Both the bath and children's room opened directly into the master bedroom. The nursery lay close by. Under the eaves, the upper floor contained both a children's play area and Renfro's atelier and workshop, where he conducted his artistic pursuits. Adult privacy and separation from the children did not rule his plan. Clearly, he intended family relations to be deliberately casual.[34]

2.9 Alfred Renfro's living room with its central, handbuilt fireplace. The hearth symbolized the primary importance of craftsmanship and familial warmth in Craftsman architecture, August 1913. Photo: Bungalow Magazine, *Seattle Public Library.*

The openness and informality of Renfro's interior space defined the beginnings of a modern domestic architecture. Victorian houses with "closed plans" featured clearly defined, usually single-use rooms to which occupants could carefully control access. Public rooms in the front, especially the parlor and the hall, served both to screen outsiders entering the house and to shield the private, family functions in the rear of the house. Typically, doors shut off all rooms from one another. By 1900, however, open plans, as in Renfro's bungalow, began to replace the Victorian layout. With his Prairie school houses built between 1900 and 1914, Frank Lloyd Wright employed an open plan centered on a massive hearth and claimed to have destroyed "the box." It was Wright's "major innovation . . . to design interior spaces that were not enclosed," argues architectural historian H. Allen Brooks, a "revolutionary concept [that] was one of the greatest contributions ever made to architecture."[35] Wright did not single-handedly invent the open plan. After all, colonial European Americans had lived in two-room, hall-parlor houses that centered on large hearths long before Frank Lloyd Wright. But Wright most successfully crystallized into architectural form the modern desire to integrate the realms of public and private, stranger and family, that Victorians had tried to keep distinct.[36]

The merging of spaces, of family members, and of functions in Craftsman homes might imply the rise of a familial sort of communitarianism. This was not the case. Craftsmen like Renfro and Stickley viewed such houses as reassertions of individuality in the face of a rampant industrialism that bred conformity and aesthetic homogeneity. Machine technology, they said, led to the outpouring of mass-produced items that smothered self-creative urges and individual uniqueness. When people bought and furnished houses with artificial, ready-made products, they became part of a faceless multitude. Only personal involvement in the entire construction process guaranteed having "an actual home which expressed your own life, . . . your own thought, your own effort to it." Here was the essence of the Craftsman movement: personal rejuvenation through individual creation.[37]

Of all the physical features of Renfro's house, the fireplace epitomized self-expression through artistic endeavor. It stood literally and symbolically at the heart of the home. "We . . . often said that we were going to have a fireplace first, then build the house around it," Renfro remembered. "This was just about the way it was done." Large and unornamented, the clinker brick fireplace occupied the center of the living room wall, directly opposite a long, handmade window seat that faced the lake. The simple slab mantle Renfro himself hewed from an old cedar log taken from Lake Washington. To build the squarish, massive structure, Renfro hired "an old mason" with a good reputation, who, "like all true artists," remained unswayed by mere "monetary reward." The fireplace became the focal point of Renfro's home, acting as "a sort of rejuvenator," as Stickley phrased it. From it radiated the warmth of family and genuine hospitality. Those viewing it, whether family or guests, could not fail to perceive its rustic artistry.[38]

An artist and craftsman, Renfro conceived and constructed much of his own furniture. Such built-in features satisfied the Craftsman dictate that interiors be "substantial, unpretentious, honestly made and sparingly adorned." In a basement workshop, Renfro fashioned bookcases, two thirteen-foot window seats, cedar cabinets with hammered copper latches and drawpulls, tables, benches, and chests. For each piece, he used "real lumber . . . [which left] nothing to come unglued or fall apart." "All of the work," he said, was "open and direct," with simplicity the keynote. "Our furniture can be leaned against, sat on, stood on, and one feels that it is not going to break or be marred." Renfro believed that true beauty arose from utilizing honest, handwrought, "authentic" materials in a straightforward, functional way. Like his houses, Renfro's furniture bespoke an anti-industrialism, a desire to return to a supposedly simpler, more unified premodern past.[39]

By building his artful, naturalistic hideaway in Beaux Arts Village, Renfro metaphorically drew a line in the sand: beyond this point, he seemed to announce, no insidious influence of corporate capitalism shall pass. But this was only rhetorical, for on another level Craftsman houses like his wholeheartedly embraced values emanating directly from the corporate world. Designers took the principles meant to organize and direct factory work—efficiency, management, planning, standardization, and functionalism—and applied them to dwellings. Craftsman homes, in other words, became domestic factories. As such, they represented the Second Industrial Revolution as much as critiqued it. This contradiction between pastoral symbolism and technological functionalism would characterize houses throughout the twentieth century, underscoring the Craftsman house's position as the first truly modern domestic architectural style.

That bungalows and factories would share a common set of design principles was inevitable, as they emerged from the same architectural context. Not coincidentally, corporate executives began to rationalize their facilities at the same time that housing reformers were reconceptualizing the home. Both movements determined to build structures appropriate for the changing functions occurring within them, and both movements succeeded in creating dramatically new spaces.

After 1900, to compete more effectively, many large-scale businesses applied the principle of efficiency to their workplaces. Greater efficiency, administrators believed, resulted from more scientific management of the overall production process. The idea was to cut out all waste—wasted material, wasted time, and wasted effort—through standardization and central control. Even the factory building itself became an efficient machine. Between 1900 and 1920, engineers began designing their plants to fit the building's function within the production process. They first reorganized the factory layout based on the principle of smooth flow of materials. They rearranged spaces to facilitate the quickest movement of goods and exert maximum control over workers. Use of concrete and steel—new and very modern materials—allowed partitionless interiors and placement of very large windows in the walls. Sunlight and air through these windows improved working conditions and thus the efficiency of workers. As much as possible, engineers mechanized production, grouping machines by function and relying increasingly on electrification to run them. This impetus resulted in a new type of "rational" factory: expansive, single-story, rectangular structures with vast, uninterrupted, interior spaces.[40]

Factory design principles seeped into domestic reform, most obviously through the burgeoning home-economics movement, but Arts and Crafts proponents also furthered the reconception of the home as a rational machine. Stickley himself called for "a radical change in the existing administration of the home." "There really is no sense," he said, "in making the home the one exception to all the industries and institutions that benefit from modern improved conditions. . . . The work of housekeeping may be carried on with no more waste of time, energy, or money than is involved in the conduct of any other well-managed business."[41] To operate like a business, reformers agreed that the home's physical structure needed transformation. Smaller, simply shaped, unelaborated bungalows with an open, flexible plan became models of efficiency and functionalism. Here, industrial principles coincided with the Craftsman architectural philosophy.[42]

The Craftsman homes in Beaux Arts Village clearly displayed this convergence. The houses invariably used simple, rectangular plans under a single gable roof. Most had all of their rooms on a single floor, although larger dwellings, like Renfro's, sometimes had secondary rooms under the roof. This layout was economical in cost and effort. Less square footage meant cheaper construction and fewer steps to complete tasks within the home. Designers put formerly "wasted" spaces to work, placing closets under stairs and building furniture into the house whenever possible. Such "convenient" features saved money and labor, allowing ease of cleaning and moving while making the most of overall diminished space. So while Renfro's "authentic," hand-built window seat embodied the craftsman's art, it also represented the contradictory industrial principle of economizing labor.[43]

To keep their occupants happy and healthy, advocates for both the Craftsman home and the rational factory called for large expanses of windows. By 1910, industrialists intent on more efficient production began constructing "daylight factories," industrial buildings with walls of multipaned windows designed to improve working conditions. Part of the industrial welfare movement, facilities with plenty of sunlight and air would attract and keep better workers, or so enlightened corporate leaders supposed. This strain of thought also pervaded early twentieth-century social-hygiene movements, including domestic reform. Better, and healthier, living conditions resulted from plenty of sunlight and air. If such wholesome environments could revitalize the poor and unhealthy, so too could they resuscitate the stultifying interiors of homes. But not just any air would do. Sunshine and ventilation had to come from the "outdoors," not from crowded, dirty urban streets.[44]

Housing designers thus wholeheartedly adopted the "daylight factory" principle. Early twentieth-century homes contained numerous, large windows, often grouped together, to give "the greatest amount possible of sunshine and air in the farthest nooks and corners." Alfred Renfro's house included such big windows facing scenic Lake Washington. In his Beaux Arts home, L. P. Tolman installed south-facing windows in groups of three so that "the lighting of each room [was] very good." Although windows satisfied the Craftsman call for integration with nature, the result was a domestic architecture that simulated the look of factories.[45]

Whenever possible, Beaux Arts Villagers incorporated the latest technological systems into their nominally preindustrial homes. As engineers had done in factories, Village builders installed new technology to make their homes efficient as well as comfortable. The most important innovation was electricity. A wired house greatly reduced household drudgery and most Seattle residents did not consider a new home "modern" unless it contained at least electric lighting. In 1916, electricity came to Beaux Arts Village at the eager request of its residents. James Ditty, who "considered himself an artist and craftsman," wired his Beaux Arts Village Craftsman home for electricity in 1911, even before electrical lines had arrived. The convenience of electricity allowed him and his family to live apart from the city in comfort.[46]

Next to electric lighting, Beaux Arts residents wanted advanced heating systems. Like most new houses, the home of engineer Clancey M. Lewis utilized a coal-fired furnace that heated the house by warming either air or water that ducts conveyed to radiators. A one-story dwelling with an open floor plan perfectly suited this type of heating. Individual stoves or fireplaces in separate rooms became unnecessary. A heating source concealed in the basement supplied evenly distributed warmth to the house's entire first floor. But Craftsman proponents carefully screened these technical systems behind overweening symbols of preindustrialism. Massive fireplaces dominated the front living spaces, yet provided little heat. The actual warmth emanated from discreetly located, unobtrusive floor registers or radiators.[47]

By the 1920s, a web of modern networks enmeshed Beaux Arts Village. Most Americans, Beaux Arts Villagers included, demanded and received the "convenience" of electric lighting, telephones, hot and cold running water, sewer or septic connections, and, in some cases, gas for cooking and lighting. Ironically, while the Craftsman architecture declared their independence from industrial capitalism, these rustic, naturalistic homes depended more than ever on advanced technologies developed and delivered from the industrial world. These same systems allowed Craftsmen like the Beaux Arts Villagers to distance themselves from the unsavory byproducts such systems produced.[48]

As redesigned factories provided a model for domestic reform, so too did newly reconceptualized hospitals. With the discovery of bacteria as the cause of disease came new standards of cleanliness. The need for an antiseptic environment led to a streamlining of interior surfaces. Inevitably, the value of sanitation moved into homes, exactly coinciding with the Arts and Crafts demand for simpler, more rational houses. To ensure family vitality, the physical structure of the house itself needed to eliminate all possible sites for disease-causing "germs." So progressive home owners banished the Victorian carpets, heavily draped interiors, elaborately tufted furniture, and ornately detailed moldings. None of the Beaux Arts Village homes featured in the 1913 *Bungalow Magazine* articles, for instance, contained carpeted interiors. Instead, area rugs with oriental or Native American motifs lay strewn on smooth, easily cleaned hardwood floors.[49]

Although reformers applied the principles of efficiency, technology, and sanitation to the entire house, they concentrated on the kitchen. As the home's primary workplace, it logically benefited most from factory-derived design. "The kitchen today," declared a *Bungalow Magazine* writer in 1915, "is the workshop of the housekeeper, managed on as hygienic, sanitary and economic a basis as the most modern hospital laboratory. Convenience, cleanliness, and ventilation are paramount."[50]

Reconceptualized as a "workshop," the modern kitchen encouraged a more productive, healthier worker. To save labor through eliminating wasted motion, modern kitchens became smaller and more compact than Victorian kitchens. In Beaux Arts Village, for example, Renfro's kitchen was eight by twelve feet, and Clancey Lewis's kitchen was only eight feet square. These efficient rooms often lacked the large, adjacent pantries of their Victorian predecessors. This required both an orderly arrangement of tools and built-in, space-saving features. Clancey Lewis's kitchen contained "plenty of built-in shelves, bins, etc." for storing commodities such as flour and sugar, compartments for pots and pans near the range, glass-doored cupboards, and drawers for linen, cutlery, and utensils. With no place for furniture, Lewis's tiny kitchen needed an adjoining breakfast room, where a "home-made fir table" rolled in and out of a recess. A nearby closet stored three folding chairs for use at the table. Not only efficient and flexible in use, Lewis's kitchen also conformed to industry's standard of smooth production flow through elimination of clutter.[51]

Like the industrial welfare movement, domestic reforms sought to keep housewives satisfied and productive by providing comfortable workplaces. Therefore, admission of light and air into kitchens became crucial. Housing experts recommended sunny kitchens with numerous windows to expel odors and to stimulate workers with fresh air. Beaux Arts Village builders invariably placed their kitchen sinks under a window. Renfro went even further, extending windows "entirely across the north and east sides" of his corner kitchen. Obviously quite concerned with air circulation, Renfro also included a somewhat unusual feature in his kitchen—a "cooler." Located on an inside wall, it drew fresh air into the room through a large pipe at its lower end. A "flue or vent" between the kitchen and second floor then sucked heated air out of the kitchen. This arrangement facilitated air circulation and dispelled cooking odors in the small room. Instead of toiling within a hot, stuffy room, housewives like Mrs. Renfro theoretically labored more efficiently and happily in bright, airy kitchens.[52]

New health standards derived from industrial laboratories demanded spotlessly clean, sanitary kitchens. Streamlined interiors, smooth surfaces, and new wall and floor materials, such as concrete, tile, and linoleum, helped maintain this level of cleanliness. White became the symbol of clinical purity. So, although Renfro carefully waxed his interior woodwork, leaving it unstained and unpainted to show its natural beauty, he painted the kitchen, pantry, and bathroom in enameled white. Overall, a Craftsman home might project rusticity, but its kitchen was a model of immaculate sterility.[53]

As main production areas, kitchens consolidated the technical systems that defined modern homes. At a minimum, a modern kitchen needed electrical lights, hot and cold running water, a sink and drain, a cooler for food, and a gas (or combination gas and coal) range. Clancey Lewis's kitchen was a good example. Before electricity arrived in Beaux Arts Village in 1916, he installed a gasoline-powered gas-generating plant in his basement. It fueled the two-burner gas plate that stood beside his coal range, and the gas lights in every room. Hot and cold water ran throughout the house and into a septic tank or (if laundry water) into a sump. In Craftsman homes, the kitchen served as a central locus of technology, indeed, functioning as the manufactory within a dwelling.[54]

Along with the kitchen, the early twentieth-century houses contained another thoroughly modern space: the bathroom. Unlike in the kitchen, however, the past offered little precedent for its design. Until the late nineteenth century, the average house rarely included a full bathroom. By about 1900, however, improved plumbing and manufacturing technology allowed for relatively easy installation of fixtures. This, and customer demand, ensured that designers placed a bathroom within the bungalow plan. Like the kitchen, this room expressed a sanitary aesthetic.[55]

Although Beaux Arts Village founders such as Alfred Renfro called for a return to nature, when nature called, they insisted on the latest sanitary technology. Community bylaws in 1909 required that all houses must have a "proper and adequate sanitary system of sewerage to be approved by the Park Board." The rules forbade permanent outhouses. Instead, a septic tank or cesspool serviced each residence. Within Beaux Arts bungalows, designers sized bathrooms smaller and located them at the rear, near the kitchen. Alfred Renfro's and L. P. Tolman's bathrooms, for instance, only measured about six by eight feet. Typically, they featured three white porcelain fixtures—a clawfoot tub, toilet, and basin—all arranged to economize space. Bigger, more elaborate residences, such as those of Lewis and Calvert, included an additional half-bath with toilet and sink. The convenience of these multiple bathrooms anticipated later twentieth-century homes in which two or more bathrooms became common.[56]

The Craftsman rhetoric of naturalness excluded bathrooms and kitchens.

In fact, such spaces contradicted the overall ideology by adhering to values of laboratory-like, antiseptic design. The Craftsman requirement of "authentic," "natural" exposed wood, for instance, had no place in bathrooms. Reformers rejected as "unsanitary" the nineteenth-century practice of wooden toilet seats, toilet tanks, and sink cabinets. After all, such an organic material could not withstand the repeated scrubbings required under the new standards of cleanliness. Instead, plumbers left metal pipes "open" (exposed with no covering) below spotlessly white porcelain sinks. Smooth tile floors and walls provided easy-to-clean surfaces. Frank Calvert went one step further in his bathroom. He lined its walls and floor with "thick cement" (apparently a form of interior stucco) over waterproofed metal lath. Household workers could literally hose it clean. In early twentieth-century bathrooms, white porcelain and white enamel paint, such as Renfro used, suggested a germless environment and starkly revealed any deviation from the ideal of hospital-like purity.[57]

Ensconced within their rustic exteriors, these industrialized, technological, factory-like spaces—kitchens and bathrooms—remained the domain of women. If the house was a machine, the kitchen supplied the drive, the "motive power" behind it, and from this room the woman as "domestic engineer" directed the flow of production—food and family—and managed the home's operation. No longer did feminine spaces connote the organic and sacred, as characterized Victorian homes. In bungalows, they symbolized the technological and mechanical.[58]

Conversely, bungalow rooms devoted to hospitality and leisure became masculine spaces. Gone were the Victorians' parlors, where women reigned and feminine symbols prevailed. Instead, large, central living rooms opening directly into dining rooms, and especially dens, emanated a manly aesthetic. Dark stained-wood paneling, hard angular surfaces, and subdued earthy colors brought characteristics of the outside, traditionally a male realm, into the room. Sometimes emblems of masculine prowess adorned the walls: stuffed animals, athletic equipment, sport pennants, and smoking paraphernalia. The rustic ambience suggested a men's club or lodge. Arts and Crafts believers banished frilly curtains, plump tufted furniture dripping with antimacassars, and soft, enveloping carpets from the living room. For example, Renfro's starkly furnished living room centered on an unornamented rough-textured fireplace and heavy, dark Mission furniture. No curvaceous, overstuffed upholstery, tasseled draperies, or lacy daintiness marred its plain, rather hard simplicity. Instead of Renfro's wife presiding over a formal parlor, Renfro himself dispensed the family's hospitality in a space exhibiting a masculine presence. He did so in front of the hearth, once considered the feminine "heart" of a home, but by 1910 largely a decorative feature anchoring a male domesticity. In Craftsman homes, the rooms considered most organic and natural were those with the most masculine qualities.[59]

Thus, the tension between the acceptance and the rejection of industrial values prevalent in early twentieth-century homes took a gendered form. Middle-class men returned to domesticity in Craftsman homes, which served as retreats from the turmoil, bureaucracy, and potential loss of power accompanying industrialization. Yet, for women, the home as domestic factory represented an extension of industrial values, an invasion of the world of work in their own kitchens and bathrooms. In subtle ways, women became imbued with the corporate values of efficiency and technology before entering the public world. The bungalow, then, helped both men and women accommodate to the Second Industrial Revolution; it offered succor to men while preparing women for a new position within the economy.[60]

The Craftsman bungalow paradox presented no dilemma or contradiction to Arts and Crafts enthusiasts such as Orrill Stapp and Alfred Renfro. Indeed, the house's very appeal rested on its ambivalence. This architecture attracted a new social group that was itself a product of the Second Industrial Revolution: the "new" professional, managerial middle class. Such people straddled a period of particularly rapid change, one foot confidently stepping forward into a new technological era, the other still reluctant to move completely from the small-town world of the nineteenth century. This class stood at a unique point of transition. While actively catalyzing change, they simultaneously lamented the passing of the world they had so fully participated in transforming. The moment would not last. Gradually, the middle class let go of its attempts to return to a pre-industrial past and, although nostalgic, accepted the modern world. Craftsman homes reflected their new outlook and helped them bridge a crucial era.[61]

This middle class arose just as the United States economy entered a new phase of corporate consolidation. As both business and government expanded after 1900, they demanded scientifically trained professionals and managers for their growing bureaucracies. As a result, a distinct class emerged, consisting of salaried managers, college-educated professionals, and white-collared office personnel. Working within large, increasingly complex organizations, these people embraced the rational ideals of order, management, and efficiency. Yet many members of the "new" middle class yearned for a sense of permanency and rootedness, which their material environments could suggest by employing distinctly pastoral designs. Further, the added pressures of functioning within the tumultuous economic and social milieu impelled managers and professionals to seek rejuvenation in nature. Craftsman homes, which embodied all these apparently conflicting impulses, most directly answered the needs of these Americans.[62]

It comes as no surprise, then, that the 1920 residents of Beaux Arts Village's charming bungalows came from this new class. In the twenty or so distinctly Craftsman or cabin-like houses lived seven families with household heads or sons who worked as salaried employees in business offices as salesmen, accountants, stenographers, or managers. Another five residents held professional occupations: two were architects, two civil engineers, and one a chemist. Four others worked in crafts associated with newspapers, as printers, photographic engravers, or commercial artists. Two ran businesses directly tied to a new service economy—a real estate brokerage and an advertising agency. Only two men associated with Beaux Arts Village were in any way skilled workers. Even several Beaux Arts women had professional or business training. One woman earned a degree in architecture, and two others (one of them married) commuted to jobs as stenographers. Not only were they solidly middle class, Beaux Arts families participated directly in fields enhanced by a burgeoning consumer and organizational economy. Thus, Beaux Arts Villagers felt the twin pressures of meeting the demands of a rapidly changing economy while also seeking solace from it in their isolated, rustic havens.[63]

Harkening back to a vaguely Anglo-European architecture seemed natural for Beaux Arts families of the professional middle class. All descended from European American, English, or Northern European backgrounds. In the twenty-three families associated with the village in the 1920 census, twenty-one men were born in the United States. Four naturalized citizens, two men and two women, originated in England and Canada. The fourteen remaining (all wives) were all native-born of American parentage or had an immigrant parent from Scandinavia, Canada, or England. Only one man of an ethnic minority (a Japanese truck farmer) lived in the census precinct, but apparently he did not reside within the village. He would not have fit in. Beaux Arts succored a special group, ethnically and economically homogenous, which, like the Craftsman bungalow itself, simultaneously benefited from and rejected the Second Industrial Revolution.[64]

One Beaux Arts villager, in particular, embodied all the tensions of the new professional middle class and its Craftsman architecture. Mixing the modern with the ancient, Clancey Lewis (fig. 2.10) erected an unusual Chinese-style, concrete-stuccoed bungalow in Beaux Arts in 1910 (fig. 2.11). To Lewis, the melding of the venerable and the modern did not seem contradictory; it epitomized perfectly his personal experience and the mindset of a trained professional in the early twentieth century.[65]

As a mining engineer, Lewis belonged to the quintessential occupation among the new middle class. In addition, he received his degree in 1899 from the Massachusetts Institute of Technology, one of the nation's foremost schools of scientific, professional training. There, Lewis encountered the latest ideas about organization, technology, and management. Later, he specialized in the research and promotion of Portland cement, a new artificial material with exciting potential for the construction industry. When he went to build a home for his family, Lewis incorporated all of the features of a "modern" dwelling (fig. 2.12). Instead of wood siding, which Craftsman adherents like Renfro considered

2.10 *A professional engineer,*
Clancey Lewis incorporated
both modern technology and
ancient symbolism in his
Beaux Arts Village home.
Photo: Frank Calvert, ed.,
The Cartoon: A Refer-
ence Book of Seattle's
Successful Men, *1911.*

2.11 *Clancey Lewis's 1910 bungalow in Beaux Arts Village featured a vaguely Chinese-inspired roof, while its walls*
consisted of the latest in Portland cement stucco, July 1913. Photo: Bungalow Magazine, Seattle Public Library.

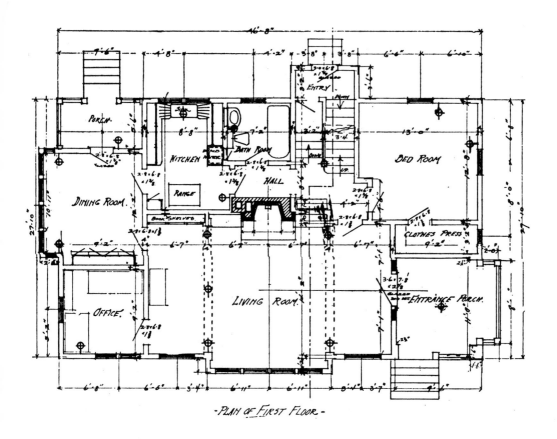

2.12 *The first floor plan of Clancey Lewis's Beaux Arts Village bungalow reveals its bungalow layout, July 1913.* Bungalow Magazine, *Seattle Public Library.*

"honest," Lewis coated his house with a Portland cement stucco. Highly technological, the house had "all of the usual conveniences common to city houses," including a coal-burning Marvel hot-air furnace, a gas generator and gas lighting, a two-burner gas plate, a septic system, and a multitude of built-ins. Hot and cold running water serviced the eight-room house's one and one-half bathrooms. Lewis clearly knew about and desired the latest in domestic technology and systematization.[66]

But, as expressed in his chosen architecture, Lewis wanted more than to merely revel in technology. He also desired a house that reflected his fascination with the preindustrial, the exotic, that he had encountered during his five years in China. There, Lewis had organized and taught mining engineering and metallurgy at Canton Christian College, and later he directed south China famine relief for the U.S government. This intimate association with a culture so different from his own greatly influenced Lewis. When designing his bungalow in conjunction with architect William J. Sayward, he deliberately

2.13 *Chinese characters on the fireplace in Clancey Lewis's living room reflect his years in China, July 1913.* Photo: Bungalow Magazine, *Seattle Public Library.*

emphasized Chinese features, most prominently in a sweeping pagoda-like roof. Inside, he decorated his massive fireplace with the Chinese characters that gave the house its name, Hong Lok (fig. 2.13). According to *Bungalow Maga-zine,* "'Hong' . . . conveys to the Oriental's mind the idea of abstract desires accomplished, while 'Lok' stands for physical appetites satisfied. Thus the idea of peace, contentment, home, paradise, heaven are evolved."[67] Lewis repeated the symbols again in the living room's large rag rug. Lewis's motif captured the paradox of Craftsman living perfectly. While Arts and Crafts idealists sought a spiritual fulfillment within resplendent nature, the most advanced household technology kept them physically comfortable.[68]

Lewis himself held to apparently conflicting ideologies. As one of the first four home builders in the early, idealistic days of Beaux Arts Village, he undoubtedly believed in many of the essential Arts and Crafts tenets. Indeed, he served as a trustee for the village park board from at least 1917 to 1924, in which he took an active hand in shaping the community's future. But if his private life adhered at least indirectly to the pursuit of fulfilling labor, his public career refuted, in fact thwarted, workers' attempts to control their own workplace. After nine years as an editor with the *Pacific Builder and Engineer,* in 1915 Lewis became the secretary of the Manufacturer's Association of Washington. Chosen for his knowledge of "organization and association work," he remained with this group for the next twenty-six years. During his tenure, the Manufacturer's Association succeeded in breaking Seattle's unions. How could Lewis not have grappled with the tension between his beliefs? Perhaps he resolved the paradox by viewing it in class terms. Unionization reflected truly working-class concerns. But "craftsmanship" belonged to those who could afford it—the new professional middle class.[69]

What Lewis really struggled with, then, was his own relationship to the tremendous changes in American economy and society. For middle-class people like Lewis, Renfro, Stapp, and others, the Arts and Crafts movement created a way to point out the most disturbing aspects of corporate capitalism and to distance themselves from them. Yet, simultaneously, they promoted the very thing they fled, the new economy that benefited them so much. Such a contradiction could not have been very easy to live with. And gradually, after the heyday of Arts and Crafts enthusiasm began to dwindle, Beaux Arts founders and their national colleagues accepted the transformation and their own contributions to it. The implicit criticism became muted and softened until it faded away entirely. In this accommodation to a modern America, Craftsman communities and architecture played a crucial role.

In the beginning, craftsman communities like Beaux Arts Village that idealists organized in accordance with Morris's idea of joyful, fulfilling worker cooperatives contained a grain of "radical perception." As historians Eileen Boris and Jackson Lears have shown, for a brief time, movement leaders believed that communities based on a small-scale handicraft economy, where workers controlled their labor, could challenge the existing capitalistic system. But it ended up being only a moment pregnant with possibility, never to be fully birthed in the United States. At its heart, Beaux Arts Village and the many others like it never truly forsook capitalism. Such utopian ventures rapidly became therapeutic, middle-class retreats from the city. The Arts and Crafts impetus transformed into the pursuit of personal rejuvenation. Craftsman homes made middle managers feel good, and thus helped them cope with their bureaucratic lives.[70]

Although Beaux Arts Village visionaries dreamed of an artists' and craftsmen's community centered on a school, the momentum soon dissipated. The colony grew slowly, and the academy not at all. Little, if any, artistic instruction ever occurred at Beaux Arts Workshop. Atelier Square remained vacant, without the workshops, camps, club building, or recreational grounds its planners had so grandly intended. Still holding a mortgage needing payments, the founders turned away from promoting Beaux Arts Village as a self-sustaining residence community for artists and instead advertised the village as a "refined community," "a homeplace for congenial people" within "natural and artistic surroundings." Home owners needed only "a love of the finer things" to qualify for membership. The academy itself became just another amenity that set Beaux Arts Village apart from other suburbs and increased the value of its homes. Gradually, the Beaux Arts Society's purpose changed from producing artists to providing a consumable lifestyle.[71]

The experience particularly furnished therapy for men. Distant from the teeming city and isolated from troublesome social problems, Beaux Arts Village revived the harried professional man and so helped him adapt to new twentieth-century circumstances. In Beaux Arts Village, *Bungalow Magazine* gushed in 1913, "the tired and nerve-wrought business man, his day done, can secure that perfect relaxation which only tranquil nature with her ozone-laden, pine-scented forest air can bestow."[72] Beaux Arts Village offered "manly health-giving sports" such as "motor-boating, automobiling, bathing, fishing, canoing, [and] rowing." Although some advertisements noted the wholesome effect of suburban life on women and children, inducements to buy Beaux Arts property rarely, if ever, directly targeted women. Clearly, its promoters saw men as the primary consumers and beneficiaries of a life close to nature.[73]

Middle-class women had less need for the solace of Beaux Arts Village's tranquil setting. Just entering the public world, women perhaps felt less ambivalence about the changes around them. Women had enthusiastically embraced the modernity of bungalow kitchens, and they hesitated to relinquish the amenities of urban living for the village's isolation. Margaret Ditty Martin, daughter of early resident James Ditty, remembered her Seattle grandmother expressing dismay at the Dittys' proposed move to Beaux Arts Village. "You can't take your family over there to the wilderness like pioneers," Martin recalled her grandmother saying to her father, "No street cars, miles from a doctor, no gas or stores to buy anything." "Oh, I would miss my Eastern Star Lodge and my church and my piano students," said Martin's Aunt Lil. "I would never consider it and glad I don't have to." Though the Ditty family's experience might not have represented all Beaux Arts women's attitudes, their apprehension further reinforced the idea of Craftsman living as an especially male enterprise.[74]

If middle-class men's rejuvenation required physical distance from the city, so too did it demand removal from disruptive social elements. Although Gustav Stickley once considered Craftsman architecture democratic, the Craftsman homes in Beaux Arts Village became part of an exclusive community. By 1913, Beaux Arts advertising attempted to lure people who desired an elite suburb. Those who wanted "good neighbors" found the village an ideal home because the society sold lots to "none but desirable people." Wealth was not the limiting factor; deeds included no restrictions on the cost of houses. The community wanted "clean livers and upbuilders of its ideals, which it believes are the leaven which makes for good, not only in the home, but in the arts and crafts of livelihood." To weed out the unworthy, by 1913 the society had instituted an application procedure. Potential home owners had to receive community approval and become members of the society to join the village. (This is still the case today.) A fence built around the grounds in 1911 further indicated the village's separateness. It prevented "intrusion from the outside," as a 1913 newspaper article noted, and allowed the society to keep the grounds as an open park. Never platted as an addition, Beaux Arts Village's grounds, streets, and parks remained entirely private. Craftsman democracy evolved into middle-class exclusivity.[75]

The leisure and solace of Beaux Arts Village, then, belonged only to "desirable people," those of the salaried and white-collar middle class descended from American or Northern European stock. No minorities or members of the new immigration lived there. But these people were no strangers to Beaux Arts Village. One black woman, "Auntie Dunn," commuted by ferry from her central Seattle home to clean the Ditty home. Helen Vogel's new maid in 1919 was a "nice Japanese girl." For servants, Craftsman houses existed as places of work, and Beaux Arts Village certainly provided no escape for them from the pressures of economic survival.[76]

But even being white and middle class did not ensure entrance into Beaux Arts Village; the community wanted only those who conformed to its brand of conventional morality. Thus, in 1915 residents unhappily beheld the arrival of Ralph De Bit and his "Christian Yoga cult." Perhaps at the suggestion of Eleanor Rininger, a community member and wealthy patron of De Bit's, nine people, along with "Dr. and Madame De Bit," moved into a large, rustic home in the growing hamlet. De Bit's purpose was a more radical version of the impulse that had sent the Western Academy of Beaux Arts to its lakeshore retreat; he apparently planned to create a yoga college that would teach his mystical beliefs. "It is a progressive exposition of religion, philosophy, and metaphysics," he explained, "with axiomatic truths as premises."[77] After Madame De Bit's legal husband snatched their five-year-old daughter from the Beaux Arts beach and began court proceedings to gain her custody, stories abounded about the immorality of the cult. Though they posed as man and wife, De Bit and Dorothy Gerber were actually unmarried. Rumors flew about naked dips in the lake and early morning strolls on the beach wearing only bathrobes. At the couple's trial for adultery, C. A. Davis, a Beaux Arts resident, declared, "De Bit tried to transform a quiet village into a red-light district."[78]

Such behavior would not do. In 1917, the Western Academy of Beaux Arts ordered De Bit to leave. After a lawsuit to evict him in 1918, a judge determined that the community could not force him from his land but could prevent him from using the private streets. Eventually, De Bit left. Though Beaux Arts Villagers themselves sought a greater fulfillment and meaning outside established institutions, they could not tolerate a less orthodox spiritual quest. They had little sympathy for the Christian yoga cult, even though its ambitions in some ways paralleled their own and derived from a similar response to the modern world. De Bit strayed too far from middle-class respectability for villagers to consider him desirable.[79]

Much as the community weeded out nonconformists, so too did it eliminate unconventional design. Beaux Arts promoters made sure that the village's architecture reflected their economic, aesthetic, and ethnic homogeneity. A building committee reviewed all construction plans, eliminating any "freak oddities" that might mar the surroundings. This procedure ensured a visual unity and guaranteed residents only beautiful neighbors. And so Beaux Arts became "not a village for artists but an artistic village," as a 1914 advertisement put it. Its "real Craftsman bungalows" signified not the productive craftsmanship of its residents but the careful consumer choices they made.[80]

As Beaux Arts Village's early idealistic purpose transformed into an act of consumption, it became a place more suited to satisfying the self than changing society. Concern for health, particularly, reflected a preoccupation with the individual's welfare, not society's. Instead of molding the character of good craftsmen, the village became an environment to be enjoyed. The outdoors, the recreational activities, and the social life around the proposed clubhouse catered to the pleasure of village residents. Beaux Arts Village belonged to "the man who can enjoy there the beauty of nature, the rest of refreshing quiet, boating, bathing and fishing."[81] In 1916, Renfro declared that the community offered itself to "those who enjoy the great out of doors, to those who have a love for the finer things, to those who are interested in building a home in better surroundings, to those who want country life but with the advantages and conveniences of the city at a minimum of cost but at a maximum of Life." Even building a Craftsman house became a matter of personal satisfaction. In 1931, Renfro wrote, "it makes no difference what you have done, where you have been, and what you have seen, you have missed the most marvelous kick which this life offers, if you have not built a house!" Renfro had come a long way from WABA's 1908 assertion that participation in crafts would produce better citizens; Craftsman homebuilding had become a consumable, therapeutic experience.[82]

Beaux Arts' shift away from its original ideals happened rather quickly. In 1913, the Beaux Arts Society began operating as a business when it officially registered itself as a joint stock corporation. As a business, it needed better exposure to a buying public than the society's acting secretary and Beaux Arts resident N. S. Leithead could give. The society hired Thomas L. Campbell, a professional real estate broker from outside the community, to manage land sales. His advertising downplayed the village as a home for artists, instead emphasizing its artistic exclusivity. Even though it was incorporated, original founders Frank Calvert, Alfred Renfro, and Donald V. Mitchell continued for a while to control the whole venture by acting as trustees for both the incorporated society and the Western Academy of Beaux Arts. But by 1916, residents must have realized the direction the village was heading. In that year, the WABA directors decided to make all property owners members of the academy. From then on, land holders voted in the five trustees who served as the Park Board, which took responsibility for roads, tax assessments, and building regulations. By 1914, the society had repudiated its earlier purpose, declaring that it was "not a colony." The dreamers who had put forth the grandiose vision of a community of craftsmen focused on a school no longer controlled it. The Western Academy of Beaux Arts recast itself as a home owner's association.[83]

Although on opposite sides of Lake Washington, the house of Orrill Stapp in Rainier Beach and the house of Alfred Renfro in Beaux Arts Village were part of the same Arts and Crafts impulse that sought succor in nature. With their stained wood siding, sheltering roofs, and low, horizontal profile, they appeared rooted in the earth, part of the rolling landscape surrounding them. Beaux Arts Village and Renfro's bungalow in particular seemed "lost in the forest primeval," as village resident Helen Vogel wrote in 1918. They did not stand so far from the urban and industrial, the degraded and ugly. These rustic shelters enclosed the most modern of spaces based on the principles of factory design. And they stood in a logged-over landscape, tied to the networks of expanding industrialization. So, too, were their inhabitants enmeshed in the Second Industrial Revolution.[84] Rugged, massive-looking Craftsman homes served as naturalistic retreats, refuges for professional middle-class men facing a much more complex and potentially alienating world than their fathers had ever encountered. Nature, and homes that seemed to blur the boundaries with nature, offered a crucial respite for those who benefited most from the modern world. Their vitality restored, such men returned to the public world not to reconstruct it but to implement and manage its transformation.

People like Orrill Stapp and Alfred Renfro believed that improvements in homes, both physically and ideally, could mitigate the deleterious effects of the Second Industrial Revolution. But they themselves stood in an ambiguous position toward the sweeping transformation. Thus, they built their ambivalence into their domestic architecture. For the rest of the twentieth century, the tension between architectural symbols of a pastoral, preindustrial past and the latest domestic technology characterized popular, middle-class housing. A visual rhetoric of antimodernism that masked an increasingly industrial house wrapped in a web of corporate networks came especially from the professional-managerial segment of the middle class. Today, when a comfortably situated suburbanite hides her television set in an antique armoire, she carries on the same equivocation that Orrill Stapp and Alfred Renfro did in the early twentieth century.

But, of course, not everyone in society felt the longing to escape, if only temporarily or visually, the intrusion of expanding capitalism. Others—plucky building contractors, opportunistic entrepreneurs, and the newly emerging petit bourgeois—saw the changes as propitious; they seized the moment, and in doing so extended the burgeoning consumer economy. For them, Craftsman houses were commodities for sale to a growing lower-middle-class market.

BUILDING THE
SEATTLE BUNGALOW

IN 1914, during Seattle's typically rainy June, crews working for the Fred Berg Building Company began to construct a house at 4203 Woodlawn Avenue. It was to be a "Craftsman" home, its artistic details celebrating the true crafts-man's skill. And, indeed, craftsmen did labor to create the future home of the Stapp family. Five and a half days a week for fifty-six cents an hour, carpenters determined its physical form.[1] With practical knowledge handed down from generation to generation, Berg and his men worked much as their grandfathers had; using their own hand tools at the site, they measured, sawed, and nailed, producing a simple, rectangular, twenty-six by fifty foot wood-frame structure. Beneath the dwelling's superficial simplicity and rusticity, however, lay complex domestic technology. Embedded in the very wood of the home, networks of plumbing, electricity, and heating snaked their way through its innards. Such complexity needed experts. Carpenters toiled alongside a new group of skilled craftsmen: plumbers, electricians, and concrete contractors. The older, contract-based work relations remained, but expanded to encompass a broad spectrum of interrelated trades.

Orrill Stapp needed new household technology. The partial basement and central heating of 4203 Woodlawn were crucial in his decision to purchase it. He wanted a flexible house with room for his small printing press and his five children and with consistent heat for music lessons that had been so lacking in his previous business location. Such technological modernity—electricity, central heating, and a basement—did not come cheaply. As inflation and expanding consumer expectations squeezed small housing contractors, they minimized, cut corners, and sought alternatives. In short, they created a simplified, less expensive form to offset the expensive domestic systems and labor. The Stapp's Craftsman bungalow, in part, resulted from this conjunction of traditional work relations and modern technology.[2]

The Stapp's Craftsman bungalow anticipated what would become a common post–World War II building pattern. It began as speculative housing constructed on the principles of mass production. Some entrepreneurial contractors employed another method of meeting rising construction costs; they practiced the economies of scale. Increased size meant lower material costs, but required more sales. As crews nailed up 4203 Woodlawn, they simultaneously constructed four other bungalows on adjacent lots. The property owner, Henry Brice, a Wallingford resident and developer, hoped to erect a hundred more homes on his large landholdings in the neighborhood. To do so, he utilized economies of scale and standardization of parts. The five Craftsman bungalows on Woodlawn, with virtually identical plans and only slightly varying facades, signaled the beginning of large-scale "merchant builders," who, after World War II, gradually whittled away the primary position of small contractors in house construction. At the cusp of this transformation stood the Craftsman bungalow.[3]

Home builders, still operating largely within nineteenth-century labor arrangements, grappled with new economic constraints and opportunities. Seeking to profit from the lucrative building boom, but facing rising costs, small contractors modified the structures they erected. They helped create a new house form: simple in shape, up-to-date in technology. The same economic forces that drove small contractors to minimalist design impelled more entrepreneurial builders toward mass production. Not only idealists, as those at Beaux Arts Village, fashioned twentieth-century domestic architecture; so too did the contractors, laborers, and technicians whose hands actually fabricated early twentieth-century homes.

While changes in the building industry lurked in the bungalow landscape, small-house contracting firms still erected the vast majority of early twentieth-century American homes. How they undertook their work and organized their work relations had a crucial influence on house design. Beginning in the nineteenth century, such enterprises operated within a system that emerged with industrial capitalism but still retained vestiges of a preindustrial artisanal work arrangement. After signing a written agreement for a completed structure at a specific cash price, usually to be paid in installments, the contractor hired his own workers, organized the building process, and obtained all necessary materials. By the time carpenters began hammering on the bungalows on Woodlawn, the contract system prevailed. Yet contractors still adhered to the basic work relations established in the artisanal period. Typically master craftsmen, they employed crews of experienced journeymen and apprentices who completed much of the construction on site.[4]

Industrialization of building components encouraged craftsmen to enter the contracting business and allowed builders with a few skilled workers to erect houses quickly and cheaply. Machines manufactured dimensional lumber, windows, molding, and doors. Railroads shipped them throughout the nation. Seattle was a center for the industrialization of lumber and building components. By 1914, as 4203 Woodlawn and thousands of structures like it went up, the city had fifty-five such firms, employing an average of 2,337 employees. Within twenty-five years, Seattle outranked all other states in production of lumber, laths, shingles, doors, and veneers, and placed a close second in the fabrication of windows and door frames, dressed lumber such as flooring, ceiling materials, and sidings. The ability to purchase all factory-made wooden components locally further simplified the building process, expediting the rise of small-time contractors.[5]

These men built Seattle's early twentieth-century neighborhoods a few houses at a time. Individual builders with some capital and a small crew erected fewer than five houses a year on average. As late as 1938, the Bureau of Labor Statistics estimated that the "average number of city houses constructed per builder was 2.2." In cities of over 100,000, bigger contractors (with between five and nine houses a year) still averaged only 6.3 houses per year. Builders with as many as ten houses per year were "relatively rare." Despite the inroads industrialization made into the house-construction business, the restricted size of these ventures reinforced a conservative work culture.[6]

Like earlier artisans, experienced craftsmen-contractors worked within a set of informal and personal relationships. They measured and cut lumber alongside their crews while supervising and training them. Though formal, legal apprenticeships sometimes funneled young men into the trade, crews commonly included the family members of building tradesmen or of the contractor himself. Typically, a small builder hired only two carpenters and a skilled laborer. To find and keep such craftsmen, the contractor used his personal knowledge of people in the industry, sometimes hiring other carpenter-builders like himself. As in the past, the builder trusted these experienced carpenters to make on-the-job decisions based on their knowledge of the building art, rather than from detailed, written plans. Even the usual method of paying employees harkened back to the artisanal system. Contractors commonly paid crews by the day, a hangover from the preindustrial period when artisans worked directly for the owner. To keep good workers or as incentive for faster completion, builders paid bonuses or extended jobs. Most used a union wage scale, and employees might belong to a union. But small contracting firms rarely hired through a union or followed union dictates. The intimate personal connections between the carpenters and contractor/foremen fostered a group loyalty that often transcended official organization.[7]

Such personal relationships marked the larger circle of building tradesmen as well. Small-time contractors apparently had few formal mechanisms or published sources for finding workers or jobs. They relied mostly on word-of-mouth referrals from other craftsmen or friendly architects. Contractors commonly established long-term relationships with skilled carpenters or subcontractors such as plumbers, hiring them repeatedly as they obtained projects. It was probably no coincidence, for instance, that the Fred Berg Building Company, which began construction on 4203 Woodlawn for the owner Henry Brice, resided only a few houses from Brice and from the construction site in the Wallingford neighborhood. Undoubtedly, the men's knowledge of one another extended beyond a purely business relationship.[8]

For twentieth-century contractors like Fred Berg, the actual circumstances of work changed little from their colonial antecedents. Nature continued to dictate the circumstances of building and of the workers' lives. Small home-building followed a seasonal cycle. When the weather warmed in the spring, around March, contractors began assembling crews and starting construction. In Seattle, this meant enduring protracted drizzle as laborers slogged through muddy building sites. By the time summer arrived, in the sunny months of July and August, work reached a feverish pace, continuing until the cold winter rains in November ended the work season. Some work continued during the winter, but it was sporadic and unpredictable. Inclement weather meant missed days of work and a truncated work year. In 1921, the federal government estimated that building workers averaged between seven and ten months of employment. Though craftsmen and laborers might receive a nominally high wage, they had to spread it over the months of no income. By the 1930s, large contractors tried to overcome weather difficulties by heating their structures to allow for interior work, but small building remained seasonal. The pattern of a preindustrial carpenter's work life continued into the twentieth century.[9]

Most small-time home builders consciously decided to keep their ventures manageable with minimal risk. Although boom times provided opportunities for contractors to expand and create relatively large businesses, most preferred to function much as had colonial housewrights. They kept administrative aspects of the job as limited as possible. Operating from their homes, small builders employed no clerks, but, like earlier artisans, might rely on wives for bookkeeping and accounting. In their "free" time, outside the working day, these businessmen managed their paperwork—payrolls, future job estimations, and bid writing. A small contractor thus had virtually no overhead office costs and operated flexibly and independently. Perhaps the most crucial legacy of the artisanal system, the desire for independence, kept many contractors small by choice. Recounting San Francisco builders in 1949, economist Sherman Maisel also described Seattle's small builders when he stated, "they take pride in their craft and like housebuilding. They enjoy working with tools and materials and are satisfied with their existing size and independence from worry and stress."[10]

In the Victorian era, such autonomous carpenters could construct astonishingly complex house forms, as nineteenth-century neighborhoods attested. However, after 1900, they consciously chose simpler structures. They did so, in part, because of new consumer and technological demands.[11]

By the early twentieth century, house buyers wanted the latest electrical, plumbing, and heating systems and fixtures for comfort and convenience. These became requirements for "modern" houses, and forced adjustments in the construction of houses. Though home-schooling guides existed to educate carpenters, little prepared them for the unfamiliar job of connecting a fully wired house to electrical lines or a fully plumbed house to its water and sewer sources. Contractors needed specialists trained in the latest technologies for installation of modern household systems. Rapidly, whole new occupations within the building trades appeared to fill the void. The U. S. census first included the category of electrician in 1900, and the numbers of these skilled tradesmen increased dramatically between then and 1930. Plumbers (including gas and steam fitters) proliferated after 1890. Even though carpenters remained the most important and most numerous craftsmen, their numbers remained basically the same in proportion to population growth. At work sites in Seattle and all over the nation, carpenters moved over to allow room for these new tradesmen.[12]

But they did not change their fundamental work organization. Instead of directly employing electricians and plumbers as part of their crews, most small builders hired expert subcontractors. Essentially, they treated subcontractors like independent peer artisans. Responsible for their own crew's training, wages, and workmanship, subcontractors and builders created a close-knit subculture of small homebuilding. Contractors established stable, long-term arrangements with their subcontractors, hiring them year after year. For instance, Maisel found that small builders in San Francisco changed fewer than one subcontractor per house built. The actual contract between the builder and subcontractor could be quite informal; cost negotiations might replace written bids. Because the builder worked near the subcontractor, he knew the process and the quality of the job done, and he needed to exert little formal supervision. Small building companies came to rely more and more on these technical experts. By the mid-twentieth century, the completion of a house took ten to fifteen specialists, and subcontracts made up the largest portion of the general contractor's costs (35 percent in 1949). Like other trades, the work of house construction became more segmented and specialized throughout the twentieth century. But in the meantime, while carpenters pounded up 4203 Woodlawn, the artisanal and traditional mixed with the complexities of modern technology.[13]

Modern houses emerged from the intersection. After 1900, expensive new systems of electricity, plumbing, and central heating forced builders to reduce labor and material costs by simplifying house forms. Uncomplicated shapes and roofs required less materials, less labor, and less time, making the shell cheaper to erect. Out of these determinants, the bungalow form materialized; low, rectangular structures open in the interior and wrapped around the virtually unseen technological systems that defined their modernity.[14]

Electricity most crucially defined a truly modern home. In 1932, the Committee on Fundamental Equipment reported to the U.S. President's Conference on Home Building and Home Ownership that "the most outstanding convenience- and comfort-producing features which make for true modernity in the home of today are provided through pipe and wire." By 1940, electricity flowed to virtually every Seattle house. Ninety-nine percent of owner-occupied dwellings received it. Lighting used most of it, although, by later standards, home electrical systems were primitive. Seattle's *Bungalow Magazine* and other publications in the 1910s ran articles on bungalows fully equipped with electrical appliances, but the actual photographs revealed a paucity of outlets and appliances. Table lamps in the pictures, for instance, received their electricity from cords running down from ceiling light fixtures. Building specifications for knob and tube wiring in a 1915 *Bungalow Magazine* called for only one base outlet each in the living room and the bedroom. Nonetheless, for people used to the soot and smell of dim kerosene lanterns, electrical lighting became an absolute necessity.[15]

However, an electrical house cost more in both labor and fixtures. The expense of wiring remained manageable if builders limited the number of outlets. In Seattle, wiring averaged 2.9 percent of the building cost in 1935–36. But the price of lighting fixtures added to the new expense of installation. Building contracts sometimes left out specifications for these, making selection the responsibility of the owner. This not only absolved the contractor of a stylistic decision but kept his price low by putting the cost outside the construction budget. Such "lighting domes, chandeliers, side brackets, globes and electroliers" were "extravagances," claimed George E. Walsh in *Bungalow Magazine*. He recommended avoiding them in bungalows, as their expense might call "for unwise economy in more vital parts of the house."[16]

As the operating costs of electricity declined throughout the first half of the twentieth century, demands for even more elaborate domestic electrical systems increased. The electrical industry campaigned energetically to advertise the benefits of a fully wired home. For instance, in 1922 and 1923, the Electrical Club of Seattle sponsored model electric homes. Wildly successful, the houses and exhibit booths showcased all the latest domestic electrical appliances "to educate the public," *Pacific Builder and Engineer* explained, "on the desirability of correct wiring and an adequate number of electric outlets in all homes, so that use may be made of the many electric aids in housework." Of course, the "municipal lighting department, the private power and light company, the manufacturers, wholesalers, jobbers, and retail dealers in electrical fixtures and appliances" sponsored Seattle Electrical Week.[17]

Under these demands, new houses acquired ever more complex and extensive electrical systems. By 1932, the National Board of Fire Underwriters recommended an electrical network that could sustain an electric range, water heater, built-in bathroom space heater, refrigerator, radio, and kitchen and laundry appliances. A new Seattle "high class" residence in 1935 had "very complete" wiring for a "fan, heating . . . refrig[erator], range, radios, [and] phone." The number of recommended outlets to handle these fixtures increased dramatically. Whereas 1910s bungalows might have only one outlet per room, in 1932 the fire underwriters advised that electricians install "convenience outlets" every twelve feet in living rooms, with at least one outlet for every separate wall space three feet or larger. And obviously, as the system expanded throughout the house, its proportional cost increased as well.[18]

At the same time that building contractors had to consider rising electrical expenses, more complicated plumbing and sewer systems increased builders' estimates for constructing even modest homes. By the late nineteenth century, both Seattle home buyers and builders desired at least a minimum level of domestic plumbing: running water, kitchen sinks, and some sort of waste water disposal system, for instance. But in Seattle's north end houses this technology remained relatively uncomplicated. In 1901, even many middle-class residents still used outhouses. That year, the city health department ordered real estate agent Frederick West to connect his home and his adjacent rental houses to city sewer lines. Until then, the residents had used outside toilets. After joining the houses to the sewer, West ordered installation of a "patent toilet and sink." The 1937 tax assessor survey indicated that a sizeable number of Seattle houses built after 1900 received plumbing fixtures sometime later. Even then, some houses constructed between the 1890s and 1906 still lacked tubs, kitchen sinks, hot water tanks, and particularly basins for hand washing. Most had toilets by 1937, but the omission of basins suggested that these structures did not originally contain fully plumbed bathrooms. Clearly, before 1906 the plumbing subcontract made up a significant new addition to construction costs, but not overwhelmingly so.[19]

Increasingly throughout the early twentieth century, however, a fully equipped, sanitary bathroom became an absolute necessity for any "modern" home. A new Seattle ordinance in 1905 codified rules for plumbing features and forced builders to include more expensive features in their building plans. The city required permits and inspections for plumbing installation and mandated that dwellings or residences contain "at least one lavatory and one sink." Indoor flush toilets rapidly became standard in both old and new houses. With the first wave of bungalow construction in Seattle after 1906, six plumbing fixtures characterized the majority of new homes: toilet, bathroom basin, kitchen sink, tub, hot water tank, and laundry trays. By 1940, 97 percent of Seattle families who owned their homes had use of a flush toilet. Less than 1 percent still relied on outside privies. Home buyers expected and received a fully plumbed house.[20]

Fixtures, too, grew more intricate and expensive in the first half of the twentieth century. Seattle houses built before 1910 included toilets with wooden seats and copper-lined wooden tanks. They might also have had copper tubs for bathing. By the bungalow era, bathrooms usually featured enamel-coated iron, free-standing tubs on claw foot legs, and wall-hung basins, toilet tanks, and toilet stools of vitreous china or the more economical enameled iron. For sanitary reasons, plumbers of this era left the pipes connecting fixtures exposed and uncovered. In the 1920s, the "pembroke," or built-in tub, took "the fixture buying public by storm," as a 1932 government report noted. By then, fashionable society considered claw foot tubs "ugly and helped to make a homely room homelier."[21] Pembroke tubs allowed for a cleaner bathroom, the report stated, because no dirt built up underneath them, as occurred with legged tubs. Showers often accompanied built-in tubs. Beginning in the mid-1920s, Seattle homes commonly included them. By 1940, only 3 percent of owner-occupied homes contained neither bathtub nor shower. Bathroom basins changed less dramatically than tubs, but many new homes in the 1920s featured the fancier pedestal basin. Such marked changes in taste forced contractors to follow the dictates of fashion and include these fixtures in their estimates.[22]

Once moved indoors, bathrooms began proliferating within new homes. By the mid-1920s, higher-cost dwellings usually included an additional half-bath with a toilet and basin. C. F. and Ruth Hughbanks in Seattle's Ballard neighborhood built both a full bath and a half-bath with "expensive" fixtures in their 1931 period-revival house. In the 1920s many families added a half-bath in remodeled basements or enclosed rear porches, increasing the network of plumbing throughout their houses. By the 1930s, some plumbers advocated additional bathrooms to ensure marital bliss. "Lack of adequate bathroom facilities," declared Joseph G. Hildebrand, a director in the Plumbing and Heating Industries Association, "is one of the causes of the increased divorce rate in the United States. The single bathtub with its order of precedence, or lack of

3.1 *In the 1920s, plumbers began installing freestanding "pedestal" sinks and "pembroke" or built-in tubs in new bathrooms. The white porcelain fixtures and white floor and wall tiles connoted a sanitary, laboratory-like purity. Photo: Museum of History and Industry, PEMCO Webster and Stevens Collection.*

it, is the cause of much family discord. All who can should have at least two bathtubs."[23] Whether or not more bathrooms fostered domestic harmony, they certainly enriched the plumbing contractors responsible for their installation.[24]

The rising expense of plumbers' expertise and the fancy new fixtures impelled a smaller, simpler house design. Providing just the basic fixtures—basin, tub, and toilet in the bathroom, kitchen sink, and laundry tubs—made up 10 percent of the budget for a $2,500 house. In 1932, the average bid to install plumbing in a modest $3,500 home reached $905—26 percent of the total cost. A Seattle survey of forty-one new houses built in 1935–36, ranging in price from $3,500 to $10,000, showed that plumbing, sewer, and side sewer made up 9.2 percent of the total cost. The more elaborate the home, the more plumbing equipment it demanded. So, within the entire plan of a new home, a comparatively small room, the bathroom, required a disproportionate percentage of the whole construction budget. But such personal features had become so crucial that house contractors cut expenses elsewhere in order to include them.[25]

Builders knew that to sell a "modern" home, with its bright lights and gleaming bathrooms, they must install a "modern" heating system. Though used widely

3.2 Along with pedestal
sinks and pembroke tubs,
showers became a common
feature in 1920s bathrooms.
The smooth, clean aesthetic
continued, although the use
of colored tiles and fixtures
began to challenge the
dominanting all-white color
scheme. Photo: Museum
of History and Industry,
PEMCO Webster and
Stevens Collection.

even into the 1930s, coal or wood stoves located in a central room failed to meet
new standards of comfort, cleanliness, and convenience. A stove's warmth did
not reach a house's hinter regions, which remained chilly and damp in Seattle's
wet winters. Stoves needed frequent attention to keep them burning, and their
ashes and fuel created a messy nuisance inside people's living quarters. After
1907, most Seattle bungalows featured hot-air furnaces as the preferred alternative to stoves. Located in the basement, these large, wood- or coal-fired, cast-
iron stoves heated air, which rose up through pipes or registers into the home.
Most common after 1907, hot-air furnaces ran ducts to first-floor (and sometimes second-floor) rooms. The first centralized heating for moderate-income
homes, such furnaces worked better in theory than in practice. In the Stapp's
bungalow, the upstairs bathroom lay directly above the furnace, and thus had
the shortest, straightest pipe leading to it. When the family opened its duct even
slightly, all the heat rose to the bathroom, leaving the rest of the house cold. The

Stapps usually did not heat their upstairs, but when they did, little warmth rose from the basement. Consequently, they supplemented the furnace by placing space heaters in some of the upstairs bedrooms. Despite their problems, though, hot air furnaces allowed a greatly desired, clean, overall warmth for the flowing, open interiors of new homes. Described by many as looking like an "octopus," a hot air furnace introduced another increasingly complicated technical system into the home.[26]

This new technology was pricey. In Seattle during 1915, a coal-burning hot-air furnace cost $125, and $100 more to install, 8 percent of a $3,000 bungalow. By 1935–1936, the cost of heating systems increased further. A survey of new homes showed that heating and ventilating networks and the oil burner furnace took 12.7 percent of the total budget. Because the price of a Roscoe oil-burner furnace remained the same ($275) for a "high-class" residence worth $10,000 or a modest dwelling of $3,500, furnaces became a much bigger consideration for contractors constructing small houses. To keep structures affordable to average Seattle buyers yet include the all-important hot-air system, builders needed to cut corners in other areas.[27]

They could not, however, eliminate basements, another expense associated with an increasingly technological house. Hot-air furnaces and coal bins required at least a partial basement. These underground spaces also created an ideal site for the home's laundry. "Modern . . . sanitary" laundry trays, usually a pair of large reinforced concrete sinks, became standard plumbing fixtures in the basement. Housewives strung clotheslines across the space, allowing the warm air to dry clothes during Seattle's lengthy wet season, most of the year. Before 1906, most average-sized houses lacked basements, but as bungalows proliferated after 1906, concrete basements became the norm.[28]

Basements commanded a high price because they needed concrete. The hole itself was relatively cheap. In 1915, home builders paid as little as $15 for the basement's excavation, probably done by hand or with a horse and scoop. However, construction of a whole concrete basement in a $2,000 bungalow cost $150, 8 percent of its total budget. Even into the 1930s, the actual labor needed in basement making cost far less than materials. Of concrete expenses, 68 percent went for materials in 1932. Such financial considerations impelled contractors to design basement shapes demanding the least amount of concrete—simple rectangles. These walls served as the foundation for the aesthetic of modern small homes.[29]

Building a "modern" home was evolving into an expensive and complex undertaking. But whereas early twentieth-century technologies and inflation squeezed small home builders, World War I and its immediate aftermath threatened to strangle them altogether. As the war curtailed or redirected crucial building materials, prices rose at an astonishing rate. Nationally, residences cost roughly 50 percent more to build after World War I. In Seattle, housing construction fell off sharply as prices skyrocketed. Whereas before the war a dwelling cost an average of $1,000 (including tent houses and temporary housing), by 1919 it ballooned to $1,760. Meanwhile, an "acute shortage" created a huge demand for housing in the city.[30]

Dramatic increases in costs for both materials and labor severely constrained addressing that demand and its potential for profit. Between 1914 and 1919, the overall cost of construction materials (excluding steel) increased by 84 percent. Even worse, the cost of cement, plumbing, heating, and electrical wiring, materials critical to modern home building, remained especially high after the war. But even if contractors could obtain expensive materials, they had to contend with a shortage of both skilled and unskilled workers and rising pay scales. Wages for unskilled laborers grew more than for skilled laborers. Between 1914 and 1918, the average hourly rate in the unionized building trades—skilled workers— expanded 28.5 percent nationally, but 37 percent in Seattle. However, wages for unskilled workers pushed total labor costs even higher. A U.S. Housing Corporation investigation found that between 1913 and 1919, labor costs for excavating and constructing concrete basements increased 100 percent, plumbing 75 percent, heating 50 percent, and sheet metal work 50 percent. More traditional sectors of building, such as plastering, lathing, carpentry, and roofing, rose less, but still increased between 40 and 67 percent. With such inflated expenses, by 1920 contractors building modest but modern houses faced a daunting financial environment.[31]

The practical solution of using a cheaper, simpler house form intersected neatly with the ideology of the Craftsman bungalow. Simple, unadorned, "natural" dwellings with open interiors cost the least to erect. In 1912, for instance, George Walsh in *Bungalow Magazine* strongly advocated simplification as a way of paring down building costs. A rectangular house with a single roof, he wrote, required less labor than an L-shaped house, because framing and timbering were simpler. Affordable houses needed a plain exterior without "a great number of columns, balustrades, cornices, pilasters, piazza and molded mill work," and room sizes that coincided with stock joist lengths. Walsh estimated that unusual timbering, selected hard woods, difficult angles, and "pretentious architectural features" could increase framing costs by "10, 20 and 30 percent. . . . Every break and bend in the roof line or the walls means extra labor and cost." Thus, he concluded, "the square or rectangular house, with simple walls and roof lines, is . . . the cheapest to build, although not always the most [satisfying] or artistic."[32] These simplifications coincided exactly with the definition of a bungalow. In its plan book circa 1911, Seattle's Bungalow Company called the bungalow "a house on one floor with any number of rooms; a low pitched roof either of shingles or composition roofing where the pitch is extremely low; . . . the exterior covered usually with rough siding, shingles or shakes; . . . a lack of fancy mouldings, grill work, etc." How fortunate for home builders! The small, simple structures they could afford to construct had become the height of fashion.[33]

For the rest of the century, these bungalow design principles for inexpensive construction characterized small-house architecture. Federal policy ensured their perpetuation. In 1937, opening the Small Home Planning Conference, Howard Leland Smith, the Federal Housing Administration's chief architect, outlined seven fundamental precepts for inexpensive homes:

1. Plan a square or rectangular-shaped house in order to get a simple floor plan.
2. Avoid unnecessary corners.
3. Plan for a minimum of hall space.
4. Use simple roof construction.
5. Use stock sizes, and standard lengths of structural material.
6. Use stock millwork.
7. Plan heating, plumbing and electrical work in conjunction with framing, and avoid long runs of pipe or ducts.

Thus, the small contractor's house of the first half of the twentieth century became codified. And, until only quite recently, its uncomplicated shape and increasingly complex technology defined popular housing.[34]

Simplifying house forms thus allowed small home builders to meet new consumer demands for modern dwellings while retaining their traditional arrangements and relationships. But though much of the builders' labor replicated a crafts-man legacy, industrialization began to creep into the business. In the beginning, it came to all home builders, big and small, with the use of machine-produced components and equipment for home shops. Orrill Stapp's bungalow and thou-sands like it consisted of factory-made parts. Milling machines, not the hands of an artisan, shaped its windows, doors, moldings, paneling, and flooring. Carpen-ters still determined house form, but they no longer fashioned the finer wooden details on site or in small shops. Joiners became virtually obsolete. Machine opera-tives in sash and blind factories replaced them. As skilled carpenters attached the elements of Craftsman styling to 4203 Woodlawn—the exposed rafter ends, the stained siding, the ubiquitous porch—they nailed up symbols of their own transforming work culture.[35]

It was much more than industrialized building components, however, that began to change the small-home builders' world of work in the early twentieth century. The beginnings of a great shift in small-home construction that cli-maxed after World War II lay embedded in cozy bungalows like the Stapps'.

The mass production of building components inexorably led to the mass production of houses themselves. Only large building firms with entrepreneurial vision could use this strategy to beat the high cost of construction in an intensively competitive business environment. While small contracting firms still erected most houses, well-capitalized developers started eyeing the immense profits inherent in the public's hunger for Seattle homes. Profit came from mass production, "practical home building," as one company termed it. The man responsible for erecting 4203 Woodlawn, Henry Brice, typified one such developer. Although not fully a "community builder" such as Levitt in the post-World War II era, Brice anticipated the future direction of home building. In 1910 he contracted Joseph Parker to construct one hundred "modern and high-class dwelling houses" in Wallingford. Four years later, he ordered construction of the five nearly identical houses on the 4200 block of Woodlawn. As the Woodlawn houses show, he erected his speculative dwellings in small units, in this case, along only one face of a block. With these bungalows, carpenters sawed and hammered much like their colonial predecessors, but here they began participating in the rationalization of home building.[36]

The bungalow form emerged partially from this call for greater industrial efficiency in home building. Herbert Hoover, for instance, hoped to establish the mass production of houses much as Henry Ford had done with automobiles. Through scientific expertise, Hoover sought to eliminate wasteful practices that resulted from "blindly following tradition and past custom."[37] To this end, in 1921 he created the new division on building and housing within the U.S. Bureau of Standards. Professional scrutiny focused on reducing housing costs through better construction methods and standardization of modern building materials.[38]

Uniformity of components, of course, had long figured crucially in industrialization, and World War I's housing crunch hastened standardization of construction materials. By the 1920s, under Hoover's aegis, a "rage for standardization" swept the industry. Hoover's experts first assessed the rationalization of plumbing, heating, lighting, clay products, interior wall finishes, and millwork. Then they considered the house as a whole, producing reports like the "Recommended Minimum Requirements for Small Dwelling Construction" in the 1920s. Trade associations joined the effort, volunteering to implement standardization cooperatively in brick and hot-water-tank manufacturing. Shingle companies around the Seattle area, for example, organized into the Puget Sound Shingle Manufacturers Association and established uniform rules for roof and sidewall shingles. After "lumber experts" estimated that waste increased cost $25 million per year, trade agreements reduced the number of finished lumber by nearly 60 percent. With uniformity came less diversity, and houses took on a more homogenous appearance.[39]

Hoover's bureaucrats also directly attacked the labor process of small-home construction itself. Efficiency and mechanization, they proclaimed, could rationalize the work routine. It only needed "pure and applied scientific research as the foundation of genuine labor-saving devices, better processes, and sounder methods."[40] New equipment for reducing building labor appeared in the 1920s: mechanical brick layers, plastering machines, and power shovels. But more wasteful than hand labor, more detrimental to the overall efficiency of home building, government officials claimed, was tradesmen's adherence to tradition. Old, useless habits of a preindustrial craft needed eradication. Reformers focused particularly on the itinerant nature of construction. Building workers typically found employment for no more than nine months a year, mostly in the three to five warm months. Unionists and workers attributed this work rhythm to the seasons and the need for mild temperatures to set mortar or concrete and to avoid harsh working conditions. But by the 1920s, rationalizers disputed the necessity of the winter "dull season," claiming that careful planning, power machinery, and heating allowed year-round construction without diminution of quality. Steady employment and full-year production created a stabilized industrial economy as a whole.[41] Only "custom, based mainly on traditional methods of building," argued Hoover's officials, prevented widespread implementation of such a logical and beneficial work organization.[42]

The business of small-home building resisted such efforts to rationalize its labor. Before World War II, small contractors remained the norm, carrying on the colonial craftsman's legacy. The informal relationships, the seasonal rhythms, the independence, and the pride instilled through a traditional work culture continued to order the world of house construction.[43]

Yet, however much carpenters might cling to traditional practices, bungalow building also marked the beginning of a great change in the industry that would bear fruit after World War II. At that time, companies like Brice's came to dominate the housing market, pushing small builders into the constricted niche of custom construction. The seeds of this transformation lay even in 4203 Woodlawn. In 1914, when Brice employed specialized crews to erect the house's frame, he adopted elements of mass production. Although never fully rationalized, these companies embraced the industrial organization and mechanization that Herbert Hoover advocated.

Rationalization attracted Henry Brice because he so clearly built for the market. To him, houses represented a lucrative commodity rather than a product of an independent craft. Building on speculation was not new in the early twentieth century. Nineteenth-century contractors might erect both a specific dwelling for a client and one or two for the market. Most small enterprises, however, lacked the flexible capital needed to wait for the house's sale. Speculating also included additional managerial burdens. Already pushing paperwork aside during the normal work day, the small operator had little time to market and supervise numerous sites. Yet Seattle's growth spurts and subsequent housing shortages created an extremely tempting and lucrative opportunity. Only a well-capitalized, well-connected dealer like Henry Brice could take full advantage of it.

Brice had to think and plan like a manager, not a craftsman, to organize such a large enterprise. Unlike a contractor/foreman, he acted as a full-time executive, directing all activities, but working separately from the crews. Following the typical pattern, Brice did have some background in construction. His firm, Andrew Peterson Construction Company, graded, paved, and curbed the streets of Wallingford. More importantly, business gave Brice his most formative experiences. He began his career in Seattle as a traveling salesman. Then, as the city burst open in the early twentieth century, he had entered real estate. Profit, not craftsmanship, motivated Henry Brice.[44]

This perspective differentiated large speculative builders like Brice from smaller, old-style builders. To erect his many dwellings, Brice employed economies of scale. Well-capitalized, he used his financial power to leverage the purchase of material in large quantities at low prices. On lots just a block from the Stapps' future home, he amassed 500,000 feet of lumber recycled from the dismantled 1909 Alaska-Yukon-Pacific exposition and anticipated adding 500,000 feet more. Very likely, this cheap wood furnished the essential structure—the joists, studs, and rafters—of 4203 Woodlawn and many other bungalows in Wallingford.[45]

Such a large enterprise demanded changes to the labor process itself. No one crew of carpenters had the satisfaction of completing 4203 Woodlawn. Carpenters working for the Fred Berg Building Company erected the frames of the five structures in June 1914. For some reason, possibly because the men had satisfied a framing contract, work halted until 1916, when, from March to June, another small contractor working for Brice, a man named P. J. Hower, finally attached siding and completed the structures' exteriors. The home at 4203 Woodlawn was unfinished when Brice sold it to the Scandinavian-American Bank in 1917. Yet a third contractor entered the picture the next year, lathing and plastering the interior. Only after five years, in 1919, did the bungalow hit the market. Though certainly not mass produced like an automobile or houses in Levittowns of post-World War II fame, 4203 Woodlawn resulted from large-scale producers' segmentation of labor.[46]

The fact that bungalows marked the first steps in the modern transformation of residential construction showed even more clearly in Seattle's Bungalow Company. The firm's predominant manager, Norman E. Coles, rose not from the ranks of aspiring carpenters, but from the world of savvy capitalists. Coles arrived in Seattle in 1909. Seeing opportunity in the popular enthusiasm for bungalows, he quickly entered residential construction, associating with Seattle's first bungalow-building firm, The Bungalow Company. This firm had begun as, the Birch Loan Company, a business venture, in about 1908. In 1909, it changed its name and list of trustees to become The Bungalow Company, yet retained the loan company's original objectives. By 1912, at age twenty-four, Coles became its president. He had little apparent practical building experience, but had studied architecture and drafting at Marquette University in Milwaukee. With O. W. Harris, who managed The Bungalow Company between 1909 and 1911, Coles established a successful business, issuing a large plan book by 1912. The two men briefly formed the office Harris and Coles, "designers and builders," before Coles absorbed it in 1914 to create Coles Construction Company. That year, claimed a 1916 biography, Coles "took out more building permits than any other [firm] in the city." Indeed, *Bungalow Magazine* frequently featured bungalows that Coles had designed and built. But, of course, Coles only directed the actual labor involved; his role was entrepreneur, not carpenter.[47]

But, in many ways, Coles did operate much as a small contractor. The Bungalow Company constructed custom housing throughout the suburban fringes of Seattle. In their plan book, the owners called themselves "general contractors" who would "build any structure you may desire," although bungalows remained their obvious specialty. For lot owners, they provided construction loans. For others, they supplied lots on "easy installments" on which their crews could build. Articles in *Bungalow Magazine* featuring their houses indicated that the company frequently built for individual clients.[48]

But Coles also constructed bungalows for the speculative market, a move too risky for the average small contractor. He used his plan book and *Bungalow Magazine* stories as advertisement. "We build bungalows for sale on easy terms," announced the 1912 plan book, "and usually have several in course of construction in different parts of the city." A good many of The Bungalow Company's contracts probably came from real estate offices. In 1910, for instance, the Puget Land Company ran an advertisement for lots in North Park, "The Beauty Spot of the North End" (today in the Greenwood neighborhood). The ad prominently displayed one of The Bungalow Company's dwellings. The Puget Land Company had apparently arranged with The Bungalow Company to erect a few speculative model homes to attract customers. Such market production put The Bungalow Company in a league beyond the common carpenter/contractor erecting fewer than ten residences per year.[49]

With size and speculation came labor reorganization. Coles obviously did not saw and hammer alongside his workers but maintained a more formal division between management and labor. Because he carried on numerous projects simultaneously, Coles specialized his crews. By 1912, The Bungalow Company claimed that its high output allowed it to undertake almost all aspects of home-building itself, eliminating subcontractors. This necessitated the business having its own plumbing and heating departments. When Coles did engage subcontractors, the firm's size helped it negotiate lower overall costs. For instance, W. W. Kellogg constructed all fireplace mantels depicted in The Bungalow Company's plan book. Knowing that he faced months of steady paychecks rather than frequent layoffs, Kellogg could afford to lower his bid. In somewhat rudimentary form, Coles anticipated the division of labor which characterized post–World War II large-scale development.[50]

Greater production also gave The Bungalow Company the ability to purchase mass quantities of materials at substantial discounts. Coles obviously had worked out such an arrangement with various Seattle suppliers. As indicated in its plan book, the firm purchased all lumber (the largest expenditure for any house) from only two Seattle-area lumber mills, the Brace and Herbert Mill Company and the Hewitt-Lea Lumber Company. The Lake Union Brick Company provided all bricks. To store its materials, The Bungalow Company maintained a "warehouse wherein we carry a complete line of building materials purchased in quantities," something small contractors could not afford. Through the economies of scale, Coles claimed to "give a high standard of work at a reasonable price." Thus his bungalows, the very symbol of creative individualism and rustic escapism, represented the nationwide trend toward the mass production of housing.[51]

An inherent conservatism in Americans' building culture, however, prevented full rationalization of homebuilding. Men like Brice and Coles introduced features of industrial organization, but they never mass-produced dwellings in an assembly-line process. Complete systematization would eventually result in identical, prefabricated houses with interchangeable parts made in factories. Contemporary modular homes come closest to this model. Americans never fully accepted these structures, associating them with loss of individuality, rootlessness, low class, and shoddy construction. The public, and certainly carpenters, thought such structures inadequate and inferior, and linked prefabricated structures to temporary housing or outbuildings, some of their early uses. Not constructed on site by skilled craftsmen, they did not qualify as "true homes" at all. So, before World II, homebuilding remained a decentralized venture.[52]

Although traditionalism continued, especially among small contract builders who erected most of Seattle's north end before the 1940s, the balance of power gradually shifted. More and more, big construction firms garnered the larger share of the market. As early as the 1920s, signs of the small contractor's dwindling importance permeated the industry. In that busy decade, speculators erected hundreds of structures. Gardner J. Gwinn, who constructed the 1922 and 1923 model electric houses, designed or built seven hundred houses between 1913 and 1925. Then he moved into apartment construction, erecting more than fifty apartment buildings throughout Seattle. Obviously, Gwinn had moved into the realm of merchant building.[53] The New Deal and World

War II further widened the distance between small custom contractors and larger speculative companies. Easier financing under the 1934 Federal Housing Act and post–World War II housing legislation allowed builders with capital to become land developers. Instead of purchasing dispersed lots, a savvy entrepreneur could buy a large tract of land beyond the city limits and build an entire community. Federal money for defense industry housing during the war exacerbated this trend. The immediate need for thousands of worker houses meeting minimum standards favored large firms that utilized more systematized, specialized production. The biggest developers became "community builders," creating whole new neighborhoods in districts such as Magnolia and West Seattle.[54]

In these new neighborhoods, houses reflected the changing work culture that produced them. In crucial ways, these homes continued principles that undergirded bungalow design, but they appeared more streamlined, more minimal, and, significantly, even more homogenous than their predecessors. Just a few miles directly west of 4203 Woodlawn, in Ballard, V. O. "Bud" Stringfellow erected blocks of houses between 1943 and 1945 (fig. 1.7) that illustrated this relationship. A former real estate dealer, Stringfellow typified those businessmen who saw the shape of future building. In 1941, he and two associates formed New Housing, Incorporated. Stringfellow brought equity in land to the company, and his main partner, C. H. Massar, contributed machinery and equipment, indicating their respective backgrounds in real estate and contracting. In Ballard, they purchased vacant land just north of the federally owned Chittenden Locks and began building residences. During the war, they constructed mainly identical duplexes, rectangular, hip-roofed dwellings with two three-room apartments. Each unit contained the minimum technology: for instance, stoves rather than hot air furnaces, showers rather than tubs. The company saved precious lumber and labor by eliminating exterior trim and porches, merely pouring concrete front steps. When the war ended in 1945, Stringfellow anticipated Americans' hunger for homes, and New Housing switched to producing single-family residences in the same neighborhood. Its houses retained the same shape, materials, and dimensions as its duplexes, but included some amenities such as basements and hot-air furnaces. Obviously, Stringfellow and Massar rationalized and mechanized their building process, creating rows of identical houses. In shape, exterior materials, interior plan, dominating roof, and household technology, New Housing's proto-ranch houses looked similar to 4203 Woodlawn and its neighbors.[55]

New Housing's Ballard homes expose the visual legacy of the bungalow form to later twentieth-century popular architecture. The bungalow exhibited the first clear statement of domestic minimalism and interior openness that characterized the proto-ranch houses constructed by New Housing. The similarities stemmed, in part, from the work world in which they emerged. On both houses, skilled craftsmen continuing traditional work patterns grappled with rising costs and advancing technologies. To resolve their competing demands, builders created a simplified, unadorned shape. Yet the differences between 4203 Woodlawn and New Housing dwellings also reveal the growing influence of large-scale, rationalized, speculative building on domestic architecture. Whereas the facades of Brice's five houses on Woodlawn varied in appearance, New Housing's structures replicated one house. This mass production could only come with the arrival of merchant builders. Yet even today, experienced carpenters still toil at the building site during a weather-related work season that in many ways resembles that of their craftsman forefathers. And small, independent house contractors who rely on an informal work culture continue to dominate custom home construction. Americans insisted on the retention of this craftsman legacy. Factory assembly lines, they believed, could never build true homes.

Who actually labored to create early twentieth-century housing mattered. The men who sweated at homesites like 4203 Woodlawn and the work world they operated in helped shape the modern domestic architectural landscape. In their adjustment to the growing consumer economy, they created dwellings like the Stapps' home. As long as small builders prevailed in the industry, however, variations in style occurred within that general form. Erecting only a few dwellings a year, small contractors operating within a time-honored tradition flexibly altered stock plans to suit their customer's desires and budgets. They built on lots scattered throughout a neighborhood, occasionally erecting a number of adjacent houses, as on Woodlawn, but rarely filling an entire subdivision. Houses created by speculative firms like Brice's looked more homogenous than those of custom builders. They relied on popular designs known to sell well, and on features of mass production, such as precut lumber and preassembled components, which conscribed design innovation. Yet, as long as such companies remained fairly small, they spread their rather bland styles over an entire district. So Seattle's early twentieth-century neighborhoods contained many different builders' houses constructed over a span of time. Even when hammered up during the same boom period, these small-builder suburbs appeared subtly diverse.[56]

Such heterogeneity gave way to a more marked uniformity when the home-building industry transformed after World War II. By the 1940s, and especially by the 1950s and 1960s, speculative building projects began to increase dramatically in size. Big developers became "community builders," acquiring large chunks of land and simultaneously erecting blocks and blocks of virtually identical houses. To do this, they employed more features of mass production and standardization. Being speculators, they more consciously marketed to an anonymous, undefined clientele. As a consequence, the diversity of housing design dwindled. The residential landscape thus created—curvilinear streets of rectangular, unadorned ranch houses—reflected the transformation of home building from a predominantly small craft to a big business.

When carpenters surveyed Seattle's early twentieth-century neighborhoods, they saw a landscape of work, of small-scale production in a time-honored tradition. Especially when compared to later suburbs, they perhaps realized that such regions marked the beginnings of a great change in homebuilding. Yet, for small operators selling houses, the streets of bungalows and period revival houses appeared as a great display of commodities. These entrepreneurs defined Seattle's northern developments as a landscape of consumption.

SELLING THE SEATTLE BUNGALOW

IN 1914, ORRILL STAPP PACKED UP HIS FAMILY—his wife, Frances, and his sons, Milton, Elbert, and Arthur—and left his hand-built Arts and Crafts home in Rainier Beach. In a reversal of his original Arts and Crafts impulse, Stapp abandoned the rusticity of life so far from Seattle's urban center and returned to the city's northern neighborhoods. As the broader Arts and Crafts movement waned, so too did Stapp's commitment to live an isolated life close to nature. Stapp could not escape his dependence on Seattle's growing consumer economy for his livelihood. He worked primarily as a music teacher, and Seattle's booming northern communities promised an opportunity to leave his difficult economic circumstances and to expand his business. By 1918, Stapp rented studio space and opened the Orrill V. Stapp School of Music, at which students received training in "voice, piano, violin, pipe organ, harmony, history of music, [and] normal training classes." For a while his venture thrived, but when World War I ended, depression ensued, and Stapp closed his academy. He decided to buy a house with space malleable enough for both family life and musical instruction. Location was much more crucial than architectural style. He needed easy access to streetcar lines, to schools and churches, and to a nearby community of customers. The charming Craftsman bungalow in Wallingford, with a living room big enough for a grand piano, met his needs. In 1922, Stapp joined the ranks of a rapidly expanding consumer class. He plunged into debt, obtained a mortgage, and purchased 4203 Woodlawn Avenue for $6,000.[1]

Stapp's signature on the mortgage papers for his Craftsman home revealed an important aspect of understanding early twentieth-century housing: bungalows functioned as commodities in the expanding consumer economy. Not a custom-built house for a discerning Progressive family, Stapp's house began as a dwelling mass-produced on a small scale for the speculative market. One of five constructed by Henry Brice, it featured the same overall dimensions, rectangular shape and dominant side gable roof as its neighbors, though their facades varied somewhat. Luring a new group of customers, including Stapp, into home ownership and debt, Seattle's small businesspeople used innovative marketing and financing techniques to sell homes like these. Because it originated as speculative housing, the very purpose of 4203 Woodlawn was to acquire monetary value on the market. Orrill Stapp typified just the sort of customer that the sellers of these Wallingford bungalows hoped to attract: white, middle-class, and willing to carry a large debt. As a music teacher and beneficiary of the nation's growing service economy, Stapp himself could fully recognize the important role of small housing entrepreneurs in creating the suburban landscape.

Even more than professional architects or planners, such diversified salespeople created the vast bungalow neighborhoods like Wallingford. They targeted the untapped market of moderate-income people and sought to extend the housing market to them. By dabbling in all phases of housing, they designed, constructed, and—most of all—sold houses to ordinary people. They did this through modern means: advertising, magazines, and installment purchasing—all methods that shaped the desires and expectations of their customers. They did not strive to attract the elite, with its need for social and aesthetic control. Instead, these housing capitalists used a particular suburban ideal that appealed to the first-time home buyer's desire for technological efficiency and family independence.[2]

As they marketed bungalows, small entrepreneurs commodified the Arts and Crafts ideal, refashioning its original meanings. Their efforts to sell houses molded the appearance of Seattle's popular residential neighborhoods. Rather than just representing architectural reform, Stapp's attractive Craftsman home also stood for the common person's deepening involvement in modern consumerism.[3]

Of these entrepreneurs, real estate agents most epitomized modern salespeople. As more and more customers eagerly sought to acquire property, the real estate profession grew in proportion. Although land sales had obviously occurred since earliest settlement, the intervention of a broker in the transactions followed the evolution of a capitalist economy in the late nineteenth century. Until then, land holders had usually sold unimproved land without an agent and thus received all the profits themselves. But rapid technological and urban growth in the late nineteenth century created a specialized field in real estate marketing. Harried landowners needed businessmen to sell their property for them. In exchange for relief from the difficult tasks of finding customers, arranging financing, and handling the paper transactions, property holders paid these brokers a commission from their sales. In turn, potential customers sought out these knowledgeable salespeople for assistance in securing property at no cost to them. Real estate agents thus helped usher in the modern twentieth-century economy based on service and consumption.[4]

Just as this economic transformation began sweeping the nation, Seattle sprang up on Puget Sound as an economically promising west coast city. Concurrent with its growth, a powerful real estate industry arose. Following a national pattern, the first businesspeople to prosper in real estate were enterprising men and women with capital who arrived early to purchase large tracts of public land. They stood poised to profit handsomely when the transcontinental railroad and massive migration caused explosive urban growth in the 1880s. Seattle's population jumped from 3,533 in 1880 to 42,837 in 1890. A frenzy of land speculation then gripped the city's capitalists. Those with land north of the commercial center particularly benefited from the boom, as expansion worked its way in that direction. Salespeople who earned their pay by uniting buyers and sellers played a central role in these myriad land exchanges.[5]

As typical throughout the nation, Seattle entrepreneurs operated at several levels of neighborhood development. Well-capitalized firms bought and platted large sections of relatively inexpensive land, often at some distance from existing settlement. When the time seemed propitious, they either improved the area, usually providing a transportation system to the central city, or sold smaller acreages to subdividers who might improve it. These capitalists generally graded and paved streets, put in concrete walks and curbs, and installed water mains and sewers. Realizing that finished houses increased the neighborhood's desirability, land speculators sometimes gave special incentives to builders constructing the first homes. When E. C. Kilbourne acquired the Denny and Hoyt addition and began the suburb of Fremont, he recalled, "We gave away 100 lots, one each to anyone who would build a home and live in it. Also two lots to a laundry, four to Kellogg's Tannery, two lots to a foundry, and 200 lots to the Fremont Mill Company, in which we were stockholders. Also two lots each to a Methodist and a Baptist Church, and three lots to the Congregational Church."[6] Smaller real estate agencies without Kilbourne's resources would buy lots in these new areas, then broker their sale and financing either to individual home builders or to small speculative contractors building a house or two.[7]

When an individual wanted a building site, he or she most commonly dealt with a general broker who worked alone or maintained a small office. Such agents made up the vast majority of real estate dealers. As late as 1936, the U.S. Census Bureau reported that real estate offices employed on average only 1.3 people. Anyone could broker real estate in the early twentieth century. Entering the field required no special credentials such as a formal education, a license, or a large initial financial outlay. In simplest terms, enterprising people (mostly men, but a few women too) needed only match up land sellers to buyers, then pocket their commission. As a result, offices proliferated during Seattle's building booms, creating an intensely competitive business environment. To survive, small-time agents mediated all sorts of real estate transactions. They sold a variety of properties, earned commissions from arranging financing and insurance, sometimes subdivided small pieces of land, and of course, hustled intensely to find customers. Creatures of consumer desire, these small dealers fed the hunger for Seattle homes.[8]

For many ambitious firms, just brokering land transactions limited money-making possibilities. Some operators who began as real estate agents diversified into industries associated with building houses. Their ultimate goal remained the same, however: to make a profit by selling. As a first, logical step, they advanced from merely selling lots or another owner's house to creating completed houses expressly for the market. After 1900, speculative building became widespread in Seattle. *Pacific Builder and Engineer* noted in 1904, "The business of building houses for the market has made marked progress during the past two years. Previous to that time those who engaged in that business had but varied success." "The ready-made house," it proclaimed, "is a better seller than the house built by individuals." When dealers moved into erecting residences, they moved well beyond just mediating property exchanges. They began to shape the built environment.[9]

Charles E. Remsberg, a prominent Fremont banker and later Port of Seattle commissioner, demonstrated how real estate provided a beginning point for speculative housing. Upon his arrival in Seattle from his native Indiana in 1889, Remsberg opened a real estate office in the newly blossoming suburb of Fremont. While working in this field, he also pursued law, and after his admittance to the bar in 1893, he formed a law partnership with George Simmonds. As the north end grew, so too did Remsberg's prosperity, so that in 1905, he joined S. P. Dixon, one of Fremont's "largest local real estate owners and business men," to open the Remsberg and Dixon Bank (later renamed the Fremont State Bank). Even though acting as both a lawyer and a banker, Remsberg never stopped selling lots, acreage, and houses on commission. Taking advantage of the north end's tremendous boom, by 1913 he had added speculative home building to his activities. That year, he wrote, "We are constantly building bungalows and houses of all descriptions. We now have six or eight under construction in different parts of the north end of the city which range in price from $1500 to $4000."[10] In appearance, Seattle's north end came to reflect the business decisions of Remsberg.[11]

As salespeople entered home construction, a few builders conversely became real estate agents. In 1905, C. E. Young erected an office in Fremont and added a real estate and loan business opportunity to his building-and-contracting operation. The *Fremont Colleague* expressed no doubt that Young's venture would be successful, as "Mr. Young is a live business man." This was probably the same Young who consolidated building, design, and selling into one office in 1909 when Youngs and Youngs, " architects, contractors and builders," affiliated with H. R. Carr, a real estate dealer active in the northern suburbs. By-passing any middle men, some small operators attempted to improve their profit margins by engaging many parts of Seattle's burst of residential building.[12]

As the Youngs demonstrated, producing architectural designs became another way that businessmen could get a bit of the cash flowing through home buying. A few of these diversified salesmen even called themselves architects. Willard W. DeLong exemplified such an entrepreneur. Apparently DeLong had little or no architectural training, though he might have had carpentry skills. However, he was a savvy businessman with long experience in riding the waves of prosperity. Born in Minnesota in 1861, DeLong first trained as a machinist, then "took up teaching as a profession" after finishing a course at a St. Paul business college. Arriving in Seattle in 1889, he continued teaching, eventually presiding over the Acme Collegiate Institute of Seattle until 1898. First serving as county clerk, he moved directly into the business field, founding the Bank of Ballard in 1901 and becoming its president in 1903. By then, the north end communities were ballooning, and DeLong wanted to be a part of it. He first erected several residences in Ballard. Then, in 1902, he incorporated the Ballard Home Building Company. A year later, he acted as an agent for the Equitable Building, Loan and Investment Association, on whose board of directors he sat. As if participating in the building and financial aspects of home building were not enough, DeLong also moved into housing design. From 1908 to 1914, the Polk City Directory listed DeLong's occupation as "architect."[13] In 1915, with his wife, Belle, DeLong published the *Seattle Home Builder and Home Keeper,* a practical and aesthetic guide to creating beautiful, modern, and moderately-priced homes. In it, he proudly and boldly advertised himself as "Principal [of the] Architectural Department Metropolitan Business College."[14]

Here, then, was a person actively shaping Seattle's northern neighborhoods and operating more than anything as a businessman. Rather than a fully trained architect with an artistic calling, DeLong personified an entrepreneur. He intended to carve out a profitable niche for himself in the flourishing home-

4.1 *From his plan book, this photo of Jud Yoho taken around 1913 accompanied the photograph of his award for the house in fig. 4.2. Photo: Craftsman Bungalow plan book, Seattle Public Library.*

building market. DeLong saw himself (at least in 1903) as a "successful business man who owes his advancement to close application, energy, strong determination and executive ability." With these values he set his mark on the suburban landscape.[15]

Without a doubt, Jud Yoho (fig. 4.1) stood out as Seattle's most flamboyant small-house entrepreneur, epitomizing the north end's diversified salesmen. This remarkable man shrewdly exploited every opportunity during the nation's bungalow craze. He mastered the art of self-promotion, so much so that today historians writing about bungalows find it almost obligatory to mention him and his publications. With flair and energy, Yoho entered into all aspects of residential construction between about 1900 and 1920, acting as real estate broker, contractor, and designer. But he went even further, publishing a national journal, *Bungalow Magazine,* that fostered sales of his particular product. Through such activities, he strongly molded consumer choice. Although his houses featured Arts and Crafts symbols, Yoho was no idealistic reformer intent on morally regenerating society. Most of all, he behaved as a modern businessman, seeking profit where opportunity lay. He considered Craftsman bungalows like 4203 Woodlawn to be commodities. As he said, he wanted "every bungalow built from my plans to prove a lasting advertisement," not an ideological statement about the degradation of work.[16]

The trajectory of Yoho's career in Seattle highlighted his primary orientation as a salesman. Typical of most diversified home purveyors, Yoho grew up in the business of building and selling. His father, John, had trundled his family across the United States as he pursued various real estate and construction ventures. By 1897, he had landed in Seattle, just as the excitement and expansion brought on by the Klondike gold rush was gripping the city. Not surprisingly, he established J. F. Yoho and Company, a seller of real estate and mines in Seattle. Working in John's office as a teenager, Jud imbibed the ethic of opportunistic salesmanship. In 1906, at the age of twenty-three, Jud opened his own real estate and insurance business. The timing was perfect. Seattle boomed with massive growth, its population leaping from 80,671 in 1900 to 237,194 in 1910. With new streetcar lines and the 1909 Alaska-Yukon-Pacific Exposition on the University of Washington's campus, Seattle's northern suburbs especially benefited during this period. Jud Yoho quickly branched into constructing "cottages" on speculation in Wallingford. Then, after the 1907 panic, he astutely refashioned his marketing to take advantage of the growing fascination with California bungalows. In 1911, with long-time business associate Guy Nelson, Yoho incorporated the Craftsman Bungalow Company. At the same time, he began calling his houses "bungalows" instead of "modern cottages." As a showcase, he erected a model bungalow in Wallingford, into which he moved with his wife and son in 1911. The cozy home thus served two purposes: warm family hearth and advertisement for Yoho's services.[17]

Yoho, of course, represented only one of a great number of entrepreneurs intent on profiting from Seattle's flourishing building environment. Competition forced small businessmen to target buyers that professional architects and large contracting firms ignored: people of modest means. Until the early twentieth century, these consumers typically had rented their dwellings or delayed purchase of a home until later in life, when they had accumulated enough money. The Jud Yohos of Seattle realized the consumer potential of these people and actively sought to extend the housing market to them. To do this, small dealers developed modern techniques of selling, advertising, and financing to induce people with modest incomes to buy houses. These methods played a decisive role in creating a particular domestic architecture.

Stock architectural plans fed the desire for stylish homes and helped families acquire them. Disseminated in mail-order plan books since the late nineteenth century, stock plans provided complete working drawings and specifications for residential construction. Earlier, plans had originated only with architects or carpenter-builders, but with a stock plan, a home builder could choose a fashionable style without an architect's fee. For speculators erecting many new suburban homes, these plans both saved money and implemented systematization in the construction process. By the early twentieth century, plan book companies became big businesses, as more speculators and home builders relied on mass-produced designs. The diffusion of plan books followed the nation's booming population growth along the transcontinental railroads, through rural free delivery routes, and into the rapidly expanding suburbs. As a result, stock plans helped break down regionalism, and popular residential architecture throughout the United States took on a more standardized, homogeneous appearance.[18]

All groups involved in the building industry, but especially small firms, used and produced plan books as a way to encourage consumption of their products. Real estate agents, contractors, material suppliers, "designers," and speculators all sold stock plans. In fact, suburban developers may have begun their widespread use in Seattle. Lumber companies, such as Hewitt-Lea-Funck, provided plan books with the assumption that customers would buy all building materials—"lumber, millwork, hardware, paint, [and] electric bell"—directly from them. Advertisements promised to save customers' money by bypassing the "middlemen."[19]

By "middlemen," they meant, of course, professional architects, who deplored the "plan factories" that they saw churning out generic, mediocre designs. But even architects themselves blurred the line between design and mass sales. Small, diversified architectural firms struggling to gain a toehold in a fast-paced economy unabashedly produced plan books. In Seattle, Victor W. Voorhees, who opened a Ballard office in 1904, published a catalogue "containing many plans of houses, apartment houses, [and] business blocks" as early as 1906. He later produced issues for "house, cottage and bungalow plans and elevations." Other architects who had expanded into residential construction, such as Frank Cruse and Elmer E. Green, also published plan books. Designers labeling themselves "architects" but apparently without professional training sold plans too. Willard W. DeLong claimed that his plan books were "not Stock Drawings nor Reprints, but PLANS drawn ESPECIALLY for YOU by experts in BUNGALOW BUILDING." Contractors who advertised as "designers and builders," such as the Distinctive Homes Company or the Herrick Improvement Company, disseminated books of plans. These small entrepreneurs did not worry about the aesthetics of the architecture they sold in such publications. Rather, they embraced plan books as an essential new tool for selling their services. In doing so, they broadcast a popular version of residential architecture.[20]

4.2 *Craftsman Bungalow plan book cover, 1913. The house depicted on this cover is the bungalow Yoho claimed was awarded a prize. It is also Yoho's copy of Arthur S. Heineman's 1909 California house. Photo: Craftsman Bungalow plan book, Seattle Public Library.*

Seattle businessman Jud Yoho mastered the new medium for housing design. Through his prolific output of plan books, he actively acquainted the buying public with new ideas in homes. He left an impressive visual and archival legacy. Yoho produced his first "booklet" on bungalows in 1911, following up with new or updated editions in 1913, 1915, 1917, 1920 and 1921 (fig. 4.2). From these, customers could purchase a complete set of plans and specifications for bungalows. Calling himself "The Bungalow Craftsman," in the 1913 "edition de luxe," Yoho stated that "the designing of an artistic bungalow of the true type requires as much skill and education as does any other branch of the architect's work. The man with the experience and training is the one to give you the best results. All of the designs in this book are bungalows pure and simple. Most of them are my own ideas." In reality, Yoho had no architectural education, but obviously understood how to exploit the housing market's unregulated nature.[21]

Yoho had clearly borrowed many of his plans directly from other sources. Ultimately, of course, he wanted to sell houses, not originate unique creations. Some photographs in his 1913 plan book included bungalows with palm trees, a plant adapted to California but not Washington. Others featured suspiciously blanked-out backgrounds. Historian Rob Anglin found that the "Bungalow which was Awarded the Prize" copied almost exactly Arthur S. Heineman's 1909 California house. Small operators such as Yoho commonly duplicated others' work, and very likely he and his colleagues brought the latest designs directly from California. Interestingly, Yoho used the models of another firm of amateur architects. Arthur Heineman and his brother Alfred had no formal training but entered the field of design from real estate and speculative building. Yoho realized that the latest fashions sold, whatever their origin.[22]

Yoho intended his stylish residences for the middle- and lower-middle class, those families that professional architects had largely overlooked. In the early twentieth century, architects charged a minimum commission of 5 percent of the total cost of "all materials and labor necessary to complete the work."[23] They made their biggest profits on expensive projects. Small residences, which cost between $1,500 and $2,000, only netted the architect $75 to $100, which professionals considered insufficient for the time involved. Big architectural firms therefore left ordinary homes to carpenters and contractors. Conversely, the additional architectural fee could determine whether families of limited means could build a house. Recognizing this potential market, plan book purveyors successfully created a new enterprise. As early as 1907, *Pacific Builder and Engineer* noted that "there is . . . a large demand for [stock plans] and it places within the reach of those with moderate means the services of a trained architect, that otherwise they could not purchase for the betterment of their home."[24]

Mail-order plan books carved out a niche in the middle class in several ways. Purveyors made plans cheap and available. In Seattle, the catalogues themselves sold from Hewitt-Lea-Funck's 10¢ version and architect Voorhees's 25¢ issue to the Herrick Improvement Company's $1.50 booklet. Blueprints and specifications, too, were affordable and complete, averaging much less than the architect's 5 percent commission, yet providing much the same service. If customers chose an average bungalow plan, it cost them about $10. Larger houses from architects with plan books, such as Voorhees, came somewhat more expensive— for example, $51 for a nine-room residence. When clients hired contractors like The Bungalow Company, plans cost nothing. Publications featured modest houses moderately priced. In the Craftsman Bungalow Company's 1913 catalogue, the average bungalow cost approximately $1,965, and the cheapest only $600. With these prices, stylish architecture entered the realm of possibility for people of limited funds.[25]

Heavily illustrated catalogues of house plans also whetted the public's appetite for houses, stimulating the desire to own a home. They acted as "wish books," placing images of desirable homes before a group hungering for the suburban family life the books depicted. Without leaving their rooms, apartments, flats, or rental houses, people could view the latest designs in housing, choosing the one that most appealed to them. This worked both to instruct potential customers in the merits of home ownership and to instill in them the longing for such a dwelling. Even when buying a house proved elusive, plan books provided dreams. As a Seattle woman related in 1909,

> The nearest we ever came to having a home of our own was a year ago, when we sent a dollar for an architect's book and, after much earnest tea table controversy, selected the plans and specifications for a six-room bungalow. I am sick of dwelling ephemerally in a castle in the air. I would rather have a little four-room bungalow with a green roof that I could call my very own. My husband's salary is small, and some way we can't seem to get more than a hundred dollars ahead to save our lives. . . .[Then] something comes up that devours our little surplus and leaves us even with the board, exactly where we started ten years ago when we married. I do envy a woman who has a little home of her own.

This woman may have already yearned for the American dream of home ownership, but access to plan books further kindled that desire.[26]

Some housing entrepreneurs took even stronger measures than stock plans to attract moderate-income families craving affordable homes. A few enterprising men and women produced magazines and publications that advertised their products and services. DeLong's book, *Seattle Home Builder and Home Keeper,* exemplified advertising disguised as instruction in home building. Published in 1915, the booklet ostensibly dispensed practical recommendations on the planning and construction of a residence. DeLong's wife, Belle, gave scientific advice for "The Wife (Cook)" on diet, recipes, and home remedies. Advertisements, however, for professional services, building material suppliers, food, and home appliances made up about half the book. DeLong encouraged readers to consider advertisements "some of the most important contents of the volume" and claimed that "their suggestions are as timely and as authoritative as the editorial matter." His own advertisement for special bungalow plans appeared opposite this pronouncement. Though DeLong refrained from directly promoting his services, he and his advertisers obviously sought to boost their businesses through such a seemingly impartial publication.[27]

With his remarkable talent for self-promotion, Jud Yoho emerged as Seattle's most adroit and celebrated purveyor of literature on popular, middle-class architecture. He achieved this fame through his *Bungalow Magazine,* a monthly periodical produced between 1912 and 1918. The magazine ostensibly sought to teach the public about the beauty of bungalow architecture. In format, it mimicked Stickley's popular *Craftsman* magazine. Well-illustrated with photographs, it mostly featured Seattle bungalows and articles about California residences, some lifted directly from *The Craftsman*. With these came recommendations for interior decorating, built-in furniture, landscaping, and technological systems appropriate to bungalows. Each month's issue included the complete plans, elevations, and material list for a specific bungalow. Advertisements for housing accessories appeared frequently—building supplies, furniture, and appliances such as coolers, furnaces, and hot-water heaters.[28]

Although it claimed to be "devoted exclusively to artistic bungalow homes," *Bungalow Magazine's* real purpose was to sell a commodity in which its creators had a major financial interest. Unlike *The Craftsman,* Yoho's journal omitted articles about the broader ideology of the Arts and Crafts movement. For instance, it never included editorials lauding William Morris's socialism or glorification of the master craftsman. In 1913, when Yoho served as president of the Bungalow Publishing Company, he also headed the Craftsman Bungalow Company, which constructed speculative housing and sold real estate in Seattle. *Bungalow Magazine* regularly featured many of these residences, with Yoho's name prominently displayed as "architect." Dolph E. Hooker, treasurer of the Bungalow Publishing Company and Yoho's business partner since at least 1907, also benefited directly from the periodical's promotionals. While editor from 1913 to 1915, Hooker operated an import-export store that advertised wicker furniture—"just the thing for bungalows." So, of course, in May 1915, the journal ran an article by Charles Alma Byers extolling "the advantages of wicker furniture for the bungalow." For Yoho and Hooker, magazine publishing functioned as advertising.[29]

Bungalow Magazine advertised not only Yoho's work but the work of a whole group of Seattle bungalow builders, architects, and real estate developers who operated in the same commercial strata as Yoho. Particularly before 1917, each issue consisted mainly of glowing descriptions and plentiful photos of Seattle bungalows. At the beginning of each article, the editors pointedly specified the architect, designer, or builder, and at the end added a business address. Some stories mentioned a client/home-owner, but most featured speculative housing. Nowhere did the journal crassly publicize houses for sale. But it obviously highlighted those firms with a marketable commodity, and greatly expanded their audience beyond common advertising methods. The journal even went so far as to unite builders and designers with new customers. It did this through a "free plan service." The name implied that readers could obtain "free" house specifications, but in reality it only provided them with sources for purchasing the plans shown in the journal.[30]

Bungalow Magazine proved particularly useful to the handful of professional architects who designed bungalows. Although the journal mainly focused on contractors or designers like Yoho, houses from a few members of the Washington State chapter of the American Institute of Architects (AIA) did grace its pages. An exclusive group established in 1894, the local AIA viewed its members as experts adhering to a code of conduct that emphasized objectivity. Artistic principles, not the crass pursuit of money, guided their work. Directly advertising services violated this standard. By the 1930s, the Washington chapter had clarified its position. It was "unethical," reaffirmed the board of directors, for AIA members to feature their work in publications that contained advertisements, or to publish brochures or catalogues that contained both their designs and advertisements. However, designs of AIA architects could appear in a "regularly published magazine or newspaper having a general circulation and containing material of general interest." *Bungalow Magazine* provided such an outlet. There, professional architects could let the public know of their houses, yet not overtly advertise them.[31]

A few of Seattle's professional architects and AIA members used *Bungalow Magazine* in just this way. Most well-known was Ellsworth Storey. Obtaining a degree at the University of Illinois, he came to Seattle in 1903, where he commenced a well-respected career in architecture. Through the 1910s, he created buildings in different fashionable styles, but retained a predilection for Arts and Crafts–inspired buildings in Prairie, Swiss Chalet, and Tudor variations. His houses appeared occasionally in the journal between 1914 and 1916. Educated at the Massachusetts Institute of Technology, the University of Pennsylvania, and Drexel Institute, W. R. B. Willcox was another AIA professional who submitted a design for a spare, modest bungalow in 1917. These men, however, thought about moderately priced dwellings only as a side issue to their more lucrative commissions. An exception was Edwin J. Ivey. A native Seattleite, he returned to practice there after graduating from the University of Pennsylvania in 1910. Though an AIA member, Ivey regularly contributed to *Bungalow Magazine* with articles and designs in "Old English," Colonial, or Dutch Colonial style. Ivey worked with developers on speculative housing. For instance, the January 1918 issue featured a block of small, individual "Colonial" houses designed by Ivey, who had a long-standing association with E. E. Harold, "one of the men most active in developing West Seattle property with really worth while houses." The magazine, therefore, provided another medium for both Ivey and Harold to advertise their speculative projects.[32]

More than just advertising the wares of builders and architects, *Bungalow Magazine* sought to shape the architectural choices of middle-income Americans. Much as Stickley's *Craftsman* tried to influence the residential habits of the professional middle class, *Bungalow Magazine* attempted to teach ordinary people a certain "taste" in their purchasing habits, a taste that Yoho and his partners could then exploit. It joined a whole phalanx of modern popular magazines that flooded the mail routes in the early twentieth century. As Christopher P. Wilson has argued, the publications ushered in a "consumerist reorientation" and spread the desire to consume deeply into society. When advertisements featured domestic architecture, then the suburban landscape itself became a symbol of this new consumer culture.[33]

Used as a promotion by salesmen like Yoho, the Craftsman handicraft ideal mutated. Yoho's formation of the Take Down Manufacturing Company clearly revealed this. Established in 1915 with Yoho's wife, Elsie, and Ralph and Loraine Casey, the new firm issued a booklet entitled "Craftsman Master Built Homes." But no master carpenters had handcrafted its bungalows, as the title implied. These were prefabricated "portable" houses. For as little as $300 to $450, families could order small dwellings in panelized sections, which, the booklet claimed, could be "erected by any one by following our simple directions without it being necessary to hire skilled labor." "Craftsman Master Built" actually meant a "method of construction" in which houses came preassembled from a factory, eliminating expensive handwork. "We have learned from experience," the owners stated, "that power driven machines can do better work at a lower cost than hand labor. This has resulted in a factory equipment that does every bit of the work with the most modern machinery."[34] A rhetoric that once glorified the traditional craftsman transmuted into a marketing slogan for factory-produced houses. The original radical meaning of Morris's alternative to industrial capitalism collapsed into an incentive to buy industrialized, prefabricated homes.[35]

But invoking a popular sentiment alone could not sell houses for Seattle's small-time housing entrepreneurs. They had to find a way that families with moderate incomes could pay for their own homes. Installment purchasing furnished the means. Housing salesmen offered their own financing, which home buyers repaid in monthly payments. These practices revolutionized lending and ushered in the modern consumer credit system. As home ownership became available to a greater part of the population, the reach of a burgeoning consumer economy widened and this fueled the suburban expansions of the 1910s and 1920s.[36]

Buying houses "on time," as people termed it, became an accepted middle-class practice in the early twentieth century, although working-class people had bought items such as furniture and sewing machines "on time" since the mid-nineteenth century. Until then, respectable society had viewed installment buying as "a sign of poverty and improvident living." Most people who could afford a house purchased it outright from savings or received small loans through personal connections. The less wealthy obtained manageable loans through a mortgage from building and loan (or savings and loan) associations, or they received more restrictive loans from savings banks. Typically, such loans covered only about half of the price, and required semiannual interest payments and a lump sum satisfaction of the principal at the end of the term (usually three to eight years). Borrowing through a mortgage provided a relatively safe, conventional way for the middle class to finance a home. And it was socially respectable. The middle class believed that cash buying reflected their core values of thrift and responsibility.[37]

Such a restrictive nineteenth-century lending system helped ensure that money for homes circulated mainly within the middle class. The way real estate agents found and secured private mortgagees clearly illustrated this. Arranging financing for clients made up an important part of salespeople's jobs. They matched up lenders looking for safe and profitable investment opportunities to credible borrowers desiring a loan to buy land or buildings. The lender advanced the cash to the broker, who drew up the necessary papers, gave the loan to the borrower, and received a fee. Even though private, such mortgages functioned much as did those given by institutions. For instance, in 1901 Seattle agent Frederick West described his policy to a woman in Washington, D.C., interested in opportunities in the city's real estate. "Interest rates vary from 6 to 8%, owing to length of time the money is [loaned] and the amount loaned, occasionally a higher rate may be had than I have named but in most cases it is on account of the security not being of the best," he wrote.[38] He commonly negotiated three-year loans with the 8 percent interest payable semiannually, terms much like the Fremont State Bank offered in 1910. Funding for these private mortgages came from the agent's connections to business networks and social organizations, and through personal referrals and family. West, for example, sold lots to a homebuilder, then arranged for his father to extend the buyer a mortgage for construction of a residence. Mostly limited to the middle class, conventional mortgages like these greatly constricted the size of the housing market.[39]

Salespeople needed more innovative financing to satisfy ordinary people's dreams of home ownership. A few sellers adopted installment payment plans pioneered for such goods as sewing machines and furniture and created a new method of financing variously called a "land contract," or "contract for deed." Sellers themselves directly provided financing, extending the ability to purchase houses to people with only limited savings. The arrangement consisted simply of a legal contract in which the buyer paid a small down payment and agreed to pay the full price in monthly installments with interest payments included. The catch was that the seller retained legal title to the property. This allowed the seller to bypass legal foreclosure and easily evict the buyer for even one missed payment. When this happened, the buyer not only lost the house but the down payment and all subsequent installment payments. Sellers could negotiate any sort of contract or terms to which both parties agreed. Thus, they could charge much higher interest rates than the legal mortgage limit during periods of housing shortages, or to customers excluded from conventional financing, such as African Americans. Some contracts contained outright fraud, especially in the sale of lots in new additions. Developers could extend contracts on land to which they did not actually hold title, taking customers' payments but leaving them without legal ownership. Or, builders' liens and debts might encumber the property, which became the new owner's responsibility with the transfer of the title at the end of the purchase period. This form of financing could prove unsafe for builders, too, as it tied up capital needed for other projects and provided only incremental returns. But despite these risks, the contract for deed burst open opportunities to acquire homes. Now, anyone with a minimal down payment and the discipline and means to make a monthly payment might potentially buy a house.[40]

Use of land contracts boomed along with Seattle's late 1880s construction expansion. In 1890, *Seattle Illustrated,* published by the Seattle Chamber of Commerce, credited the real estate firm of F. J. Monroe and Company with introducing "the innovation of selling land upon instalment [sic] payments . . . [which] immediately became popular throughout the State." The publication noted that this new practice had extended the land market, saying it had "worked so satisfactorily to the person with small means in hand, and who had hitherto been almost shut out from having his lot in common with those of money in hand. We can attribute to this fact alone the possession of land by the laborer, who otherwise could not have had his own house and lot."[41] (Monroe also began the use of newspaper display advertising for real estate in Seattle.) Indeed, firms in the 1890s, such as E. C. Kilbourne, often advertised sale of lots on "easy terms." As housing construction intensified in the early twentieth century, developers increasingly applied installment buying practices to erected dwellings as well as lots. By 1908, real estate agents sold moderately priced homes in northern neighborhoods by advertising a down payment of about $100 to $300 and the "balance like rent." Even when owners wanted half the price in cash, they offered "easy terms" for the remaining portion. Sometimes they accepted down payments as low as $25 or $50, with $25 to $30 monthly payments. Within a few decades, installment purchasing revolutionized home financing and home ownership. Through its use, moderate-income families became important components in shaping the suburban landscape.[42]

More than anyone else, small building entrepreneurs like Jud Yoho instigated this home financing revolution. Always alert for ways to make a profit, they used contracts for deed to attract a new group of buyers that they claimed as their own. By 1910, agents in Seattle's north end sought to lure first-time home owners. H. F. Sharpless's 1910 ad for Wallingford and Green Lake homes queried, "Why pay rent when such homes can be bought on easy monthly payments?" House payments under a contract compared favorably to paying rent, as Yoho frequently pointed out. For instance, in 1909, a Wallingford-area landlord advertised a four-room modern cottage for rent for $15 a month and a seven-room "modern house" for rent for $20 a month. Two years later, S. P. Dixon of Fremont sold "modern" five-room bungalows in Wallingford for only $25 down and $15 a month. Claiming that "anybody can buy," these small dealers, not the increasingly big and powerful developers with access to conventional funding sources, appealed to Seattle's middle-income populace.[43]

With enticements such as affordability and easy terms, salespeople like Yoho created a distinct ideal that resonated with their intended clientele. Through newspaper advertisements, plan books, and publications, these housing businessmen advanced an image of independence, modern technology, and urbanity. Yoho promised his consumers secure homes, free from the intrusions of pushy employers or nosy landlords. For those families fleeing apartments, this must have been alluring. Small-time dealers stressed an image of individual homes closely tied to technology and the larger consumer economy. Yoho relentlessly called his houses "modern," meaning they contained the latest household technology. By 1912, the *Seattle Post-Intelligencer* declared that "certain conveniences are now in such general use that their omission would render the building practically unrentable, e.g., electrical equipment, modern plumbing, gas ranges, ice machines, etc."[44] Advertising emphasized access to urban systems such as streetcar lines and convenient location near workplaces, schools, and the city center rather than a naturalistic setting. Magnificent views and beautiful landscaping mattered less than neighborhood "improvements" such as concrete sidewalks, paved streets, and water mains. Freedom, technology, urbanity—the savvy salesmen of the built environment used these ideals to market their products.[45]

Of course, the promise of lower-middle-class suburban home ownership failed to materialize in quite the way advertising promised. Buying houses on time imposed a rigid financial discipline that tied workers to their jobs and the mercy of their employers. Dependency on advanced technical systems instead of individual wells and wood stoves further bound owners to consumption by compelling them to buy their heat, light, and water and by encouraging purchases of household appliances. Many streets that gridded the north end's densely built blocks of logged-off land remained unpaved into the 1920s. The supposed freedom and independence assured in sales literature came with qualifications. Nonetheless, in such neighborhoods, families of moderate means could acquire their own homes.[46]

Small-time housing salesmen knew well how to attract the aspiring lower middle class; they themselves came from this group and desired the same suburban ideal. Jud Yoho's life could easily represent that of his fellow businessmen and his customers. Like so many of his cohorts, Yoho grew up in economic volatility and understood life's vagaries. He spent much of his young life on the move. His father, John Yoho, a restless man with little or no formal education,

20¢ THE COPY   JULY 1913   CANADA 25¢

BVNGALOW
MAGAZINE

UPPLEMENT °BVNGALOW

4.3 Jud Yoho's 1911 house at 4718 Second Avenue Northeast in the Wallingford neighborhood served as both dwelling and advertisement, appearing in both the July 1913 Bungalow Magazine *and Yoho's* Craftsman Bungalow *plan book.*

had gradually worked his way west, earning a living in such ventures as real estate. Financial stability eluded him, however, and after the 1890s financial collapse in Denver and the nation, he made his way to Seattle. Although he arrived at a propitious time, hard luck followed him. He died in 1908 at the age of fifty-one, without ever achieving entrepreneurial success. John left to Jud his business savvy and, importantly, the desire to maintain middle-class security. From life with John, Jud understood how to appeal to those on the financial edge, those who appreciated a sense of domestic permanence in unpredictable times.[47]

Yoho could advance an image of suburban independence and freedom because he understood firsthand the ups, downs, and desires of his lower-middle-class market. His company built Craftsman bungalows, mostly in Seattle's north end suburbs, so Yoho logically chose to locate his family's first permanent home there. In 1910, he moved his wife, Elsie, and their baby out of a rental, and in 1911, after a brief stay in one of his speculative houses, into a model Craftsman bungalow at 4718 Second Avenue NE (fig. 4.3). In Wallingford, his primary place of speculative building, Yoho joined a community of people much like himself. Here, mostly closely packed, moderately sized bungalows constructed between 1906 and 1915 lined the gridded streets. Salespeople, accountants, clerks, and agents like Yoho most often selected these bungalows. Although many occupational groups—professionals, managers, and skilled workers, for instance—also lived in bungalows, they did not choose them as exclusively as did the sales class. Like Yoho, most were probably first-time home owners, taking advantage of easier home financing, incurring a large debt to purchase their dwellings. In 1920, 44 percent of the families within a portion of Wallingford held mortgages. The Yoho family certainly did. In 1918, when Yoho's Seattle ventures and his marriage began to unravel, he defaulted on his loan with the Martin Investment Company. King County foreclosed, and he lost his lovely home. As a salesman and consumer at the whims of the new economy, Yoho fully grasped the vision of suburbia that would appeal to others like him. Together, sellers and buyers like Yoho created neighborhoods that reflected a burgeoning consumer culture embraced by an expanding group of service-sector participants.[48]

Small-scale housing purveyors like Yoho demonstrated such success in shaping early twentieth-century cityscapes that newly emerging building professionals in real estate, construction, and especially architecture decisively moved to shut them out of the lucrative market. These experts sought greater control over a chaotic, unregulated, and destructively competitive field. In the first two decades of the twentieth century, nothing but individual economic restraints prevented enterprising go-getters from entering all aspects of the housing business. As Seattle flourished, people flooded in, calling themselves contractors, architects, or real estate agents without needing any legal proof of their expertise. To compete, struggling salespeople undercut one another, pushed commissions lower, and lured customers away from other firms. Worse yet from many professionals' view, "fly-by-night" operators threatened legitimate enterprises by besmirching their reputations. Big, influential real estate firms like Seattle's West and Wheeler complained of the "irresponsible men" intent on defrauding naive buyers. Magnates in well-capitalized contracting companies decried the diminishing profits and shoddy work that resulted from periodic influxes of both competent and shady builders. [49]

Professional architects had special reason to desire curtailing small operators like Yoho. As in real estate and building, anyone with some knowledge of construction could adopt the title of architect and set about designing structures. The competition from such entrepreneurs potentially pushed down fees and stole work from experts who had acquired specialized training or advanced education. In addition, architects saw themselves as artists, the sole stewards of landscape beauty. As Portland architect Charles C. Rich proclaimed, the architect is "an expert, trained by years of study in school and travel and practice; an expert builder, plus an artist in design and planning. He may never have lifted a saw or a hammer, and yet he is a craftsman in the largest and truest sense; indeed the chief craftsman."[50] Only such formally schooled professionals had the necessary understanding of the "immutable design principles of unity, harmony, balance and repose" that produced truly beautiful, unique design. The Yohos of the field who dispensed architectural services without any "expert" credentials threatened this artistic supremacy.[51]

To an emerging elite in the home-building industry, the street after street of bungalows and period revival houses put up by small, diversified operators like Yoho often failed to meet burgeoning professional standards. More painfully, these prolific entrepreneurs hurt profit margins. Some big, influential firms—often including contractors, architects, and real estate agents—sought order by becoming "community builders." They acquired large tracts and created and sold planned, elite residential suburbs where developers controlled all aspects of physical design and marketing. Their size grew dramatically, as such ventures required a large staff of clerks and salespeople organized into coordinated but specialized departments. Company owners acted like chief executive officers, moving beyond their initial roles as salesmen.[52] But most professionals still faced continual pressure from their small competitors. To eliminate this threat, they utilized their most powerful tactic: they created professional organizations to influence legislation protecting elite interests.

In 1903, determined to "raise the standards of the industry," and, of course, to keep commissions from falling, Seattle's most prominent and wealthy agents created the Seattle Real Estate Association. Its first important campaign worked to restrict competition from small, undifferentiated entrepreneurs. In 1912, the group lobbied for a state law to require licensing of real estate agents. As magnate James Wheeler saw it, this exclusivity provided a way to "prevent a man who was not qualified [from] operating as a real estate agent."[53] Finally, in 1925, a state registration law succeeded. From then on, "brokers"—defined as anyone who negotiated real estate deals for other people—had to apply to a state real estate director for a license. The new law closed the field to those without some financial base and ties to the community. But in reality it did not prevent the entry of small entrepreneurs with some capital. It only threw up a few hurdles. Small enterprises continued to make up the majority of real estate offices.[54]

Big building contractors, too, moved quickly to cut off entry into their field. Although it existed as early as 1906, the Seattle Master Builders' Association formally organized in 1914. By 1919, it advocated the licensing of contractors, claiming this would deprive irresponsible contractors of "a chance to prey upon the public."[55] A stiff licensing fee would distinctly favor the master builders. For years, the group lobbied the state legislature, but with little success. For justification, it argued that licensing would curtail bad building by unscrupulous operators who discredited home ownership. *Pacific Builder and Engineer* declared in 1931 that "jerry-built" houses meant double payments for purchase and costly upkeep. The public could be assured of "properly designed and constructed" homes only if "the progenies of Jerry [were] eliminated through adequate licensing."[56] The Contractors Registration Act became law in 1963, but not before the courts had ruled it unconstitutional at least once. Its relatively weak provisions required little more than a $2000 surety bond and proof of public liability and property damage insurance. Home construction by small outfits, "the progenies of Jerry," continued apace.[57]

Architects worried most about the deleterious effect of nonprofessionals like Yoho on the appearance of cities taking shape in the early twentieth century. In 1894, prominent Seattle architects formed the State of Washington Society of Architects. A few months later, they affiliated with the American Institute of Architects (AIA) to become the Washington State chapter of the AIA. Uniting architects "in fellowship . . . for their mutual protection," they opened their ranks only to those deemed "worthy of membership" by two members and with five years' or more direct employment as architects. By 1900, new members needed a degree from an approved architectural school or to pass an AIA examination. Regulating its own members did not solve the problem of entrepreneurs like Yoho, however. Finally, after years of AIA lobbying, in 1919 the Washington legislature passed an architect's licensing law. It mandated that all new persons calling themselves architects had to pass an exam administered by the newly created state board of architect examiners composed of powerful AIA members. From then on, small business people like Yoho who dabbled in housing design could no longer call themselves architects.[58]

Try as they might, though, professional architects could not curtail the influence of small housing entrepreneurs on the domestic landscape. Home builders did not need professional architects to acquire attractive house designs. In fact, few trained architects even bothered with modest dwellings. Professionally trained architects disdained the mass production of domestic architecture originating in plan books or copied by small builders. Plan books, they asserted, reflected the poor taste of popular fashion rather than the elite, cultivated standards of original art. Only with the intervention of architects could small houses reflect "either originality of design, artistic beauty or be structurally attractive." The results of "plans . . . usually taken from 'ready cut' catalogues or designed by local carpenters" were "dull, drab American small town homes."[59]

The huge surge of suburban building after World War I prompted professional architects to try wresting residential design from the small diversified entrepreneurs. Eyeing this rich new source of revenue, architects realized that entrepreneurial builders had cornered the market. In 1919, prominent Seattle architect and AIA member Carl F. Gould decried the ugly neighborhoods he saw peppering the landscape. "The speculative builder procures some cheaply worked out plans from some overworked book on home plans, probably prepared by the son of a carpenter builder who happened to have a knack at mechanical drawing. Something should be done," he demanded, "to offset these extravagant speculative building projects." This was necessary, he added, because "within a few years the world will see one of the largest output of individual homes ever produced in the history of the world." Architects wanted to gain the upper hand in this development and stop the spread of stock plans to large and expensive houses, the architect's bread and butter.[60]

Responding to the challenge, the AIA moved onto the turf of entrepreneurs like Yoho and formed a stock plan service of its own, the Architects' Small House Service Bureau of the United States. Clearly, a practice initiated and mastered by businesspeople had trickled up to professional architects. Although the bureau's stated purpose was "altruistic in its nature . . . to improve the architecture of the small home," it copied the tactics and designs of common plan books. Despite its claims of beautifying suburbs with artistic structures, the AIA's efforts had little visual influence on the built environment. Its designs proved too similar to stock plans, and too few plans reached the public for any noticeable transformation to occur. By 1926, the bureau had sold only 4,000 plans. Historian Thomas Harvey estimated that of the eight million new dwelling units constructed in the 1920s, fewer than five thousand originated with bureau plans. By the Great Depression, the AIA, with disastrously declining sales and construction, conceded the field to the entrepreneur/builder. In 1934, it withdrew its support of the bureau, which officially dissolved in 1942. The small-time housing dealer remained the most important creator of the suburban landscape.[61]

The professionals could not control the built environment where most people lived, the "hundreds of poorly designed structures that have been classed as the type called 'quick-sellers.'"[62] The big development firms turned to planned communities, where they could carefully regulate both design and residents. There they could impose an order and unity that seemed so lacking in the neighborhoods created by small diversified brokers. In 1907, Seattle's Mount Baker Park marked the beginning of community building, a trend that gathered momentum throughout the twentieth century. Although existing alongside the neighborhoods of Yoho and his cohorts, places like Mount Baker Park expressed a markedly different vision. Planned by the famous Olmsted brothers, John Charles and Frederick Law Olmsted, in design it replicated a "natural garden," with curvilinear streets, scenic boulevards, parks, and open green areas.

Building restrictions mandated relatively expensive dwellings (over $2,000 or $5,000, depending on the locality within the district) designed by architects to be "as distinctive and individual in character as possible." The Mount Baker Park Improvement Club, the home owners' association, ensured that residents included only "those of the most critical taste." The club's idea of "congenial companions" did not include African Americans, and developers refused to sell lots to black families. This kind of overt, advertised, formal architectural and social control was impossible in Seattle's northern regions.[63]

In fact, such elite developments demonstrated the hold that small-time entrepreneurs maintained within the urban environment. As such dealers widened consumption through modern sales techniques, middle- and upper-class Seattleites pulled away from what they perceived as the commodified, cheapened landscape. Planned communities provided a means of expressing nuances of class within a rapidly growing consumer economy. Individually, many of the homes in Mount Baker Park did look much like the Craftsman bungalow in Wallingford that Orrill Stapp could barely afford. Yoho even built a few. But overall the two neighborhoods looked different, which even the most casual observer could perceive. With its curving streets, hilltop location, and lush open areas interspersed among the large, architect-designed homes, Mount Baker Park stood apart from the city. Like Beaux Arts Village directly across Lake Washington, it exuded refinement, wealth, and removal from the hubbub of twentieth-century urban living. Wallingford, on the other hand, reveled in its participation in the new urban environment. Streetcars headed straight for Seattle's center rumbled down its gridded streets, past rows of small houses only slightly separated by slim strips of green. Wallingford's setting appeared more technological than naturalistic, its control more individualistic than communal. Here, a different social vision prevailed, one that appealed to a different class of people. It was a place for those just entering the full pleasures of the consumer society, not those attempting to project a loftier position within it.[64]

Understanding the landscape of Seattle's north end, then, is not simply a matter of seeing the values and architectural ideals of the upper classes filtered down to the lower classes. With their elegant homes and abundant records, planned, exclusive communities have lured many historians of early twentieth-century architecture. But such handsome suburbs as Mount Baker Park can not speak for all of the urban environment. Indeed, they exist as islands within a vast ocean of modest, unassuming, relatively unplanned neighborhoods. There, in the first half of the twentieth-century, small-time entrepreneurs built and sold this landscape, and they did so for a new group of eager but struggling consumers. Rather than merely responding to a watered-down elite ideal, sellers and buyers of ordinary bungalows created something new, a landscape of consumerism.

LIVING IN THE
SEATTLE BUNGALOW

For TEN YEARS, Orrill Stapp, Frances, and their three young sons had attempted to create the cozy, intimate family in their Rainier Beach Craftsman house that Stickley and others had advocated. By 1914, however, practical realities surmounted idealism. Living the "simple life" proved difficult, as financial worries weakened his ability to live close to nature. Rainier Beach's scarce population of paying customers who valued classical music apparently forced Orrill to commute 30 minutes by streetcar to downtown Seattle. Though small printing jobs augmented his income, "times were rough," his son, Stan, wrote later. When Orrill moved his family to Seattle's northern neighborhoods, economic necessity trumped ideology.[1]

For a while, it seemed that Stapp would successfully assimilate his school of music into the expanding consumer economy of Seattle's north end. Two more children joined the family, enlarging it to seven. All seemed rosy. But, perhaps caught in the downturn after World War I, Stapp left his school's rented quarters for a house that could accommodate both his family and his students. In 1922, when he gazed upon the Craftsman bungalow at 4203 Woodlawn Avenue that looked so similar to his Rainier Beach house, he undoubtedly warmed to its overt symbolism as a nurturing refuge for an informal nuclear family and companionate marriage. But pragmatic considerations competed with these idealistic thoughts as Stapp faced growing financial pressures. The bungalow in the Wallingford neighborhood contained utilitarian space; a huge, open living room perfect for monthly recitals and piano lessons, a basement for his small printing press and for storage, and rooms for his children, including a teenaged son, Elbert, bedridden with encephalitis. Stapp purchased the house and merged his family life and business.[2]

Mixing music lessons and domesticity in 4203 Woodlawn marked only the first stage of the Stapp family's manipulation of home. The negotiation of space within the Stapp's home gradually intensified as a new and more demanding venture came to dominate the household. Beginning in 1922, Milton, Orrill's oldest son, began publishing a small newspaper from the house just two years after graduating from high school. Before long, the business blossomed into a weekly neighborhood publication, drawing in most of the Stapp family and a permanent staff. It took over the entire remodeled basement and portions of the first and second stories, remaining in the domicile until 1970, when the newspaper finally moved to its own building. The Stapps crafted a modern sort of household economy with their newspaper. From their home they manufactured a product particularly central to the new consumer economy. Their house served as a tool for this transformation. The Stapps used their space flexibly, modifying and reinterpreting its rooms as needed to help them survive and prosper as their world changed around them.[3]

Although unusual in their choice of home-based enterprise, the Stapps represented families all across North American who used their houses to meet the economic challenges and opportunities of the early twentieth century. In cities such as Los Angeles, Detroit, and Toronto, working-class suburbanites grew truck gardens, raised livestock, took in boarders and laundry, and operated small businesses from their homes. Even a few affluent households in exclusive suburbs contained lodgers and raised animals, according to historian Mary Corbin Sies. In Seattle, north-end families undertook these "production-oriented lifeways," as historian Andrew Wiese calls them, in structures articulating certain architectural precepts and domestic assumptions. As the exemplary Craftsman dwellings in Beaux Arts Village and Stapp's house in Rainier Beach revealed, reformers meant for homes to assert a new, modern domestic ideal. But most Seattleites, like Orrill Stapp, did not feel limited by those principles. When they manipulated their homes, in a process that architectural historian Kingston Heath has called "cultural weathering," they helped shape popular twentieth-century domestic architecture.[4]

Seattle and the rest of the nation contained many ordinary families, who saw the creation of a home as a dynamic process. Often their use and choices coincided with the ideology embedded in their homes' physical structures, but they also contested reformers' idealism. Ordinary people did not necessarily feel committed to the values designers expressed, and sometimes chose to ignore them altogether. Houses might offer them succor and refuge from a hostile outside world, but they also served as a hedge against economic instability and a source of independence and opportunity. As they faced the transformation from the nineteenth century to the twentieth, this flexibility, this pragmatism, assisted them and prepared them for a modern society and a modern economy. As they reshaped their dwellings, they helped redefine the meaning of home.

Because their architecture looked the same as the typical bungalow, and because they articulately expressed Arts and Crafts principles, the utopianists in Beaux Arts Village appeared to speak for all of Seattle's myriad bungalow dwellers. But the average, moderate-income families of Seattle's north end used their dwellings differently than did Beaux Arts Village's idealistic founders. Men like Alfred Renfro and Clancy Lewis sharply divided their lives, physically and emotionally, putting Lake Washington between their work lives and their homes. Both the cultural values and the income from a professional, middle-class career made this possible. They shared their architecture, but the residents of Seattle's north end did not or could not share Beaux Arts Villagers' desire for such stark isolation from the city.

Indeed, Arts and Crafts ideology had little to do with the creation of Seattle's bungalow neighborhoods. Despite all of Stickley's rhetoric about homes set in a removed, sheltering nature, Craftsman bungalows became the ubiquitous suburban dwelling after the early 1900s, packed close together in expanding developments. Because Seattle experienced a wave of suburban building following the 1890s depression, its landscape displayed the Craftsman bungalow in abundance. Much of the growth occurred north of the central business district, spurred on by an extensive, industrially produced infrastructure of bridges, streetcars, and improved roads. By the 1920s, a vast swath of homes filled the denuded, logged-off region north of the Lake Washington Ship Canal, stretching from Puget Sound on the west to Lake Washington on the east. Here, modest, builder-produced dwellings faced a decidedly unromantic street grid that undulated over the hilly topography. Small yards fronted wood-framed houses containing (on average) five rooms, usually arranged in the open bungalow plan. Such abodes made no pretense of harmonizing with the land or encouraging a rural, handicraft ethic, as Craftsmen like Stickley advocated. Rather, they existed because of the easy proximity to Seattle proper.[5]

Many of these dwellings arose in the same era as Beaux Arts Village, with the most dramatic growth taking place between 1900 and 1915. In originally independent communities such as Ballard, Green Lake, and Fremont, most houses appeared between 1900 and 1910, and among them stood nineteenth-century

Victorian homes. But, except for Ballard, bungalows made up the largest single group of pre-1920s houses. Wallingford's initial development came from small booms between 1906 and 1915 and between 1918 and 1919, just at the heyday of pre-1920s bungalow building. It featured bungalows almost exclusively. Ballard contained the least number of bungalows, featuring many more plain, gable-fronted residences constructed in the first decade of the twentieth century. In general, though, most north-end dwellings shared Beaux Arts Village houses' bungalow rectangular shape and open plan.[6]

North-end and Beaux Arts Village residents also shared a general similarity. In 1920, the average north-end dwelling contained a middle-aged married couple and two of their children. Except in Ballard, where Scandinavian immigrants made up the majority, residents were usually American born and of Northern European or North American descent. Virtually all of the immigrants in the northern neighborhoods came from the British Isles, Scandinavia, Canada, or Germany. Only a few families represented the "new" immigration from eastern and southern Europe, and hardly any Asian or black Americans resided north of the canal. As might be expected, most wives worked within the home as housewives. Despite the architecture and demographic resemblances between the north end and Beaux Arts Village, overt Arts and Crafts principles did not always explain life in the north end.[7]

Class determined the difference. This meant that each of the two groups faced early twentieth-century circumstances with differing financial means, opportunities, and cultural values about domesticity. A new well-educated, professional middle class resided in Beaux Arts Village, one of the groups most benefiting from the corporate capitalism it helped usher in. With more supervisory or professional careers, these people could afford to bifurcate their lives, to have Lake Washington separate work and home, at least overtly. People in Seattle's north end varied much more widely, ranging from unskilled mill workers in Ballard to professors at the University of Washington further east. If home ownership defined middle-class status, as some historians have contended, we might label these neighborhoods "middle class" too. But class as a category entails far more than home ownership, and not all north enders lived or thought like Beaux Arts Village professionals. For practical reasons, North Seattle families chose homes much nearer their places of work.[8]

To working families, a house meant more than just class status; it meant a certain level of autonomy. Debt-free houses conferred a crucial independence from outside authorities, like lenders and landlords, to those more economically vulnerable, and served as a sort of insurance in hard times. As various geographers and historians have shown, blue-collar workers gave particular importance to home ownership and viewed their homes as useful tools. In Seattle's north end in 1920, laborers made up the largest percentage of those who owned their houses free and clear of debt. They tended to own older Victorian houses and small cottages built before 1910 that included fewer technological amenities. Although older, such dwellings cost less and were easier to acquire than new houses. (This may also reflect families further along in the life cycle, who had lived longer in the area.)[9]

A closer look at Ballard reveals the crucial importance workers gave to owning their homes. A large working class resided in Ballard, where shipyards, fisheries, and lumber processing plants focused the community on its industrial waterfront. Whenever possible, Ballard's laborers bought their own homes. Ninety-three percent in Ballard's southern neighborhood owned outright or were buying a house in 1920. Seventy-one percent of the neighborhood's skilled workers and foremen, who comprised the majority there, owned or held a mortgage. The area's older, less expensive dwellings made this possible. Although Ballard experienced its biggest pre-1920s building boom in the same period as did Green Lake and Fremont, it featured markedly fewer bungalows and many more plain, gabled residences. Clearly, Ballard workers, like all people of limited means, valued owning a home, even if not the most stylish or "progressive," far more than following the latest fashions and ideologies in domestic architecture.[10]

Ballard's overwhelming immigrant population also helps explain its high rate of home ownership. As historian Olivier Zunz has shown, "owning a home . . . was not a middle-class phenomenon, nor was it a sign of any movement into the middle class. . . . [It] was more an emblem of immigrant working-class culture than of the established middle-class native white American culture." Scandinavian and especially Norwegian immigrants found a haven in Ballard. In the blocks northwest of Ballard's commercial district in 1920, 53 percent of household heads and their spouses were immigrants, mostly from Norway and Sweden. There, they bought and built homes, establishing a cultural autonomy through home ownership.[11]

For Ballard immigrants, inclusion in an ethnic community far outweighed adherence to any architectural ideology. In fact, for one immigrant Ballard family, home design apparently meant nothing at all. On Ballard's west side, a masonry contractor, Frode Frodeson, and his family lived in a 1926 period-revival house (fig. 5.1), a dwelling that mimicked an idealized English heritage. Norwegian immigrants, the Frodesons worked hard to keep their family's ethnicity, playing a very active part in Norwegian organizations and maintaining the Norwegian language and rituals such as a traditional Norwegian Christmas. Inga, Frode Frodeson's wife, was "more or less the heart of the Norwegian-American community in her prime, the mid '30s until 1957," her daughter Anne Marie Frodeson Steiner remembered. President of the Daughters of Norway, she sang for the *Lundquist Lilly Hour* (a Scandinavian radio program), participated in the Norwegian Hospital Association, and helped found the Norse retirement

5.1 Norwegian immigrants, the Frodesons occupied the vaguely Tudor-style dwelling of 1926 at 6416 Thirty-sixth Avenue Northwest in Ballard, 1937. Photo: Puget Sound Regional Archives.

home in Ballard, where she was called "the Mother of Norse Home." For the Frodesons, their house achieved its significance from its location in a culturally autonomous ethnic community, not from any ideas that distant designers might have ascribed to its appearance.[12]

Along with workers and immigrants, entrepreneurs in the north end bought homes whenever possible. This group, which included contractors in various aspects of the construction industry, clearly preferred to own property, and was the least likely to rent. Like workers, entrepreneurs perceived home ownership as a means of independence. However, for them, houses could serve as financial, not emotional, investments. Owners could liquidate quickly when they needed cash. For some entrepreneurs, houses stood as demonstrations of their goods and services for sale, as exemplified by Jud Yoho. Although home ownership marked both workers and entrepreneurs, north-end working people clearly valued the security they received from clear titles to their properties far more than did the entrepreneurs. While entrepreneurs eschewed renting, they willingly acquired large mortgages to finance their homes. In contrast, in 1920, 37 percent of laborers in the city's neighborhoods owned their dwellings outright.[13]

For working people in Seattle's north end—laborers, skilled craftspeople, and foremen—houses and home ownership represented older republican values of independence, thrift, and property. But as the United States shifted toward a consumer economy and value system, some people in new occupations showed less concern about incurring heavy debts in order to acquire their own homes. The two groups that grew most dramatically from the early twentieth-century economic transformation had the lowest percentage of debt-free homes in Seattle's north end. In 1920, 48 percent of sales, accounting, and clerical household heads and 41 percent of professionals, managers, and engineers paid on a mortgage. Those people heavily involved in the new bureaucratic and retail economy seemed significantly more willing to procure large mortgages to pay for their homes. Perhaps a modern business outlook, a view that debt itself was a tool and not a stigma, pervaded this growing class of people. Or, just entering the economic world, they had acquired more easily available mortgages and had only begun paying on them. Nonetheless, they readily accepted the imposed rigors of paying off a burdensome debt to an outside institution in order to acquire homes.[14]

A heavy debt load accompanied salespeople's housing and neighborhood choices. Perhaps reflecting aspirations for greater social mobility, those in sales wanted newer, more expensive structures, particularly bungalows and the boxy four-squares, as did the professionals and entrepreneurs. Priced higher than older structures, such dwellings of course often required mortgages. They sprang up rapidly in Fremont, Green Lake, and especially Wallingford, where the highest percentage of those working in sales, accounting, clerical, professional, and management jobs lived. Willingness to go into debt for modish, up-to-date houses in a modern neighborhood symbolized salespeople's inclusion in the new consumer society. Their new values that accepted debt in return for home ownership thus marked the suburban landscape.[15]

Whether owned outright or with debt, homes provided moderate-income people with a major asset that they could use in times of need. Unlike their counterparts in Beaux Arts Village, families in Seattle's northern neighborhoods were realists when it came to domestic spaces. No doubt they comprehended the subtle ways the dwellings' architecture attempted to prescribe their behavior and fashion a certain domestic ideal. But as economic and family circumstances changed, north enders felt few qualms about physically altering their dwellings or reinterpreting their domestic environments. Sometimes necessity meant defying understood notions of "home." At other times, it required only a temporary adjustment. In both cases, however, the houses themselves helped Seattleites weather economic shifts or take advantage of new opportunities in the world that was emerging in the 1920s.

Ideologically, the home stood at the opposite pole from income-producing work in the public world, especially for the professional middle class. As Stickley put it, homes give "a sense of peace and comfort to the tired men who go back to them when the day's work is done." For the most part, north enders too divided the realms of home and work. But without the same sorts of financial resources as Beaux Arts Villagers, such families took a much less rigid view of the separation. When a family needed money, it could readily accommodate public, economic ventures in its home. Income-producing activities ranged from services such as laundering or boarding that merely extended domesticity to paying customers, to outright manufacture, as most represented by the Stapps' newspaper. Some ventures required much more physical restructuring of the dwelling than others. All home-based businesses, however, allowed families to survive or exploit new circumstances. A house used flexibly thus helped ordinary people adapt to a fluid and mercurial economy.[16]

Boarding remained the most widespread income-producing activity within Seattle homes. In 1920, a significant number of sample households—14 percent—included unrelated boarders (or roomers) and the occasional servant. In this practice, nonfamily members lived in the midst of the supposedly private home. Boarders rented space in all kinds of houses—including bungalows, which housing reformers had specifically claimed for nuclear families. In Wallingford, for example, most boarders resided in bungalows. Their bungalow's small size and large attic spaces encouraged home owners to remodel more often than in larger, Victorian dwellings or four-square houses. Clearly, when possible, Seattleites wanted physical divisions when boarders or tenants used their homes.[17]

The childhood home of Harry Jacobsen at 4136 Baker Avenue (fig. 5.2) in the Phinney Ridge neighborhood between Fremont and Ballard showed how one family made such a division. Constructed in 1907, the small, one-and-a-half story house featured three rooms on the first floor and three bedrooms in the attic. Sometime before 1926, Harry's father, recently divorced and working as a streetcar driver, cut a door on the south side to allow independent access to the second floor attic. There he lived while renting the first floor to a Canadian family. Having no formal bedroom, the Canadians slept in the living room that opened directly into the dining room. Because the house had only one bathroom, Harry's father apparently shared the facility with the couple and their newborn. With his remodeling, Harry's father created a sense of spatial separation from his tenants. Yet the two realms—the private, domestic and the public, income-producing—overlapped in the bathroom. The congruence of the two proved temporary. When Harry and his sister moved back in with their father in 1926, the house returned to a single-family dwelling.[18]

The Jacobsens' situation deviated from the usual pattern because the home owner, a single man, occupied the peripheral regions and gave the renters the main rooms. Usually a family rented an attic or second-story rooms to single lodgers. This happened with the Boitano family, a large, Italian-American family with seven children that owned a 1904 four-square at 5018 Seventeenth

5.2 *Constructed in 1907, the Jacobsen family residence at 4136 Baker Avenue at one time housed Jacobsen in the upper floor and tenants on the main floor, 1937. Photo: Puget Sound Regional Archives.*

Avenue NW in Ballard (fig. 5.3). The second floor contained all of the home's five bedrooms and a second bathroom. John Boitano remembered one boarder living with his family after some of his older siblings left home, probably in the 1920s or 1930s. An Italian immigrant, John's father maintained a garbage-hauling contract in Ballard. Boitano's boarder, a Greek man who ran a grocery store in the Ballard Hotel, had similar Mediterranean roots. He "liked our family," John remembered, and with their roomy, two-story house, the Boitanos needed no remodeling to accommodate him in one of the second-floor bedrooms. The separation between outsider and family blurred, the realms converging and dividing on a continual basis.[19]

Lodging houses further extended the way ordinary people could use a residence to produce revenue. In these situations, a family, often headed by a woman, both lived and produced its livelihood. Providing room and board to outsiders extended the architecture's domestic intent into the commercial realm. This arrangement, however, often required more physical reshaping to maintain distance between roomers and the home owners. Even then, the dwelling might remain middle class in appearance, but shelter a family that mingled with strangers.

5.3 Four-square in plan, the Boitano's 1904 house at 5018 Seventeenth Avenue Northwest in Ballard contained a large Italian-American family and occasionally boarders, 1937. Photo: Puget Sound Regional Archives.

A glimpse into the world of Hugh Miracle gives some idea of how Seattle families managed the space within a lodging house. In 1918, Hugh's mother, Kathryn, purchased a large four-square house in Seattle's University District and turned it into a rooming house. In this eighteen-room dwelling, she provided only "housekeeping rooms" for college students—renters had to find their meals elsewhere or they had to use the gas plate provided in the rooms. Probably built from a lumber company plan, the house's original design intended its use as a single-family home. In 1909, when carpenters hammered up the house, the University District had experienced a tremendous building boom sparked by the Alaska-Yukon-Pacific Exposition held that year on the nearby University of Washington campus. Many boarding houses appeared in the area, including the Miracles', which always housed lodgers or some sort of fraternity. By the time Hugh's mother acquired it, a previous owner had completed a two-story rear addition, increasing the amount of rentable space.[20]

For Hugh and his divorced mother, this profit-making structure also constituted "home." They established a general line of demarcation between the public and private spaces that changed with their economic circumstances. In the 1910s and 1920s, they occupied the downstairs portion of the house, including the dining and living rooms. As a youngster, Hugh slept in a small bedroom behind these rooms. Renters lived on the second and third floors. Although this might appear to have made the realms distinct, the two often mingled. An

5.4 *Four-square structures like Dr. Aloyce Pierrott's 1905 house at 1538 West Sixtieth Street could easily accommodate small medical clinics, 1937. Photo: Puget Sound Regional Archives.*

only child, Hugh remembered that the college students in his house included him in many of their leisure-time activities. The single-family plan also forced an intimacy between the family and its tenants. The house contained only one bathroom on the second floor, the whole household apparently sharing the only tub. A toilet and basin on the third floor and an additional sink in the second floor hall alleviated some of the pressure on the single bathroom.[21]

When Hugh's mother found it increasingly difficult to support herself and her son, she carved deeper into her domestic space to gain badly needed cash. Probably in the early 1920s, she increased the number of rentable rooms by creating two basement rooms from a storage area, one of which Hugh occupied. Later in the 1920s, she enclosed a portion of her front porch and opened a real estate office in it. Around 1930, when the Depression began cutting into her rent receipts, she walled off a portion of the living room, acquiring yet another "housekeeping" room. When necessary, Hugh's mother ignored the intention architectural ideologues decreed for her home and marketed domestic space as a commodity.[22]

Medical care also fit appropriately into residential spaces. In an era when women nursed ill family members at home, extending this service for pay within a home merely stretched a basic domestic activity. Four-square houses, in particular, suitably morphed into small hospitals. In 1905, for example, Dr. Aloyce Pierrott erected an eight-room four-square in Ballard at 1538 West Sixtieth Street (fig. 5.4). For a few years, he ran a medical office and hospital from the house while he (and presumably his family) lived there. The floor plan facilitated these two functions and allowed a division between public and private activities without much renovation. A large entrance and front stair provided access to the second floor bedrooms, bypassing the family domains of the living and dining rooms. Dr. Pierrott apparently used the front room of the house as his office. Family members reached the upper stories (and single bathroom) by a rear stair. By keeping patients in the house's front regions or in the upper bedrooms, Pierrott could screen his family spaces, keeping them functionally separate. The only alteration necessary consisted of a speaking tube from the front upstairs bedroom to the front porch, apparently so outsiders could converse with patients in times of quarantine. Merging a home with a hospital in a four-square required so little change that when Dr. Pierrott sold the house in 1908, its new owners converted it to a single-family dwelling without any apparent remodeling.[23]

Hard times pushed some families to use homes as temporary workplaces. The Great Depression, particularly, compelled many families to make products in or offer services from their homes. Typically, they separated these ventures from interior spaces by utilizing their basements for sales activities. In the 1930s, beneath her rooming house, Hugh Miracle's mother sometimes made chocolate confections and canned spaghetti to sell. After Eileen McElhoe Wolgamott's father lost his blacksmith shop in the Depression, he ran a saw filing business from his workbench in the family's basement at 2602 Northwest Fifty-ninth Street (fig. 5.5). The Ballard lumber mills brought their huge saws to him for his expert attention. Even when stability returned and he acquired a government job at the Ballard locks, Eileen's father continued this sideline, essentially keeping a portion of his home for commercial activity. Mr. McElhoe used his domestic space to survive a particularly revealing transformation; as his artisanal craft eroded, his home enterprise carried him through until he could acquire the relative security of a bureaucratic government position, a thoroughly modern occupation.[24]

The Stapp family at 4203 Woodlawn illustrated the accommodation between domesticity and business that so many north side families made. Commercial activities in the Stapps' Craftsman bungalow totally defined some spaces, particularly the basement. Other areas, though, shifted meanings when the functions within them changed, defying overt architectural ideology. When the family gathered in the living room, the domain fulfilled its intended purpose, but it became a commercially productive site when Stapp wrote and edited the newspaper in his overstuffed chair. The Stapps used their beautiful, progressive

5.5 Although constructed in 1904, the McElhoe's home at 2602 Northwest Fifty-ninth Street featured a 1918 remodeling that added a Craftsman porch and detailing, 1937. Photo: Puget Sound Regional Archives.

architecture flexibly, sometimes adhering to its underlying ideology, but always it was a tool for the family's economic survival.

If anyone should have been aware of the Arts and Crafts rhetoric that separated domesticity from the degraded industrial world, it was Orrill Stapp. In about 1906, Orrill deeply criticized what he saw as a commercialized, degenerate, urban society in his rambling essays for his artistic journal, *The Triton*. But with his activities at 4203 Woodlawn, he moved further from his earlier beliefs and closer to the consumer economy that so troubled him as a young man.[25]

At first, Stapp limited his commercial use of domestic space and thus undertook no physical alterations. In the living room, he conducted a music studio, giving classical music lessons on his grand piano (fig. 5.6). Periodically, the family hauled out chairs and placed them before the piano, transforming the room into a recital hall. Students entered the house through the enclosed porch and remained in the living room, while family members avoided the front regions of the house during lessons. Business and family functions only overlapped in the shared bathroom, and then sometimes with some confusion. Stan Stapp remembered frantically pounding on the bathroom door under the assumption that his younger sister was monopolizing the bathroom. Hollering "Let me in! Let me in!" he found to his chagrin that "two rather upset young ladies, piano pupils of Father's music studio" emerged from the room. But in all, the Stapps' domestic life and their income-producing activities existed peacefully side by side, as happened in many bungalows where people offered services like music lessons.[26]

5.6 *Orrill Stapp's living room, with his grand piano and mohair chair, at 4203 Woodlawn. According to Stan Stapp, Orrill hand built the music cabinet behind the piano. Although the room retained its domestic functions, it also served as a recital hall for Stapp's music students, circa 1928. Photo: Stan Stapp, private collection.*

Gradually, however, the Stapp family became even fuller participants in the consumer economy. Their home mutated into a site of production, a sort of modern household economy, but one inextricably tied to consumption. Their newspaper, the *North Side Outlook,* a weekly neighborhood publication supported by advertising, precipitated the transformation. Although the outward appearance of the house changed relatively little, interior spaces underwent both remodeling and reinterpretation.

As we might expect, the Stapps' newspaper began in their basement. Milton's small printing operation moved into the partially dirt basement when the Stapps bought 4203 Woodlawn. As the enterprise took off, another son, Arthur, joined Milton, and the paper became a "regular newspaper." Together, the brothers dug out a complete basement and skidded a new and larger press through the house, into the kitchen, and down into the basement, where it dominated the lower level. Orrill, too, began devoting time to the publication, taking the jobs of editor and publisher. Around 1925, an even better cylinder press—a linotype machine—and a folding machine necessitated a new outside entrance and base-

5.7 Beneath the living room of the Stapp bungalow at 4203 Woodlawn, a business and production flourished. Here, in 1928, employees of the Outlook *composed the paper and operated the linotype. Milton Stapp appears on the far right, circa 1928. Photo: Stan Stapp, private collection.*

ment window (fig. 5.7). Within several years, the business flourished, printing weekly several additions of sixteen to twenty-four pages and reaching 15,000 residences.[27]

The house still looked like a Craftsman bungalow, and in many ways it still functioned entirely as Craftsman idealists intended. Stan Stapp, the youngest son, remembered his home as being divided into "'upstairs,' where I lived with my family . . . and 'downstairs,' [where he] helped produce the *Outlook*." But the two realms of work and family did not separate so distinctly. On the inside, commercial functions outcompeted domestic uses. Machinery cluttered the open basement space. Under the front porch, secretaries answered calls in a narrow "front" office (fig. 5.8). The main floor included another office in the "guest room" off of the big living room (fig. 5.9). Even the bedrooms on the upper level stored paper for the press. Rooms that still appeared totally domestic mutated into commercial space when their occupants shifted their attention to newspaper work. Frances, for instance, often proofread galleys in the dining room bay window (fig. 5.10) or in her "office," the breakfast nook. Orrill, who had given up teaching music by 1928, claimed a corner of the glassed-in front porch for his writing and editing (fig. 5.11). Newspaper employees also entered

5.8 In 1928, secretaries for the Outlook worked in the office dug out under the porch of 4203 Woodlawn, circa 1928. Photo: Stan Stapp, private collection.

the ostensibly private spaces, such as the house's single bathroom. For newspaper workers, this meant a trip from the basement through the kitchen, dining room, and living room, up the main stairway, and into the second-story bathroom. Eventually, the Stapps installed another toilet in the basement, near the laundry trays. Public and private, family and business, production and consumption all overlapped and merged in the Stapp home. The veneer of Craftsman architecture overlaid it all.[28]

Of course, the Stapps' bungalow represents an unusual example of early twentieth-century houses serving as sites of production. But it reveals how ordinary people constantly negotiated the relationship between the embedded social ideology and their actual use of space. Architectural design might impel certain behaviors, but people continually pushed these boundaries, blurring the distinctions that the physical design laid out. Families moved between expected behavior and the very real necessities that dominated their lives. To them,

5.9 *Intended for purely domestic activities, the "guest" room next to the living room on the first floor of 4203 Woodlawn became the Outlook's office in the mid-1920s, circa 1928. Photo: Stan Stapp, private collection.*

a malleable domestic space acquired different meanings as use, behavior, and occupants changed. For ordinary families, "home" was a dynamic, ever-changing process, not a static construction.

As we have seen, most of Seattle's north enders fit their families into bungalow plans that encouraged the blurring of categories and spatial realms. These arrangements helped break down barriers between previously-accepted dichotomies. Such a layout influenced internal social dynamics. For instance, no parlor or hall sequestered outsiders from the family's center, the living room. Once in the house, guests faced no obstacles, other than perhaps low built-in bookcases or pillars, that inhibited free movement into the open dining room. The edges of public and private blended. Bedrooms on the first floor next to a single bathroom consolidated family interactions into a smaller area, especially as more personal hygiene moved from bedrooms and into bathrooms. The arrangement forced familial mingling, if only in squabbling for the bathroom. A breakfast nook in the kitchen brought the male householder into a traditionally female domain. Clear-cut gender separation as the Victorians conceived it began to melt at the edges. Indeed, at least to some degree, reformers' intentions in the bungalow design carried over into actual conduct.

But the physical layout of a house could only direct behavior, and thus imple-

5.10 *The Stapp's dining room at 4203 Woodlawn, along with the kitchen, became the domain of Frances Stapp, circa 1928.*

ment ideology, to a certain extent. Overtly progressive houses could shelter a variety of lifestyles, even some contradictory to the stated architectural intentions. Take, for instance, the asserted goal of early twentieth-century domestic theorists to return men to their rightful place at the center of the home. When the spheres of public and private had begun to diverge in the early nineteenth century, so too had the spaces associated with male and female, masculine and feminine. The Victorian middle-class house became enshrined as a woman's proper place, with domesticity and femininity synonymous characteristics. Architectural idealists believed that early twentieth-century housing reform could merge the masculine and the feminine, build a home of gender coequals, and create a more equitable society. Arts and Crafts dwellings, especially, sought to bring men and masculinity back into traditionally female-controlled dwellings. Yet, in one way or another, most houses remained stubbornly associated with women.[29]

However, the amount of authority early twentieth-century women actually wielded in the home depended upon the individual family. The Langes, for instance, included independent women who not only directed the household but took responsibility for actively purchasing their Seattle dwelling. In 1924,

5.11 Orrill Stapp undertook his work for the Outlook *in his work corner of the enclosed portion of the front porch, circa 1928. Photo: Stan Stapp, private collection.*

the Langes and their four youngest children moved from Seattle to Vancouver, British Columbia. Ruth Lange Fall remembered that the following year, her mother, Hattie, decided that the family had better return to the United States. Her mother came to Seattle looking for a house to buy. She chose a new Colonial bungalow (fig. 1.6) in the Wallingford neighborhood and moved her family there in 1925. Mr. Lange, a pattern maker in a foundry, apparently left this major decision totally up to his wife, who handled the family's finances. When circumstances delayed departure from Canada, the Langes' two oldest daughters set up the household without much, if any, contribution from their father. These two, Mildred and Bernice, had already charted independent lives in the mid-1920s. While their parents lived in Canada, they had rented rooms near downtown Seattle. In an era when many women never learned to drive, Mildred, who worked for a hat company, drove her own Ford car. While she kept books at a surveying firm's office, Bernice pursued a civil engineering degree from the University of Washington, graduating as one of the school's first women civil engineers. She went on to design bridges in the Seattle City Engineer's office.[30]

The Lange women clearly illustrated how some women broke down the older

Victorian conceptions of women's confinement to the home. They acted much as Progressive reformers thought they should in a Colonial bungalow, gaining certain powers as the chief consumers in the household, participating actively in the public world, and, in the case of Bernice, stepping into the male realm of work. Conversely, the Lange women showed how, for some families, older conceptions of patriarchal authority over the family shifted in the early twentieth century.[31]

In other families, though, progressive architectural design could not override older cultural dictates. Despite the gender-blurring implicit in the open floor plan, some families continued to follow a traditional patriarchal model of household space well into the twentieth century. The Boitanos in Ballard were one such family. Mr. John Boitano adhered to values reflecting an Italian immigrant heritage. His son, John, remembered him as "conservative, frugal ... [and] hardworking." He probably purchased his relatively new 1904 four-square residence (fig. 5.3) outright without debt. As the father, Mr. Boitano clearly filled the role as household head and breadwinner, the dominant figure who made the family's important decisions. He insisted that his wife stay attached exclusively to the private domestic sphere. She, in turn, enjoyed little independent public life. John recalled a revealing incident in the late 1920s. His mother had left the house to see a movie. In the meantime, his father came home to find her absent. Upon her return, he "gave [her] hell," and his mother "never went to the show after that for her entire life." Even though women had made many advances into the outside world by then, the Boitanos continued to equate Mrs. Boitano's role with the private, interior, domestic realm ultimately under clear patriarchal control.[32]

Most north-end families, however, stood midway between the Langes and the Boitanos when it came to equating domesticity with women. Separate spheres did not really disappear, as most married women remained at home with their children in the space demarcated for women, but in this era, women made great strides into the workforce and into educational institutions. Doubtless, in some ways, the blending of spaces within bungalows mirrored a larger societal breakdown of barriers to women. Charlotte Williams Lenz's mother, for instance, received a pharmacy degree in 1907 from the University of Washington. For a while, she practiced as a professional pharmacist while living with her brother. After 1919, when she married Lewis Williams, a Seattle attorney, she quit her job and raised their three daughters in a Craftsman bungalow (fig. 1.4) in Ballard. Charlotte's mother represented middle-class women in transition. Although acquiring a professional degree, after her marriage she chose (or was compelled) to remain in the private realm long associated with women. Yet, while she still functioned within a patriarchy that limited access to professional life, for a time she had moved into the public world of men.[33]

Even when removed from economic production, housewives such as Mrs.

Williams still retained limited power within their families. In many families, women's intimate association with the home and their position as chief consumer gave them at least some authority over its direction. Charlotte Williams Lenz recalled that her mother made most of the household decisions and all decisions concerning her daughters. Such wives commonly controlled family finances. Eileen McElhoe Wolgamott's mother handled the family's money and household management. Her husband relinquished his paycheck directly to her. As might be expected, Mrs. Lange not only purchased the Lange's new house in 1925, she selected the furniture, determined the place of residence, and controlled family finances in general. In about 1940, after Mr. Lange retired, he took to socializing at the local tavern. Mrs. Lange disapproved, so she made the decision to quash this situation by moving to Lake Forest Park, a suburb quite distant from Wallingford and away from bad influences. For these women, the equation of domesticity with women conferred authority, and men played a decidedly subordinate role in decisions concerning the household.[34]

In some ways, the bungalow's design goal of restoring masculine domesticity succeeded. As we saw in Beaux Arts Village, some men did create definably male interiors—stark, rugged, and unadorned. With the loss of the traditionally female-controlled parlor, many houses featured spacious masculinized living rooms with boxy, unpadded furniture, coarse fabrics, and sometimes even furs or stuffed animals on the walls. However, a true blurring of gendered spaces did not occur in all early twentieth-century dwellings. Gender divisions continued much as before. In particular, the rear, private spaces—kitchens, bathrooms, and bedrooms—remained female. Arts and Crafts–inspired architecture might lure men back into domesticity, but only to the most obviously public realms.[35]

This enduring division appeared most distinctly in the Stapp family. By the 1920s, tensions between Orrill and Frances began to destroy their marriage. To cope with living in the same house, they increasingly divided their spaces. Orrill dominated the front of the house, especially the large living room, where he both slept and wrote at a portable desk laid across a mohair easy chair near the fireplace (fig. 5.6). This was "HIS domain," his son Stan wrote much later, "and from his seat he [could] observe the comings and goings of everyone and just about everything that took place on the main floor." Frances's bailiwick centered on the dining room, at the heart of the house, where she combined her newspaper duties and domestic responsibilities (fig. 5.10). "This was HER domain," Stan observed, "where [she] served our meals, sewed our clothes on her pedal-operated New Home sewing machine, and often proofread the Outlook [newspaper]." The kitchen, too, belonged to her. It served as "Grand Central Station," the home's nexus, where family and business merged. Sometimes she used the kitchen's breakfast room as "her office," where she read newspaper proofs. She often interacted with newspaper employees there, as the basement door led to the kitchen in the early days. From the kitchen, Frances supervised household activities. Small children ran in and out, deliverymen brought in goods, and employees traipsed through to use the upstairs bathroom—all while Frances bustled about preparing family meals and sometimes food for the newspaper staff. Orrill's intrusion to shave in the kitchen sink every morning "was a bother" to Frances, an encroachment of the male into female-controlled space. For her, this was too much masculine domesticity.[36]

The modern, open, parlorless plan could not compel a companionate marriage and family. In fact, a few families defied outright the prescribed middle-class behavior and continued a truly patriarchal order. The Boitanos showed how this worked. The living room did not serve as a place of familial and gender mixing. Instead, the Boitanos used their "fancy room," as John called it, like a parlor. There they entertained guests with a player piano and radio, but children did not play there. The family maintained the dining room, too, as purely formal space, with "nice" furniture and a china cabinet for display. They ate there only for elaborate Sunday meals or when guests visited. The Boitano family activities centered almost exclusively on the kitchen, the most private and most feminine of the downstairs rooms. They "lived in the kitchen," John recalled, the parents and seven children eating most of their meals at a big, round table. This family ignored their rooms' design and intent and imposed an older, working-class model upon their home, where feminine production centered a household under patriarchal control.[37]

Indeed, try as they would, architectural reformers made little headway in changing certain deeply embedded conceptions about how people should use their domestic space. Arts and Crafts spokesmen like Gustav Stickley envisioned an informal home centered on an undifferentiated living space where the public and private merged, parents and children comprised a democratic family, and the realms of the male and female blurred. Although they tried to encourage such activities through architectural design, a persistent hierarchy of gender, age, and class structured behavior within most American's early twentieth-century homes.[38]

More than any other characteristic, gender prescribed how families conceived of and used their spaces. Children learned early that the house, and especially its interior, equated with women and femininity. Cleaning fell to girls. "It was considered a girl's job to help around the house," Anne Marie Frodeson Steiner recollected. Boys usually attended to outside duties or heavy tasks like shoveling coal into coal bins and furnaces, and yard work such as lawn mowing. In the Stapp family, Stan, the youngest son, "never did anything in the kitchen," while his younger sister, Pat, helped with such tasks as washing dishes.[39]

Gender further defined the home's private spaces, especially the bedrooms. Small children of both sexes might share a bedroom, but when youngsters reached a certain age, these spaces became distinctly separate. Boys and girls slept in different bedrooms. Generally, little gender overlap occurred between the private spaces of older children. Harry Jacobsen recalled that his sister did not go into his bedroom, and Anne Marie Frodeson Steiner "never remembered one of [her] brothers ever coming into her room." Occasionally, children jealously guarded these personal realms. Stan Stapp created a "hide-out, or den, or office" in an upstairs bedroom closet. To prevent "intruders (such as my sister and her friends)," he constructed "a home-made alarm system that would ring an old very loud doorbell" if they entered. The gender line between children's spaces could hardly have been clearer.[40]

Although intended to promote an informal, affectional family togetherness, open floor plans remained subject to a distinctive hierarchy of age. When children were very young, parents sometimes did share their bedrooms with small children, blurring age distinctions, as did the Hughbanks family. For several years after beginning construction of their Tudor Revival house (fig. 1.5) in Ballard in 1931, C. F. and Ruth Hughbanks and their two small children together occupied the downstairs bedroom while the second floor neared completion. However, when carpenters completed the second floor about the time their youngest child was born, the family moved into separate bedrooms. Perhaps the physical closeness of the family did foster a companionate family, but such blending of parental and children's private spaces did not last long.[41]

Usually adults clearly distinguished their own private spaces from their children's, continuing a nineteenth-century physical division within homes. The oldest and most powerful members of the family, the parents, could access any part of the entire dwelling, but kept certain private spaces for themselves. Most parents usually occupied larger, spatially demarcated bedrooms that lay apart from other bedrooms, such as on the first floor or to the front of the house. Generally, children slept in second-story rooms. When Mr. and Mrs. Lange moved into their new Colonial bungalow in 1925, they slept in the downstairs bedroom near the only bathroom, and their six children shared the three upstairs bedrooms. In the Williams's bungalow, which had two bedrooms on the first floor, the parents used the one in the front and placed their small daughters in the rear.[42]

Ironically, when the separation was not complete, when the bungalow's most informal spaces actually merged private and public functions, it often indicated some sort of upheaval. A simple case of crowding pointed this out. In the late 1920s, Eileen McElhoe Wolgamott's family consisted of the parents, three young children, three uncles, and an aunt in a three-bedroom house (fig. 5.5). Doubling up allowed most family members to have bedrooms. The baby slept in the parent's room, Eileen with her aunt, and the young men in the third bedroom. But Eileen's younger brother slept on a cot in the dining room, flouting its intended public use. Here, informality became lack of privacy, one of the Progressives' greatest laments about cramped, working-class housing.[43]

Instead of fostering an easy familial democracy, the very openness of bungalow interiors sharply exposed family lives gone awry. Too much mixing of children and adults, of public and private, might reveal troubled marriages. This was the case in the Stapp family. With five children (one completely bedridden) and only three upstairs bedrooms in their bungalow, Orrill and Frances put their two youngest in their own room. Stan slept in his parent's bedroom until he was at least eight years old, then shared a room with his older brother Art. His younger sister, though, remained in his parents' bedroom. Eventually Stan's parents became estranged, his father sleeping on the living room couch, and Stan's mother and sister occupying the upstairs front bedroom. In this case, greater informality between family members did occur within an open floor plan, as reformers hoped. But the Stapps did not necessarily see that as a beneficial feature. The inability to make bungalow living rooms more private when needed by shutting them off completely, as Victorians could do with parlors, only accentuated a family's failure to achieve the domestic ideal.[44]

Progressive reformers wanted informality to extend to outsiders as well as family members. They deplored the stiff, formulaic rituals of receiving callers in extravagant but little-used parlors, so they eliminated them from bungalows. Yet, as with Victorian dwellings, bungalows and other houses of the period retained a basic division of public rooms to the front and private spaces to the rear. Lacking a front hall and formal parlor, the bungalow's wide entry and open plan brought visitors right into the midst of the family. But only certain people gained admittance to the front rooms: invited guests, adult friends and peers, and extended family. Strangers might stand waiting on the porch. Once inside, adult guests moved freely in the living room, where formal functions and rituals usually occurred. In this respect, living rooms took over the ceremonial activities of nineteenth-century parlors, places designated as appropriate for "company." Here, parties, weddings, and Christmas celebrations focused the interactions of invited outsiders and family. In the spring of 1936, for instance, Ruth Lange Fall's older sister Bernice was married in the family living room before a fireplace decorated with pear blossoms. The Stapp's twenty-seven-foot living room allowed Milton Stapp to have a small band and dancing at his engagement party in 1923. Such events often flowed into the dining room. But both powerful customs and the plan itself prevented any further incursions by strangers. Doors closed to kitchens and bedrooms, limiting guests not intimate with the family to the front part of the house.[45]

Working-class strangers, however, saw a truer informality than middle-class guests who arrived at the front door. Penetrating the private regions, service workers came and went through people's houses, observing and entering back rooms. They did not commonly receive the hospitality of the front rooms. Families like the Hughbanks, who could afford servants, often housed them in the rear, next to the kitchen and bathroom. These nonfamily members populated the very regions denied to front-room guests. Icemen frequently resupplied the iceboxes in homes. If the box lay within the house, the iceman had to bring large chunks of ice, dripping water and debris, from his wagon, through the back porch, and into the kitchen, where he could see and smell messy household activities. People often built outside doors to their iceboxes or placed iceboxes on their back porches to avoid this situation. Laundrymen collected people's wet wash, milkmen delivered milk (sometimes leaving it inside), and fish, produce, and bread-sellers brought their groceries to people's back doors. A person of the laboring class knew to enter at the back, and that propriety prohibited going beyond the dining room door. So a person's class and function helped determine which side of the dining room door he or she would see.[46]

With workers, youths experienced more fully the informality of bungalow plans. Less concerned with how they and their homes appeared to children, many parents allowed outside youngsters in all areas of the house. As might be expected, organized entertainments such as birthday parties took place in living rooms. Most children's play, however, occurred in dining rooms, a sort of transitional space between formality and informality, family and outsider. The room's central table facilitated activities such as doll play, cards, studying, and casual conversation. Often the dining room was the warmest room because of its proximity to both the basement furnace and the kitchen range. Neighborhood children had ready access to kitchens and back porches too. Preadolescent youngsters entered through back doors connected to kitchens, possibly never using the front door. In fact, these realms sometimes became the designated places for children and their friends (as well as women). In the Boitano household, children socialized predominantly in the kitchen, as did the family, because they considered the dining room more "formal."[47]

Before adolescence, children of both sexes entered such semipublic spaces. In bedrooms, however, gender governed admittance. Neighborhood children sometimes visited each other's bedrooms, the most private region withheld from the purview of adult outsiders. Many families did not permit children's friends to play in bedrooms, but when they did, inclusions depended on gender. A clear line of division among preteen-agers excluded boys from girls' bedrooms or girls from boys' bedrooms.

Once young people reached adolescence, they began to follow the rules of adult outsiders. Social custom, more than the floor plan, provided the cues on how they should behave. Charlotte Williams Lenz remembered her childhood male and female friends socializing everywhere in her bungalow but the bedrooms. But when teenage boys began to date her and her sisters, they called in the living room, "never . . . the kitchen." The age and intentions of these young men reduced their freedom to move about within homes. When boys who had raced through the Williams' kitchen became suitors, propriety relegated them firmly to the most public space. Essentially, the bungalow's big living room then took on a formal courting function and appearance. When Eileen McElhoe Wolgamott's aunt wanted the living room to look attractive for the young men she entertained there, she purchased a davenport and chair set. As they grew up, young people had to ascertain new behavioral expectations associated with static spaces.[48]

Age, class, and gender structured behavior despite what reformers or architects might have envisioned. Domestic spaces never became totally informal. The open plan did provide freer access into the house and countered the spatial rigidity and control built into nineteenth-century parlors. But it still expressed distinctions of public/private and formal/informal. A person learned to negotiate the seemingly undiversified space, to follow unwritten codes of conduct that changed relative to his or her personal characteristics. More than spatial cues, social roles and conventions placed responsibility on individuals for acting properly.

Teaching these social values, of course, remained within the purview of the family. Architectural reformers imagined a particular kind of family inhabiting their creations, nurturing the nation's future citizens. They attempted to structure a new type of middle-class, egalitarian, companionate, two-parent family through the home's physical space. They did so partly out of fear, as they perceived an erosion in the stability of middle-class families. Modernized bungalows that reified this family ideal could prevent this decay.[49]

The ideal masked the reality. Despite restrictive laws, divorce rose in the early twentieth century, increasing fifteenfold between 1870 and 1920. Divorce and loss of a parent through death caused the numbers of single-parent families to expand markedly in the early twentieth century. Seattle's north end reflected this national pattern. There, 13 percent of the heads of household in 1920 were either widowed or divorced. Women made up 11 percent of these. In such families, children usually remained the responsibility of the mother. It appears that single mothers with children remarried less frequently than did single fathers. Needing income and having few options, many single mothers put their homes and domestic skills to commercial use by taking in lodgers or running boarding houses, so that they could earn a living and watch over their children too. The Miracles illustrated such an arrangement. Hugh's mother began operating her rooming house in the University District only after she and Hugh's father divorced in 1918. Obviously, she and other women in similar circumstances had to ignore the ideal of cozy domesticity centered on a companionate husband and wife. Without adult male challenge, the entire dwelling became their province.[50]

Divorced or widowed men with children more quickly reestablished a household with both sexes. Their jobs usually gave no option but to remain absent from home most of the day, necessitating some sort of housekeeper to tend children. For instance, Harry Jacobsen and his sister lived with their father after

5.12 The Purves family house at 158 West Eighty-first Street was constructed between 1910 and 1916; 1937. Photo: Puget Sound Regional Archives.

their parents' divorce in the early 1920s. Harry's father had been the captain of a Puget Sound steamer. When he and his wife split up, he took a job ashore as a streetcar driver that eventually allowed him to keep his children. Harry's father hired a succession of female housekeepers to help out when the children were young. Widowers and divorced men with children had an immediate incentive to remarry quickly. This happened in the Purves family (fig. 5.12). Left with two small youngsters after the death of his wife, D. S. Purves, a Scottish immigrant and master bookbinder, soon married a young Norwegian woman. They then had two sons of their own. The arrangement of families with single fathers more quickly conformed to the ideal than did those of single mothers.[51]

This did not mean, however, that blended families reenacted the domestic bliss designers thought their interior environment could determine. Harry Jacobsen recalled a troubled relationship with his Swedish stepfather, which may explain his living apart from his mother and her husband. Ironically, the open plan might have exacerbated the tension inherent in bringing two families together. Just as undifferentiated space might enhance a close family, it might also increase hostility in a troubled one. It gave family members few places to get away from one another when situations became tense. After her step-mother arrived, Betty Purves Bostrom remembered "unpleasant times," which she escaped by burying herself in books instead of distancing herself physically. Clearly, architecture alone could not always create the homes idealists visualized as snug sanctuaries. As the numbers of complicated, blended families expanded in the twentieth century, people had to find ways to adapt tangled family relations to structures designed for a static paradigm.[52]

Such adaptation provides the key to understanding how the lives of ordinary people contributed to creating the modern home. Most people felt little particular inclination to adhere strictly to the ideological assumptions embedded in their houses' designs. People of modest means took the most important resource available to them, their house, and began a process of continually adjusting their domestic space to meet their needs. This fluidity of domestic space marked the lives of average Americans in their early twentieth-century homes.

If we focused only on the overt symbolism of Orrill Stapp's charming home, we might conclude, along with many architectural historians, that the ideology of Beaux Arts Villagers stood for all occupants of Craftsman bungalows. However, the domesticity that defined the professional middle class did not necessarily apply to families in Seattle's north end. These families' use of domestic space revealed little ambivalence about the new world emerging from the Second Industrial Revolution. They frankly embraced the advantages of technology: the streetcar lines to work, central heat, the latest plumbing. They worried little about living a simple life close to nature. Indeed, they viewed bungalows as a step up from apartments or from the "simpler" life in cottages without toilets or furnaces. Certainly, ordinary people allowed economic production in domestic spaces without much agonizing. Although both Beaux Arts Villagers and north end families sought control over their homes and communities, the type of control differed subtly. Beaux Arts Villagers originally tried to create a model community showing how they, and, by implication, others, should live. They created regulations that ensured conformity. Even if they wanted to, north end residents could only exert informal controls. But their high rates of home ownership reveal that they greatly valued individual control over their own homes. As assets and refuges, autonomous homes provided independence, both to thwart the intrusions of idealists telling them how to live, and to react with resilience to economic and social circumstances of the early twentieth century. When we view the far-flung neighborhoods of small bungalows that stretch across Seattle and the United States, we should see them not through the lens of Arts and Crafts ideology but as artifacts of ordinary people's resourceful and pragmatic experience of home.

6

LEGACY OF THE
SEATTLE BUNGALOW

THE SERENE ARTS AND CRAFTS BUNGALOW at 4203 Wood-
lawn Avenue stood facing the future, the light of each new day filtering through
its large front windows. The home stood on the cusp of change, decisively
turning away from the nineteenth century and ushering in twentieth-century
modernity. It provided the pattern for homes to come, the low, horizontal ranch
houses with their ubiquitous open plans that so marked the post–World War II
residential landscape. Tens of thousands of cozy bungalows sheltered families
like the Stapps, ordinary Americans rethinking, selling, building, and modifying
their domestic spaces to better accommodate a transforming world.[1]

As the first modern popular house type, the bungalow thus served as a transitional dwelling signaling a clear shift in domestic architecture. Whatever
fashionable symbolism garbed them, houses from the 1910s until the end of the
twentieth century featured the essential characteristics that began with bungalows: an open plan, advanced-comfort technology, a streamlined minimalism,
and an increasingly industrialized building process. Bungalows introduced this
modern design and prepared Americans for how their suburban landscapes
would look for much of the century.

Twentieth-century popular domestic architecture also eased Americans into a new economy and society in which consumerism took on a steadily growing dominance. Bungalows helped people make a transition into this new world. Through them, Arts and Crafts adherents could reclaim the past in order to face the future. They initiated small builders and housing entrepreneurs into the intricacies of juggling customer demand, mass production, innovative financing, and imaginative advertising. Most of all, bungalows provided ordinary people with a flexible site from which to negotiate the future.

Orrill Stapp made that adjustment only partway. Despite his attempt to remake himself into a modern man, Stapp proved unable to adjust fully to the new world he had helped fashion. Espousing the ideas of Arts and Crafts, social-ism, and his own unique spiritualism, Stapp embraced new ways of thinking. But he could not reconcile himself to other aspects of modern culture. He never learned to drive a car, preferring to walk or travel by city bus; never played con-temporary music on his grand piano, only classical; and remained removed from popular culture as a whole. He stood caught between two worlds.[2]

Stapp's struggle to fabricate a different kind of home and person from the vestiges of the previous age took its toll. He found it increasingly difficult to cope. The domestic patriarchal authority he had extolled while living in his Rainier Beach Craftsman home began to slip away. His sons, Milton and Arthur, and then Stan (in the 1930s), actually managed and operated the newspaper, though Stapp remained as titular head through the 1930s. As his paternal power declined, so too did his relations with his wife. By the late 1920s, Orrill and Frances were "estranged," though they continued to live together in the house. The power dynamic shifted between the two. In 1906, for instance, Stapp argued strenuously that women must place the needs of their families first and remain ensconced in the home, retaining the sanctity of the family. But by the 1920s, the Stapp home no longer served as a merely domestic sphere, and Fran-ces spent more and more of her time assisting the newspaper. In what may have been a tug-of-war for her attention, Stapp lost. He slept on the couch while Frances and her small daughter occupied the front upstairs bedroom. All of these changes, coupled with economic hard times, came crashing down on Stapp. In the early 1930s, no doubt accelerated by economic setbacks, he suffered a "nervous breakdown" and, according to Stan, both his musical and newspaper careers ended for good. He remained at 4203 Woodlawn, however, as a sort of deposed patriarch, whiling away his time in increasingly eccentric activities. He became obsessed with discovering hidden meanings that substantiated his theory of a double world and his theory of determinism. From then on until his death in 1968, Stapp contributed little to the family economy, filling his days researching and writing at the Seattle Public Library. Although he wrote volu-minously, including "several books of fiction, several of non-fiction, numerous poems, and millions of words devoted to his personal diary," he produced no published text. In the 1940s, the family moved Stapp and his piano out of 4203 Woodlawn and into a series of rentals in the Wallingford neighborhood. Frances remained, living quietly above the printing presses in her basement. In the end, Stapp did remake himself, but not in a manner that dovetailed with the realities of modern life.[3]

While the bungalow at 4203 Woodlawn failed to help Orrill Stapp accommodate to twentieth-century life, it nurtured his son, Stan. From it, Stan emerged as a modern man fully capable of negotiating the consumer economy. The Arts and Crafts–inspired home had done its job. It had assisted in the formation of an individual with a place in and comfortable with a new economy.

Having participated in newspaper publishing since the age of four, when his family moved into 4203 Woodlawn, Stan literally grew up in that industry so crucial to consumerism. While his older brothers and father built up the community newspaper from a small advertising bulletin in their basement, Stan worked his way up through the printing process. As a small boy, he began as a general clean-up helper, then took over delivering newspapers, running a folding machine, and working as a "printer's devil," or apprentice. By 1933, city directories called Stan a printer, and as a teenager he learned to hand-set type and feed the huge presses, including the Linotype, that pounded away in the Stapp's basement. Stan never entered college, though he lived close to the University of Washington. He preferred to write and edit for the family's newspaper, the *Outlook.* In 1954, he took over as publisher and sole owner from his brother, Milton. Even after his mother's quiet death in her wicker rocker in 1963, the business pumped out the *Outlook* from the basement of 4203 Woodlawn. For virtually his entire life, until his fifties, Stan negotiated the consumer economy from this Craftsman bungalow, facilitating its growth with advertising, mediating its reach into north Seattle neighborhoods.[4]

The domesticity Stan Stapp learned growing up in his bungalow taught him skills necessary for success in this new world. He felt no particular adherence to an ideology that might cast doubt on the economic function of his home. If publishing from a house created problems, they stemmed more from the practicalities of space than from ambivalence about the separation of home and business. The Stapps' pragmatic view of domestic space allowed them to grab opportunities that the consumer economy presented them, to carve out a niche in it rather than distance themselves from it by retreating to nature. As domestic flexibility became valued, so too did malleable people who could blur categories while adjusting to rapidly changing circumstances.

Stan's youth in a bungalow also prepared him for the later twentieth-century homes he would inhabit. When he married in 1946, he and his wife moved into a 1940 house with a contemporary look near the suburb of Lake City, directly

Fig. 6.1 *After they married in 1946, Stan Stapp and his wife occupied this 1940 house at 2122 North 117 Street. It is a good example of a so-called minimum house, with its simple plan, eaves flush with the walls, and lack of front porch, 1940. Photo: Puget Sound Regional Archives.*

north of his childhood dwelling (fig. 6.1). Sleek and spare, the small home wasted no materials on wide eaves or welcoming porches. A "minimum house" advocated by planners and government officials to solve the problem of adequate but low-cost housing, it contained only four rooms. For Stan, its multifunctional interior would not have seemed so different from what he had always known. After all, his early life in 4203 Woodlawn had acquainted him with living in an interior space where activities and spaces flowed together. The Lake City home's rectangular shape, requisite fireplace, and diminutive size revealed its debt to the first modern, popular domestic form, the bungalow.[5]

This small house served only as an interlude for the Stapps. By 1955, Stan and his family joined millions of other Americans who were purchasing their dream homes in new suburbs well beyond the city limits. Of course, his new abode in the Sheridan Hills addition close to Lake Forest Park was a ranch house (fig. 6.2), the classic symbol of 1950s middle-class success. It represented a home construction industry transforming itself in the face of extraordinary expansion and opportunity. The era of small home-building firms was slipping away. With the federal government's aid, large-scale companies increasingly dominated the vast construction industry after World War II. They operated on purely business, not craftsman, principles. Often combining design, construction, and real-estate departments under a central organization, "merchant builders" employed as much mass production and prefabrication of components as possible. They employed specialized crews of less-skilled subcontractors who

Fig. 6.2 Stan Stapp and his family moved into this new ranch house at 16718 Thirty-seventh avenue Northeast in 1955. Its location near Lake Forest Park required Stapp to commute by automobile to the newspaper office in Wallingford, 1955. Photo: Puget Sound Regional Archives.

labored with power tools to cut and shape new materials such as plywood and plaster board. In Stapp's ranch house, they glued down vinyl flooring, plumbed two bathrooms, set in a clothes washer and dryer, tarred and graveled the gently sloping roof, and installed an oil furnace. Ubiquitous now were garages like Stapp's, up front and integrally attached to the house, visually confirming the auto-mobile's new reign of power. The suburban landscape became more uniform in appearance than ever before.[6]

Yet, despite the changes in the industry, the essential features of its bunga-low antecedent still shone through in Stapp's ranch house: the horizontal wood siding (though wide now), the living room's "Oregon" stone fireplace, the same basic domestic technology, the concrete basement, and, most of all, the unre-stricted movement through the spacious public rooms. Here, designers had merely modified the bungalow's plan, turning it on its side, spreading out all six rooms on one level. In this house, Stan, the offspring of an Arts and Crafts enthusiast, came home to the architectural offspring of the Arts and Crafts house his father had chosen decades earlier. For almost his entire life, he had interacted with modern homes, and by the 1950s, Stan clearly showed his ability to negotiate successfully modern life.[7]

Like his ranch house, Stan himself harkened back to an Arts and Crafts ante-cedent. Perhaps following his father's example, Stan handcrafted useful and beautiful furniture, though without any apparent adherence to an accompanying ideology. When the *Outlook* finally moved from the Stapp bungalow in 1970, Stan purchased a remodeled office building at 4273 Woodland Park Avenue North, just six blocks away. Inside, Stan himself fashioned "all partitions, counter tops, production work areas, and desks." Though a modern red brick structure with multicolored windows, the *Outlook*'s new home integrated the fruits of Stan's handicraft alongside the noisy newspaper machinery. The melding of technology and preindustrial symbolism characterized both the modern home and the modern man.[8]

As the Stapps and their houses so clearly showed, houses, especially bungalows, stood squarely at the center of a new social and economic order emerging in the early twentieth century. They served in many capacities: as retreats, income producers, commodities, and symbols. These homes oscillated between the poles of high-minded domestic ideology and the practical demands of economic need. They acted as sites of continual adjustment to an ever-changing set of familial and economic demands. Not all people responded to the new circumstances in the same way. We cannot necessarily extrapolate the lives and minds of ordinary people from the actions and writings of elites, who publicly articulated their values. By necessity, all Americans ultimately would become deeply embedded in a modern consumer culture, but nonelites made the transition on their own terms and not necessarily as architectural ideals might prescribe. As they negotiated the changing economy, ordinary people participated in shaping the emerging domestic landscape. Such is the story of the Stapp family and their houses, and such is the story of countless Americans, who, by making modern homes, helped craft modern life.

APPENDIX

All tables derive from the author's architectural and demographic database of Seattle's north-end neighborhoods. Percentages have been rounded, and may not total 100.

TABLE 1

HOUSE SHAPES (percentage of houses built in four sample areas)

	Irregular	Square or Rectangular	2+ Stories	1 or 1½ Stories
1890s–1906	28	71	16	84
1907–1960s	6	94	10	90

TABLE 2

ROOF SHAPES (percentage of houses built in four sample areas)

	End Gable	Side Gable	Intersecting Gables	Hip	Other
1890s–1906	29	9	20	37	5
1907–1960s	36	30	8	21	5

TABLE 3

HOUSES WITHOUT BASEMENTS
(percentage of houses built in four sample areas)

1890s–1906	53
1907–1911	24
1912–1930	6

TABLE 4

PLUMBING FEATURES IN 1937 (percentage of houses built in four sample areas)

	6 Features*	No Laundry Tray	No Tub	No Sink	No Basin	+$\frac{1}{2}$ Bath
1890s–1906	44	53	3	2	9	1
1907–1912	62	26	< 1	0	1	2
1913–1930	81	5	0	0	< 1	4

* tub, toilet, basin, sink, hot water tank, and laundry tray

TABLE 5

HEATING SYSTEMS IN 1937
(percentage of houses built containing each heating system in four sample areas)

	Stove	Pipeless	Hot Air	Hot Water	Steam
1890s–1906	63	9	20	6	< 1
1907–1912	43	10	44	5	< 1
1913–1930	5	8	67	8	1

TABLE 6

FIREPLACES IN 1937
(percentage of houses built in four sample areas)

1890s–1906	13
1907–1912	31
1913–1930	86

TABLE 7

GENERAL ARCHITECTURAL DESCRIPTION OF 1920 HOUSEHOLDS
(expressed in percentages)

	Wallingford	Fremont	Green Lake	Ballard
Victorian	8	19	12	19
Transitional	7	14	18	13
Bungalow	64	38	40	25
Workers cottage*	7	6	5	4
Four-square	8	8	5	9
Hip bungalow	–	7	12	8
Colonial	5	5	5	< 1
Other/plain gable	2	2	2	19

* one-story, square or rectangle, with hip roof

TABLE 8

DATES OF CONSTRUCTION FOR PRE—1920 HOUSES
(percentage of houses built in each period)

	Wallingford	Fremont	Green Lake	Ballard
1890s	4	7	2	5
1900–1905	10	28	31	32
1906–1910	36	38	35	44
1911–1915	35	16	18	12
1916–1917	2	2	6	3
1918–1919	14	8	9	3

TABLE 9

PLACE OF BIRTH FOR 1920 HOUSEHOLDERS AND SPOUSES
(expressed in percentages)

	Wallingford	Fremont	Green Lake	Ballard
United States	72	71	68	45
British Isles	5	4	5	3
Canada	5	4	5	5
Norway	6	6	5	21
Sweden	5	9	11	13
Denmark	2	< 1	2	1
Germany/Austria/ Switzerland	4	3	4	2
Iceland	–	–	–	3
Finland	–	–	–	5

TABLE 10

OWNERSHIP AND HOUSEHOLD HEAD OCCUPATIONAL GROUP IN 1920
(summary of four sample areas, expressed in percentages)

	Own Free	Own with Mortgage	Rent	Own w/ or w/o Mortgage
Laborers	41	37	22	78
Skilled workers/foremen	34	40	26	74
Salesmen/accountants/clerks	23	48	29	71
Professionals/managers/engineers	30	41	30	70
Entrepreneurs	36	46	18	82

TABLE II

OCCUPATIONAL GROUPS IN 1920 COMPARED TO STYLE OF RESIDENCES
(summary of all four sample areas, expressed in percentages)

	Victorian	Transitional	Bungalow	Workers Cottage	Hip 4-Square	Bungalow	Colonial	Other
Laborers	40	10	23	10	5	0	3	10
Skilled workers/foremen	17	17	35	6	7	9	3	7
Salesmen/accountants	8	8	54	7	10	4	5	4
Professionals/managers	11	10	45	3	8	13	8	2
Entrepreneurs	11	11	48	7	11	4	7	0

TABLE 12

OCCUPATIONAL GROUPS IN FOUR NEIGHBORHOODS IN 1920
(expressed in percentages)

	Wallingford	Fremont	Green Lake	Ballard
Laborers	3	8	6	16
Skilled workers/foremen	25	27	27	41
Salesmen/accountants	21	21	17	4
Professionals/managers	17	12	14	10
Entrepreneurs	11	10	7	4

TABLE 13

BALLARD SAMPLE AREA 1920 OCCUPATIONAL GROUPS AND HOME
OWNERSHIP (number surveyed in parentheses, expressed in percentages)

	Own Free	Own w/ Mortgage	Rent	Own w/ or w/o Mortgage
Laborers (15)	53	40	7	93
Skilled workers/foremen (57)	32	39	30	71
Salesmen/accountants (8)	38	25	38	63
Professionals/managers (6)	50	33	25	83
Entrepreneurs (1)	0	0	100	0

TABLE 14

BOARDERS, EXTENDED FAMILY, AND SERVANTS IN DIFFERENT HOUSING TYPES (in four sample areas)

	Houses w/ Boarders et al.	Remodeled Houses w/ Boarders et al.
Victorian/plain	38	9
Transitional	17	2
Bungalow	72	19
Workers cottage	5	0
Four-square	19	2
Hip bungalow	6	0
Colonial	8	3
Other	6	0

TABLE 15

FOUR-SQUARE HOUSES (in four sample areas)

	Wallingford	Fremont	Green Lake	Ballard
Total # in sample area	8	14	8	12
Number with boarder or extended family	6	6	4	2
Percentage with boarder or extended family	75%	43%	50%	17%

TABLE 16

DIVORCED OR WIDOWED PEOPLE WITHIN 1920 SAMPLE HOUSEHOLDS
(includes householders, children, and boarders)

	Wallingford	Fremont	Green Lake	Ballard
Divorced men	0	0	1	0
Divorced women	3	2	2	2
Widows	10	14	20	18
Widowers	3	3	3	3
Total households	109	137	133	115
Percentage of households				
w/ divorce/widow	15%	14%	20%	20%

GRAPH 1

TOTAL HOUSES BUILT EACH YEAR IN ALL FOUR NORTH-END SEATTLE
SAMPLE AREAS, 1890–1929

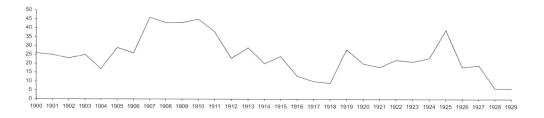

NOTES

1 BLUEPRINTS FOR "THE SEATTLE BUNGALOW"

1. Calvin Schmid, *Social Trends in Seattle* (Seattle: University of Washington Press, 1944), 165–90; Janice Reiff, "Urbanization and the Social Structure: Seattle, Washington, 1852–1910," (Ph.D. diss., University of Washington, 1981).

2. The leading works that examine this architectural transformation are Gwendolyn Wright, *Moralism and the Model Home: Domestic Architecture and Cultural Conflict in Chicago, 1873–1913* (Chicago: University of Chicago Press, 1980); Clifford Clark, *The American Family Home, 1880–1960* (Chapel Hill: University of North Carolina Press, 1986); Margaret Marsh, *Suburban Lives* (New Brunswick: Rutgers University Press, 1990). The terms "Victorianism" and "modernism" refer to historic periods, cultural systems, and groupings of architectural styles. Historians generally delineate the Victorian period of U.S. history as stretching roughly from the Civil War to the early twentieth century; a particular middle-class culture reigned during this time that has inspired much scholarly examination. Victorianism as a cultural system emphasized a hierarchal social order of rigidly defined and clearly separated categories. At the top of this "natural" hierarchy, the most "civilized" (white, middle-class, Protestant, native-born men) distinguished themselves from the lower, increasingly "animalistic" (women, African Americans, and the poor) by their rationality, self-control, discipline, and morality. Scholars have written voluminously about many aspects of Victorian culture and society, especially women and material culture. A good place to start is Daniel Walker Howe, "Victorian Culture in

America," in *Victorian America*, ed. Daniel Walker Howe, 3–28 (Philadelphia: University of Pennsylvania Press, 1976); and Thomas J. Schlereth, *Victorian America: Transformations in Everyday Life, 1876–1915* (New York: HarperCollins Pub., 1991). Works on Victorianism that were important for me are T. J. Jackson Lears, *No Place of Grace: Antimodernism and the Transformation of American Culture, 1880–1920* (New York: Pantheon, 1981); Katherine C. Grier, *Culture and Comfort: People, Parlors, and Upholstery, 1850–1930* (Rochester: Strong Museum, 1988); Kenneth L. Ames, *Death in the Dining Room and Other Tales of Victorian Culture* (Philadelphia: Temple University Press, 1992); and Clark, *American Family Home.* Victorian domestic architectural styles accompanied the Victorian era and culture. The most widely used stylistic guide, *A Field Guide to American Houses*, places Second Empire, Stick, Queen Anne, Shingle, Richardsonian Romanesque, and Folk Victorian styles under "Victorian Houses" arising between 1860 and 1900. Irregularly shaped, the floor plans of such houses reflected the Victorian cultural values of well-defined, hierarchal, separated spaces. See Virginia McAlester and Lee McAlester, *A Field Guide to American Houses* (New York: Alfred A. Knopf, 1984), 238–315. Historians commonly demarcate the modern period of U.S. history from the beginning of the early twentieth century (or World War I) until about 1970. During this time, a modern culture appeared as the United States transformed economically and socially. (See notes 21 and 22 for works on the Second Industrial Revolution.) This new mindset appeared particularly in art and literature, but its values also permeated the twentieth century as a whole. As Daniel Singal defines it, the modernist world view sought to break down the rigid hierarchy and formality of Victorian categories and to integrate and mesh the previously separate social and cultural groupings. Instead of a fixed order dependent on universal laws, modernists saw a relativistic, constantly changing universe. They desired authenticity, lived experience, and a realism that engaged the world. For the best brief definition of modern culture, see Daniel Joseph Singal, "Towards A Definition of American Modernism," *American Quarterly* 39 (Spring 1987): 7–26. See also Lears, *No Place of Grace,* and Stanley Coben, *Rebellion Against Victorianism: The Impetus for Cultural Change in 1920s America* (New York: Oxford University Press, 1991). As with Victorianism, a set of domestic architectural styles reflected this modernist cultural system. The definition of modern architecture is slippery. Traditionally, art historians consider modern architecture as the consciously reformist work of early twentieth-century European avant-garde idealists that rejected past precedents and unnecessary ornamentation and adopted a streamlined, industrial aesthetic. For example, see Alan Colquhoun, *Modern Architecture* (New York: Oxford University Press, 2002). Many recognize that Craftsman bungalows played a transitional role in ushering in modern architecture of this sort. McAlester lumps the Prairie, Craftsman, Modernistic, and International styles under "Modern Houses." Mark Gelernter calls the Chicago school, Arts and Crafts, and Prairie styles "proto-modernist movements" in Gelernter, *A History of American Architecture: Buildings in their Cultural and Technological Context* (Hanover, NH: University Press of New England, 1999), 191. As one of the first types of modern architecture, Craftsman bungalows reflected a modernist world view. Vincent Scully argues that the Shingle style (not Arts and Crafts architecture) provided a late-nineteenth-century precedent for Frank Lloyd Wright and twentieth-century modernism in *The Shingle Style: Architectural Theory and Design from Richardson to the Origins of Wright* (New Haven, CT: Yale University Press, 1955). I agree that this style was an important transition between Victorian styles and those like Wright's in the twentieth century. However, Shingle style's irregular plan, usually featuring a parlor, seems to me more Victorian than modern. Therefore, I agree with McAlester's categorization.

3. The idea that Arts and Crafts architectural design filters down from architects is the standard interpretation of all popular housing. For a current architectural history of the United States that illustrates this idea, see Gelernter, *History of American Architecture*, 214–25; Marcus Whiffen and Frederick Koeper, *American Architecture*, vol. 2, *1860–1976* (Cambridge, MA: MIT Press, 1995), 12–31; and McAlester, *Field Guide to American Houses*, 454. Vincent Scully claims that California bungalows were just builders' versions of Greene and Greene architecture. Scully, *Shingle Style*, 157, n6.

4. Mary Corbin Sies, "Toward a Performance Theory of the Suburban Ideal, 1877–1917," in *Perspectives in Vernacular Architecture*, vol. 4, ed. Thomas Carter and Bernard L. Herman (Columbia: University of Missouri Press, 1991), 197–207; Mary Corbin Sies, "North American Suburbs, 1880–1950: Cultural and Social Reconsiderations," *Journal of Urban History* 27 (March 2001): 313–46; Mary Corbin Sies, "The City Transformed: Nature, Technology, and the Suburban Ideal, 1877–1917," *Journal of Urban History* 14 (November 1987): 81–111. Most works explaining this architecture argue that professionals conceived it before it trickled down to the masses. See McAlester, *Field Guide to American Houses*, 454; Clark, *American Family Home*, 131–92; Wright, *Moralism and the Model Home*; Gwendolyn Wright, *Building the Dream: A Social History of Housing in America* (Cambridge, MA: MIT Press, 1981), 158–76; and Derek Holdsworth, "House and Home in Vancouver: Images of West Coast Urbanism, 1886–1929," in *The Canadian City: Essays in Urban and Social History*, ed. Gilbert A. Stelter and Alan F. J. Artibise (Ottawa: Carleton University Press, 1984): 196. Some architectural historians, however, refute the idea that the bungalow was a creation of just architects. For instance, see Robert Winter, *The California Bungalow* (Los Angeles: Hennessey and Ingalls, 1980); Anthony King, *The Bungalow: The Production of a Global Culture*, 2nd ed. (London: Routledge and Kegan Paul, 1984); and Barbara Rubin, "A Chronology of Architecture in Los Angeles," *Annals of the Association of American Geographers* 67 (December 1977): 521–37. Howard Davis, *The Culture of Building* (New York: Oxford University Press, 1999), and Robert Gutman, *The Design of American Housing: A Reappraisal of the Architect's Role* (New York: Publishing Center for Cultural Resources, 1985), place architecture in a much larger economic and technological context.

5. These authors provide the best understanding of how consumerism flourished in the early twentieth century. See Daniel Horowitz, *The Morality of Spending: Attitudes Toward the Consumer Society in America, 1875–1940* (Baltimore: Johns Hopkins University Press, 1985); Roland Marchand, *Advertising the American Dream: Making Way for Modernity, 1920–1940* (Berkeley: University of California Press, 1985); Stewart Ewen, *Captains of Consciousness: Advertising and the Social Roots of the Consumer Culture* (New York: McGraw-Hill Book Co., 1976); Lears, *No Place of Grace*; William Leach, *Land of Desire: Merchants, Power, and the Rise of a New American Culture* (New York: Vintage Books, 1993). Lawrence B. Glickman, ed., *Consumer Society in American History: A Reader* (Ithaca: Cornell University Press, 1999), and

Lendol Calder, *Financing the American Dream: A Cultural History of Consumer Credit* (Princeton: Princeton University Press, 1999), 18–19, give a broad overview of consumerism in the United States. Although the history of consumerism is a burgeoning field, few architectural historians use it to understand the spread of architectural design. The best summary of how material culture in general meshes with consumerism is Ann Smart Martin, "Makers, Buyers, and Users: Consumerism as a Material Culture Framework," *Winterthur Portfolio* 28 (Summer/Autumn 1993): 141–57. Smart's article shows that most such scholarship focuses on the seventeenth through nineteenth centuries and on artifacts other than houses.

6. Social histories that view cultural change as emanating from the bottom up that have been particularly influential for me are Kathy Peiss, *Cheap Amusements: Working Women and Leisure in Turn-of-the-Century New York* (Philadelphia: Temple University Press, 1986); Peiss, *Hope in a Jar: The Making of America's Beauty Culture* (New York: Henry Holt and Co., 1998); Roy Rosenzweig, *Eight Hours for What We Will: Workers and Leisure in an Industrial City, 1870–1920* (New York: Cambridge University Press, 1983); Jim Cullen, *The Art of Democracy: A Concise History of Popular Culture in the United States* (New York: Monthly Review Press, 1996); and Steven J. Ross, *Working-Class Hollywood: Silent Film and the Shaping of Class in America* (Princeton: Princeton University Press, 1998). Two works particularly important for me that show the influence of working-class housing on twentieth-century popular architecture are Joseph C. Bigott, *From Cottage to Bungalow: Houses and the Working Class in Metropolitan Chicago, 1869–1929* (Chicago: University of Chicago Press, 2001); and Thomas Hubka and Judith T. Kenny, "The Workers' Cottage in Milwaukee's Polish Community: Housing the Process of Americanization, 1870–1920," in *People, Power, Places: Perspectives in Vernacular Architecture,* vol. 8, ed. Sally McMurry and Annmarie Adams (Knoxville: University of Tennessee Press, 2000), 33–52.

7. In their broadest sense, suburbs are those residential regions developed beyond the city. Although suburbanization, which reached a frenzy after World War II, is commonly considered a postwar movement, the impetus to create suburbs from the cheap land adjoining cities began in the nineteenth century. During the economic and transportation revolutions of the late nineteenth century, the modern suburb appeared. Speculative developers bought large tracts of land connected to the center of the city by streetcar lines. Lured by both a suburban domestic ideal and affordable prices, home owners began to fill in the developments with houses. Then, usually impelled by infrastructure needs, either residents requested annexation to the city or the municipal authorities incorporated the suburb into its city limits. These regions that began as suburbs then became neighborhoods. However, they retained their suburban characteristics: yard-surrounded single-family residences accessible to the distant urban center by streetcar or automobiles. Seattle's development followed this pattern. By 1907, the city had annexed most of the suburban developments and independent communities surrounding it that had originated earlier. Therefore, I have used the terms "suburb" and "neighborhood" to refer to Seattle's northern regions. See Schmid, *Social Trends in Seattle*, 41–80. The history of suburbanization is large. I have relied on Clark, *American Family Home;* Marsh, *Suburban Lives;* Sam Bass Warner, Jr., *Streetcar Suburbs: The Process of Growth in Boston (1870–1900)* (Cambridge: Harvard University Press, 1962); John R. Stilgoe, *Borderland: Origins of the*

American Suburb, 1820–1939; and Kenneth T. Jackson, *Crabgrass Frontier: The Suburbanization of the United States* (New York: Oxford University Press, 1985) as basic sources. I drew from Mark S. Foster, "The Western Response to Urban Transportation: A Tale of Three Cities, 1900–1945," *Journal of the West* 18 (July 1979): 31–39; Carol A. O'Connor, "A Region of Cities," in *The Oxford History of the American West,* ed. Clyde Milner II, Carol O'Connor, and Martha Sandweiss (New York: Oxford University Press, 1994), 535–63; Howard R. Lamar, ed., *The New Encyclopedia of the American West* (New Haven, CT: Yale University Press, 1998), 212–14; and John Findlay, *Magic Lands: Western Cityscapes and American Culture After 1940* (Berkeley: University of California Press, 1992), to explain the western pattern of urbanization. In a recent work, Diane Shaw argues that new eastern cities of the early nineteenth century such as Rochester, New York, broke away from an older, walking city model. Built during the burgeoning market economy, "sorted" cities with distinct commercial, civic, and industrial areas resulted from the new middle class's desire for order and control. The spatial divisions these entrepreneurs created reinforced bourgeois power and privilege. See Diane Shaw, *City Building on the Eastern Frontier: Sorting the New Nineteenth-Century City* (Baltimore: Johns Hopkins University Press, 2004).

8. John M. Faragher, in "Bungalow and Ranch House: The Architectural Backwash of California," *Western Historical Quarterly* 32 (Summer 2001): 149–73, argues that the western bungalow form served as a model for later ranch houses. Alan Gowans, in *The Comfortable House: North American Suburban Architecture, 1890–1930* (Cambridge: MIT Press, 1987), provides the best coverage of new suburban houses in the early twentieth century. For the best work on the Arts and Crafts movement, including Craftsman communities, see Eileen Boris, *Art and Labor: Ruskin, Morris, and the Craftsman Ideal in America* (Philadelphia: Temple University Press, 1986). For a clear definition of the Craftsman architectural style, see McAlester, *Field Guide to American Houses,* 453–63. For a discussion of the bungalow house type, see *The Craftsman*; Clay Lancaster, *The American Bungalow, 1880–1930* (New York: Abbeville Press, 1985); Winter, *California Bungalow*; and Anthony D. King, *Bungalow.*

9. King, *Bungalow,* 26.

10. King, *Bungalow,* and Clark, *American Family Home,* give good overviews of the bungalow's origins. To see how the bungalow spread from California, see Robert M. Fogelson, *The Fragmented Metropolis: Los Angeles, 1850–1930,* 2nd ed. (Berkeley: University of California Press, 1993), 78; Jeffrey Ochsner and Dennis Alan Andersen, *Distant Corner: Seattle Architects and the Legacy of H. H. Richardson* (Seattle: University of Washington Press, 2003), 30; Winter, *California Bungalow;* Deryck W. Holdsworth, "Vernacular Form in an Urban Context: A Preliminary Investigation of Facade Elements in Vancouver Housing," (master's thesis, University of British Columbia, 1971); Deryck W. Holdsworth, "Regional Distinctiveness in an Industrial Age: Some California Influences on British Columbia Housing," *American Review of Canadian Studies* 12 (Summer 1982): 64–81; King, *Bungalow;* Lancaster, *American Bungalow;* M. Jeff Hardwick, "Homesteads and Bungalows: African-American Architecture in Langston, Oklahoma," in *Shaping Communities: Perspectives in Vernacular Architecture,* vol. 6, ed. Carter L. Hudgins and Elizabeth Collins Cromley (Knoxville: University of Tennessee Press, 1997), 21–32; and Susan Mulchahey Chase, "Rural Adaptations of Suburban Bungalows, Sussex County, Delaware," in *Gender, Class*

and Shelter: Perspectives in Vernacular Architecture, vol. 5, ed. Elizabeth Collins Cromley and Carter L. Hudgins (Knoxville: University of Tennessee Press, 1995), 179–89.

11. Roger Moss, *Century of Color: Exterior Decoration for American Buildings, 1820–1920* (Watkins Glen, NY: American Life Foundation, 1981). For regional variations of bungalows, see Marsha Weisiger, *Boosters, Streetcars, and Bungalows* (Phoenix: Roosevelt Action Association, 1984); Winter, *California Bungalow;* Holdsworth "House and Home"; Rubin, "Chronology of Architecture"; and Diane Maddox, *Bungalow Nation* (New York: Harry N. Abrams, Inc, 2003).

12. Lisa Mighetto and Marcia Montgomery, *Hard Drive to the Klondike: Promoting Seattle During the Gold Rush* (Seattle: University of Washington Press, 2003), 56; Maddox, in *Bungalow Nation,* features Seattle as an archetypical bungalow city.

13. Researchers can find descriptions of Seattle's physical growth and appearance in Ochsner and Andersen, *Distant Corner,* 19, 28, 30, 57; Schmid, *Social Trends in Seattle;* Jeffrey Karl Ochsner, ed., *Shaping Seattle Architecture: A Historical Guide to the Architects* (Seattle: University of Washington Press, 1994), xvii–xxxii; Matthew Klingle, "Urban by Nature: An Environmental History of Seattle, 1880–1970" (Ph.D. diss, University of Washington, 2001); Lawrence Kreisman, *Made to Last: Historic Preservation in Seattle* (Seattle: Historic Seattle Preservation and Development Authority, 1985), 1–7. Mighetto and Montgomery, *Hard Drive to the Klondike,* 1–17, 56, provide the best overview of Seattle's growth, with census statistics, of the early twentieth century.

14. Leslie Blanchard, *The Street Railway Era in Seattle: A Chronicle of Six Decades* (Forty Fort, PN: Harold E. Cox, 1968), 30, quote on 32; Richard C. Berner, *Seattle 1900–1920: From Boomtown, Urban Turbulence, to Restoration* (Seattle: Charles Press, 1991), 101–2.

15. Schmid, *Social Trends in Seattle,* 72, 222; Ochsner, *Shaping Seattle Architecture,* xix.

16. Schmid, *Social Trends in Seattle,* 63, 69; Folke Nyberg and Victor Steinbrueck, "An Inventory of Buildings and Urban Design Resources: Ballard, Wallingford, Fremont, University District, Mount Baker Park" (Seattle: Historic Seattle Preservation and Development Authority, 1975).

17. Schmid, *Social Trends in Seattle,* 216–17; John Owen, "The Evolution of the Popular House in Seattle" (master's thesis, University of Washington, 1975), 41–105; Ochsner and Andersen, *Distant Corner,* 207–51; Bigott, *From Cottage to Bungalow;* and Hubka and Kenny, "Workers' Cottage," 33–52.

18. Owen, "Evolution of the Popular House," 86–96, 137; Schmid, *Social Trends in Seattle,* 75.

19. Berner, *Seattle 1900–1920,* 60. See especially chapter 7, "The Framework of Life in the City," 56–106. See Reiff, "Urbanization and Social Structure," for the best discussion of Seattle society before 1910.

20. Quoted in Roger Sale, *Seattle, Past and Present* (Seattle: University of Washington Press, 1976), 196.

21. Classics in the economic transformation at the turn of the twentieth century remain Robert Wiebe, *The Search for Order, 1877–1920* (New York: Hill and Wang, 1967); Samuel P. Hays, *The Response to Industrialism, 1885–1914* (Chicago: University of Chicago Press, 1957); and Alfred D. Chandler, Jr., *The Visible Hand: The Managerial Revolution in America* (Cambridge, MA: The Belknap Press of Harvard University Press, 1977). A good synthesis is Maury Klein, *The Flowering of Third America: The Making of an Organizational Society, 1850–1920* (Chicago: Ivan R. Dee, 1993).

22. A growing bibliography now deals with American society during the Second Industrial Revolution. Particularly useful are Lears, *No Place of Grace*; David Montgomery, *The Fall of the House of Labor: The Workplace, The State, and American Labor Activism, 1865–1925* (New York: Cambridge University Press, 1987); Olivier Zunz, *Making America Corporate, 1870–1920* (Chicago: University of Chicago Press, 1990); Burton Bledstein and Robert D. Johnston, eds, *The Middling Sorts: Explorations in the History of the American Middle Class* (New York: Routledge, 2001); and Ronald Edsforth, *Class Conflict and Cultural Consensus: The Making of a Mass Consumer Society in Flint, Michigan* (New Brunswick, NJ: Rutgers University Press, 1987). See Sale, *Seattle, Past and Present*, 180, 196, and Berner, *Seattle 1900–1920*, 21–32, 29, 172, 175, especially chapter 3, "The Economy, 1900–1914"; Reiff, "Urbanization and Social Structure"; and Kathryn Morse, *The Nature of Gold: An Environmental History of the Klondike Gold Rush* (Seattle: University of Washington Press, 2003).

23. Foster, "Tale of Three Cities," 33; Mighetto and Montgomery, *Hard Drive to the Klondike*, 56.

24. Wright, *Moralism and the Model Home*, has the best discussion of how the bungalow resulted from the conjunction of various reform movements by professionals and architects in the Progressive period. See also Boris, *Art and Labor*; Gustav Stickley, *Craftsman Homes: Architecture and Furnishings of the American Arts and Crafts Movement* (New York: Dover Publications, 1979; reprinted from New York: Craftsman Publishing Co., 1909); and Gwendolyn Wright, "The Progressive Housewife and the Bungalow," *Building the Dream: A Social History of Housing in America* (Cambridge: MIT Press, 1981), 158–76.

2 IDEALIZING THE SEATTLE BUNGALOW

1. Stan Stapp interviews, 13 September 1991 and 8 June 1998, Seattle, Washington; Polk Seattle City directories, 1900–1905; *The Triton*, vol. 1. (n.d.), two copies in possession of the author, originals in possession of Stan Stapp; obituary of Orrill V. Stapp, *North Central Outlook* (Seattle), 12 September 1968.

2. Tax assessor form for 10143 66 Avenue South, Puget Sound Regional Archives, Bellevue, Washington; Stapp interview, 8 June 1998. Next to a small photograph of his Rainier Beach home in his photo album, Orrill Stapp wrote, "Home, Rainier Beach, upon which, grading, planning, carpentering I labored so much first decade." From this, I assume that Stapp himself built at least parts of the house himself. Photo album in possession of Stan Stapp.

3. Ronald Edsforth, *Class Conflict and Cultural Consensus: The Making of a Mass Consumer Society in Flint, Michigan* (New Brunswick, NJ: Rutgers University Press, 1987), and T. J. Jackson Lears, *No Place of Grace: Antimodernism and the Transformation of American Culture, 1880–1920* (New York: Pantheon, 1981) examine how working- and middle-class Americans weathered the Second Industrial Revolution. A good overview of the Second Industrial Revolution is Maury Klein, *The Flowering of Third America: The Making of an Organizational Society, 1850–1920* (Chicago: Ivan R. Dee, 1993).

4. Eileen Boris, *Art and Labor: Ruskin, Morris, and The Craftsman Ideal in America* (Philadelphia: Temple University Press, 1986), 10. This is the best book on the movement within the United States. One of the best brief summaries of the Arts and Crafts movement in both the United States and Great Britain is Elizabeth Cumming and Wendy Kaplan, *The Arts and Crafts Movement* (London: Thames and Hudson, 1991).

5. Cumming and Kaplan, *Arts and Crafts Movement,* 10. On the British influence on the American movement, see Wendy Kaplan, "The Lamp of British Precedent: An Introduction to the Arts and Crafts Movement," in *"The Art that is Life": The Arts and Crafts Movement in America, 1875–1920,* ed. Wendy Kaplan (Boston: Museum of Fine Arts, 1987), 54. See also Eileen Boris, "'Dreams of Brotherhood and Beauty': The Social Ideas of the Arts and Crafts Movement," in *"The Art that is Life,"* 208–22, for a concise discussion of the reform ideals of the movement.

6. Boris, *Art and Labor,* 28; Boris, "Dreams of Brotherhood and Beauty," 208–22.

7. Leland Roth, *American Architecture: A History* (Boulder, CO: Westview Press, 2001), 299. Robert Winter likened the movement to a religious revival in "The Arts and Crafts as a Social Movement," in *Aspects of the Arts and Crafts Movement in America,* ed. Robert Judson Clark, *Record of the Art Museum, Princeton University* 34 (1975): 36–40. Janet Kardon, ed., *The Ideal Home, 1900–1920: The History of Twentieth-Century American Craft* (New York: Harry N. Abrams, Publishers, 1993), and Robert Winter, ed., *Toward A Simpler Way of Life: The Arts and Crafts Architects of California* (Berkeley: University of California Press, 1997), discuss the design ideology of Arts and Crafts. Boris, *Art and Labor,* 28–31. While architectural historians such as Boris and Roth usually credit the Boston Society of Arts and Crafts, founded in 1897, as the first organization, historian Mark Hewitt places the first exhibition most appropriately in San Francisco in 1895–96. See Mark Hewitt, *Gustav Stickley's Craftsman Farms: The Quest for an Arts and Crafts Utopia* (Syracuse: Syracuse University Press, 2001), 2–3.

8. Much has been written on the Arts and Crafts movement's effect on American architecture and the influence of Gustav Stickley. The most influential for me were Boris, *Art and Labor,* and Hewitt, *Gustav Stickley's Craftsman Farms.* See also Barry Sanders, *A Complex Fate: Gustav Stickley and the Craftsman Movement* (New York: John Wiley and Sons, 1996), for a biography of Stickley. H. Allen Brooks, *Frank Lloyd Wright and The Prairie School* (New York: George Braziller, 1984), 12.

9. Quote from "Western Academy of Beaux Arts and the Beaux Arts Workshop" promotional brochure, n.p., n.d. (circa 1908), in Beaux Arts Village scrapbook #1, 1908–64, Beaux Arts Village Archives, hereafter cited as WABA pamphlet.

10. See Boris, *Art and Labor,* 82–98; Wendy Kaplan, "Regionalism in American Architecture," in *The Arts and Crafts Movement,* 125; Hewitt, *Gustav Stickley's Craftsman Farms,* 71–78; and Wendy Kaplan, "Spreading the Crafts: The Role of the Schools," in *"The Art that is Life,"* 298–306, for discussions of Arts and Crafts schools. Joan Draper, "The École des Beaux-Arts and the Architectural Profession in the United States: The Case of John Galen Howard," in *The Architect: Chapters in the History of the Profession,* ed. Spiro Kostof (New York: Oxford University Press, 1977), 211, 216, explains the École des Beaux-Arts method of instruction. On the workshop's goals, see WABA pamphlet; "The Society of Beaux Arts," unidentified newspaper copy, n.p., n.d. (circa 1909), Beaux Arts Village scrapbook #1, 1908–64, Beaux Arts Village Archives, hereafter cited as Society of Beaux Arts pamphlet; and Frank Calvert, ed. *Homes and Gardens of the Pacific Coast,* vol. 1, *Seattle* (Beaux Arts Village, Lake Washington: Beaux Arts Society Publishers, 1913; reprint, with new forward by Christopher Laughlin, n.p.: 1974). Early pamphlets mentioned very little about the art of home-building, emphasizing the Beaux Arts Society's object as "to develop art and its appreciation here in the Northwest."

11. Quotes in WABA pamphlet, n.p., and Society of Beaux Arts pamphlet, n.p. Boris contends that the American Arts and Crafts movement from the beginning contained two divergent purposes. More idealistic members held "anticommercial" beliefs attacking modern industrial production. Others were essentially "tastemakers" who advocated handicrafts as a means of returning beauty to production. Apparently, Beaux Arts Society members were predominantly tastemakers. See Boris, *Art and Labor,* 28–31.

12. WABA pamphlet, n.p.; Renfro and Calvert could have been the men H. B. Staley remembered as members of the Seattle Press Club who helped Frolich form the society. See *Seattle Post-Intelligencer,* 6 June 1958, clipping in artists scrapbook #90, Fro–Fz, Fine Arts Department, Seattle Public Library, Seattle, Washington; biographical information on Frolich, Renfro, and Calvert in the Beaux Arts Village scrapbook #1; Calvert, *Homes and Gardens* reprint; Society of Beaux Arts pamphlet, n.p.

13. "Articles of incorporation of the Western Academy of Beaux Arts," 1908, #12040, Puget Sound Regional Archives; Beaux Arts Village scrapbook #1, n.p.; quote from clipping on Frolich from *The American Review of Reviews,* n.d., Beaux Arts Village Archives; Calvert, *Homes and Gardens,* n.p.; Mrs. Travis Thompson to Margaret Guilford, 13 August 1984, in Beaux Arts Village scrapbook, 1981–1984, Beaux Arts Village Archives.

14. Quote from WABA pamphlet, n.p.; excerpt from *The Argus,* 18 December 1909, in Calvert, *Homes and Gardens* reprint; unidentified newspaper clipping of advertisement entitled "Village of Beaux Arts," n.d., in Beaux Arts Village scrapbook #1. One indication of this shift was Frolich's withdrawal from WABA. In 1909, he became commissioner of sculpture for the Alaska-Yukon-Pacific (AYP) Exposition, which was about the same time a civil engineer named Donald V. Mitchell replaced him as a Beaux Arts trustee. Frolich never lived in Beaux Arts Village. Shortly after the AYP, Frolich left for California where he established a successful career in sculpture. On Frolich, see artists scrapbook #90, Fro–Fz, n.p., Fine Arts Department, Seattle Public Library; Frolich clippings, Beaux Arts Village scrapbook #1, n.p.; "Origin of Beaux Arts Village and the Western Academy of Beaux Arts, 1908–1928 Plus," Beaux Arts Village Archives; undated speech by Joshua Vogel, in Beaux Arts Village Archives, hereafter cited as Vogel speech.

15. On the British and American communitarian impulse, see Elizabeth Cumming, "Sources and Early Ideals," in *The Arts and Crafts Movement,* edited by Elizabeth Cumming and Wendy Kaplan (London: Thames and Hudson, 1991), 28; and Hewitt, *Gustav Stickley's Craftsman Farms,* 48–70. Boris, "Dreams of Brotherhood and Beauty," 208–22, generally includes Hubbard's Roycroft community, and George E. Thomas, "William Price's Arts and Crafts Colony at Rose Valley, Pennsylvania," in *The Ideal Home,* 125–35, discusses Price's venture. For the best coverage, see Boris, *Art and Labor,* 156–68.

16. Quote from "Beaux Arts Village, Home of the Beaux Arts Society," pamphlet, n.d., Special Collections, University of Washington Libraries, Seattle, Washington, 4. My description of the early growth of Beaux Arts Village comes from these primary sources: *Seattle Post-Intelligencer,* 28 May 1909, clipping in Beaux Arts Village scrapbook #1, n.p.; unidentified newspaper clipping, 9 May 1909, Beaux Arts Village scrapbook #1, n.p.; Vogel speech; Alfred Renfro, Acting Secretary, Beaux Arts Village Park Board, "Beaux Arts Village," undated brochure (circa 1916), Beaux Arts Village Archives, 9–14.

17. On the seemingly contradictory mix of antimodernism and capitalism, see Marie Via

and Marjorie Searl, eds., *Head, Heart and Hand: Elbert Hubbard and the Roycrofters* (Rochester: University of Rochester Press / Memorial Art Gallery, 1994), and Boris, *Art and Labor*, 146–50. Eileen Boris, in "Crossing Boundaries: The Gendered Meaning of the Arts and Crafts," in *The Ideal Home*, 32–45, has the best discussion of how those contradictory impulses facilitated accommodation to a new economy.

18. For further reading on the Craftsman movement within the broader impulse for the simple life, see Boris, *Art and Labor;* David Shi, *The Simple Life: Plain Living and High Thinking in American Culture* (New York: Oxford University Press, 1985); and Miles Orvel, *The Real Thing: Imitation and Authenticity in American Culture, 1880–1940* (Chapel Hill: University of North Carolina Press, 1989). Gustav Stickley's ideology is easily accessible in Gustav Stickley, ed., *Craftsman Bungalows: Fifty-Nine Homes from "The Craftsman,"* with a new introduction by Alan Weissman (New York: Dover Publications, 1988), v–vi; and Gustav Stickley, "A Craftsman House Founded on the California Mission Style," in *Craftsman Homes: Architecture and Furnishings of the American Arts and Crafts Movement* (New York: Craftsman Publishing Co., 1909; reprint, New York: Dover Publications, 1979), 9. Two sources fully explain Craftsman architectural ideals. See Gustav Stickley, "Als Ik Kan, The Craftsman Idea in Homebuilding," *The Craftsman* 24 (April 1913): 129, and Hewitt, *Gustav Stickley's Craftsman Farms.*

19. "Beaux Arts Village, Home of the Beaux Arts Society," 2.

20. Alfred Renfro, "We Built Our House on the Shore of Lake Washington," *Sunset Magazine* (September 1931): 13; Hewitt, *Gustav Stickley's Craftsman Farms,* 117–35, 154–58.

21. "Distinguishing Features of Craftsman Houses," *The Craftsman* 23 (March 1913): 727–29.

22. "Beaux Arts: The Community Problem Solved," *Bungalow Magazine* 2 (August 1913): 32; Renfro, "We Built Our House," 13.

23. "Porches, Pergolas and Balconies, and the Charm of Privacy Out of Doors," *The Craftsman* 9 (March 1906): 843–45; Charles Alma Byers, "The Message of the Western Pergola to American Home- and Garden-Makers," *The Craftsman* 22 (August 1912): 474; "Beaux Arts," *Bungalow Magazine* 2 (August 1913): 41.

24. "Beaux Arts," *Bungalow Magazine* 2 (August 1913): 41; Renfro, "We Built Our House," 14

25. Renfro, "We Built Our House," 14.

26. "Beaux Arts," *Bungalow Magazine* 2 (August 1913): 40.

27. Stickley, "Als Ik Kan," 129.

28. "Beaux Arts," *Bungalow Magazine* 2 (August 1913): 33.

29. "Beaux Arts," *Bungalow Magazine* 2 (July 1913): 14–15.

30. Ibid.; tax assessor card for 2811 106 Southeast, Ditty house, Puget Sound Regional Archives; "A Country Home for the Business Man: A Second Visit to Craftsman Farms," *The Craftsman* 19 (October 1910): 56; Stickley, "Als Ik Kan, The Craftsman Idea in Homebuilding," 129; "Home With a Personality," *Bungalow Magazine* 4 (January 1915): 3; Stickley, "The Value of Permanent Architecture as a Truthful Expression of National Character," *The Craftsman* 16 (April 1909): 80.

31. "An Education in Home-Building: The Need and the Opportunity of Studying This Art in America," *The Craftsman* 26 (April 1914): 78; Stickley, "The Craftsman Idea of the Kind of Home Environment that Would Result from More Natural Standards of Life and Work," Stickley, *Craftsman Homes,* 198.

32. Renfro, "We Built Our House," 14; "The Living Room, Its Many Uses and Its Possibilities for Comfort and Beauty," *The Craftsman* 9 (October 1905): 59; "Distinguishing Features of Craftsman Houses," *The Craftsman* 23 (March 1913): 727. For a full discussion of parlor ideology that Craftsmen like Renfro reacted against, see Katherine C. Grier, *Culture and Comfort: People, Parlors, and Upholstery, 1850–1930* (Rochester, NY: Strong Museum, 1988), 287–300.

33. "The Dining Room as a Center of Hospitality and Good Cheer," *The Craftsman* 9 (November 1905): 229; "Distinguishing Features of Craftsman Houses," 727; Renfro, "We Built Our House," 15.

34. "Beaux Arts," *Bungalow Magazine* 2 (August 1913): 33.

35. Gabrielle M. Lanier and Bernard L. Herman, *Everyday Architecture of the Mid-Atlantic: Looking at Buildings and Landscapes* (Baltimore: Johns Hopkins University Press, 1997), 10–51, have an excellent discussion of the open and closed plans. Kenneth L. Ames, "First Impressions," in *Death in the Dining Room and Other Tales of Victorian Culture* (Philadelphia: Temple University Press, 1992), 7–43, discusses the importance of closed spaces to Victorians. Daniel Joseph Singal, "Towards a Definition of American Modernism," *American Quarterly* 39 (Spring 1987), 7–26, shows that integration, in this case, of spaces, was a hallmark of modernist culture. Brooks, *Frank Lloyd Wright*, 18.

36. James F. O'Gorman, "The Prairie House," in *American Architectural History: A Contemporary Reader*, ed. Keith L. Eggener (London: Routledge, 2004), 267–80; Vincent J. Scully, Jr., *The Shingle Style: Architectural Theory and Design from Richardson to the Origins of Wright* (New Haven: Yale University Press, 1955).

37. "An Education in Home-Building: The Need and the Opportunity of Studying This Art in America," *The Craftsman* 26 (April 1914): 78; "The Craftsman Idea of the Kind of Home Environment That Would Result from More Natural Standards of Life and Work," Stickley, *Craftsman Homes*, 198; Lears, *No Place of Grace*, 42; Winter, "Arts and Crafts as Social Movement," 36–40.

38. Renfro, "We Built Our House," 14; "Some Craftsman Chimneypieces, Any One of Which Might Furnish the Key-note for an Entire Scheme of Decoration," *The Craftsman* 12 (April 1907): 39–50; "The Heart of the Home: The Value of the Open Fireplace in Modern House-building," *The Craftsman* 22 (July 1912): 444; "Distinguishing Features of Craftsman Houses," 728; *Pacific Builder and Engineer* 12 (9 September 1911): 105.

39. Renfro, "We Built Our House," 14; "Distinguishing Features," *The Craftsman* 23 (March 1913): 728; "Beaux Arts," *Bungalow Magazine* 2 (August 1913): 32–41.

40. Lindy Biggs, *The Rational Factory: Architecture, Technology, and Work in America's Age of Mass Production* (Baltimore: Johns Hopkins University Press, 1996), 29–30.

41. "The Modern Home and the Domestic Problem," *The Craftsman* 10 (January 1907): 453.

42. On the concept of efficiency and functionalism in the home, see Gwendolyn Wright, *Moralism and the Model Home: Domestic Architecture and Cultural Conflict in Chicago, 1873–1913* (Chicago: University of Chicago Press, 1980), 150–71; Susan Strasser, *Never Done: A History of American Housework* (New York: Pantheon, 1982): 202–23; and David P. Handlin, "Efficiency and the American Home," *Architectural Association Quarterly* 5 (October/December 1973): 50–54. For an interesting biography that puts the home economics movement into the Progressive Era context and shows this emphasis on efficiency, see

Janice Williams Rutherford, *Selling Mrs. Consumer: Christine Frederick and the Rise of Household Efficiency* (Athens: University of Georgia Press, 2003).

43. "Beaux Arts," *Bungalow Magazine* 2 (August 1913): 23, 28–29; Jud Yoho, "Built-In Conveniences for the Bungalow," *Bungalow Magazine* 4 (January 1915): 42; Nancy C. Dunlea, "Don'ts for for [sic] the Home Builder," *Bungalow Magazine* 6 (April 1917): 213; "Three Low-Cost Bungalows All in a Row," *Bungalow Magazine* 3 (September 1914): 562.

44. For discussions of the importance of fresh air, see "Open-Air Rooms and Sleeping Porches: The Revolt Against the Shut-In Houses of Our Forefathers," *The Craftsman* 24 (July 1913): 434; Ester Matson, "The Romance of the Window: How it Can Be Used Practically to Redeem Modern City Dwellings from Monotonous Ugliness," *The Craftsman* 12 (July 1907): 439; Persis Bingham, "Buttressed Openings Between Rooms in Bungalow Made to Serve Many Useful Purposes," *Bungalow Magazine* 5 (October 1916): 647; Bliss Carman, "The Use of Out of Doors," *The Craftsman* 10 (January 1907): 424; Stickley, "Als Ik Kan," *The Craftsman* 27 (October 1914): 110; Harlan Thomas, "Possibilities of the Bungalow as Permanent Dwelling," *The Craftsman* 9 (March 1909): 859–63.

45. "Beaux Arts," *Bungalow Magazine* 2 (August 1913): 41; Biggs, *Rational Factory,* 96–97.

46. For electrification in bungalows, see "Bungalow Equipped with Many Electric Devices Attracts Much Notice at Big Exposition," *Bungalow Magazine* 4 (August 1915): 505; Herbert C. Moss, "Electric Cooking in the Bungalow," *Bungalow Magazine* 2 (December 1913): 48–55, 41; "September Supplement Bungalow," *Bungalow Magazine* 4 (September 1915): 545. For biographical material on J. S. Ditty, see Roger Downey, "Tales of the Wild Eastside," *Seattle Weekly* (29 May–4 June 1985): 33–39; and "Meet Your Neighbor," *Bellevue-Mercer Islander,* 26 November 1953. For the best overview of the electrification of the home, see Ronald C. Tobey, *Technology as Freedom: The New Deal and the Electrical Modernization of the American Home* (Berkeley: University of California Press, 1996).

47. Charles Hart Nichols, "The Choice of a Heating System for Your Home," *The Craftsman* 28 (April 1915): 132–35; Wright, *Moralism and the Model Home,* 239; "Beaux Arts," *Bungalow Magazine* 2 (July 1913): 23.

48. *Bungalow Magazine* 2 (July 1913): 23; Wright, *Moralism and the Model Home,* 237; *Pacific Builder and Engineer* 10 (24 September 1910): 123.

49. "Modern House Furnishing," *Pacific Builder and Engineer* 5 (14 September 1907): 10; W. L. Claffey, "The Passing of the Carpet," *Bungalow Magazine* 6 (November 1917): 666–67; Wright, *Moralism and the Model Home,* 118–19; Grier, *Culture and Comfort,* 289.

50. "Modern Kitchens More Convenient and Sanitary than Those of Olden Days," *Bungalow Magazine* 4 (April 1915): 236; Lucy M. Salmon, "Our Home Department; Philosophy, Art and Sense for the Kitchen," *The Craftsman* 10 (September 1906): 811.

51. Biggs, *Rational Factory,* 108–14, discusses efficiency in factories, while these Craftsman writers discuss the same in homes; Stickley, *Craftsman Homes,* 143; "Modern Kitchens," *Bungalow Magazine* 4 (April 1915): 236, 238; Charles Alma Byers, "A Suggestion of Kitchen Planning," *Bungalow Magazine* 7 (January 1918): 41; "Beaux Arts," *Bungalow Magazine* 2 (July 1913): 23, 27, features Lewis's bungalow.

52. "Beaux Arts," *Bungalow Magazine* 2 (August 1913): 38–39; "Modern Kitchens," 237–38; Stickley, *Craftsman Homes,* 143.

53. Renfro's bungalow, see "Beaux Arts," *Bungalow Magazine* 2 (August 1913): 36; "Respect for the Kitchen," *The Craftsman* 28 (April 1915): 130; Salmon, "Our Home Department," 812; Stickley, *Craftsman Homes,* 143.

54. "Beaux Arts," *Bungalow Magazine* 2 (July 1913): 23, 29.

55. Maureen Ogle, *All the Modern Conveniences: American Household Plumbing, 1840–1890* (Baltimore: Johns Hopkins University Press, 1996). This is the most recent work on household plumbing.

56. Bylaws of the Western Academy of Beaux Arts (1909), in Renfro, "Beaux Arts Village," 13; "Beaux Arts," *Bungalow Magazine* 2 (July 1913): passim.

57. "Beaux Arts," *Bungalow Magazine* 2 (July 1913): 20. See May N. Stone, "The Plumbing Paradox: American Attitudes Toward Late Nineteenth-Century Domestic Sanitary Arrangements," *Winterthur Portfolio* 14 (Autumn 1979): 283–309; "The New Built-In Sanitary Bathroom," *The Craftsman* 24 (April 1913): 109–11; "'The Order of the Bath': Comfort and Hygiene in the Modern Bathroom," *The Craftsman* 28 (April 1915): 126–28.

58. Edwin J. Ivey, "Kitchen Coolers to Preserve All Kinds of Perishable Foods Necessary for the Modern Bungalow," *Bungalow Magazine* 5 (January 1916): 43; Gwendolyn Wright, *Building the Dream: A Social History of Housing in America* (Cambridge: MIT Press, 1981), 158–76.

59. Stickley, *Craftsman Homes,* 129, 137: Cheryl Robertson, "Male and Female Agendas for Domes-tic Reform," *Winterthur Portfolio* 26 (Summer/Autumn 1991): 134–138, has the best expla-nation of gendered bungalow spaces. Charles Alma Byers, "Planning the Bungalow Den," *Bungalow Magazine* 5 (March 1916): 175; "The Inglenook," *Bungalow Magazine* 6 (May 1917): 293. For discussion of middle-class concern changing from the parlor to the living room, see Grier, *Culture and Comfort,* 287–300; and Margaret Marsh, *Suburban Lives* (New Brunswick, NJ: Rutgers University Press, 1990), 83–89. Robert Blair St. George, "'Set Thine House in Order': The Domestication of the Yeomanry in Seventeenth-Century New England," in *Common Places: Readings in American Vernacular Architecture,* ed. Dell Upton and John Michael Vlach (Athens: University of Georgia Press, 1986), 336–64, influenced me to see the hearth as traditionally gendered as feminine.

60. Eileen Boris, "Crossing Boundaries: The Gendered Meaning of the Arts and Crafts," in *The Ideal Home* (see note 6), 32–45.

61. Boris, in "'Dreams of Brotherhood and Beauty,'" explicates this idea of accommodation to the modern world.

62. For a discussion of the "new" middle class, see Daniel Horowitz, *The Morality of Spending: Attitudes Toward the Consumer Society in America, 1875–1940* (Baltimore: Johns Hopkins University Press, 1985); Olivier Zunz, *Making America Corporate, 1870–1920* (Chicago: University of Chicago Press, 1990); Burton J. Bledstein and Robert D. Johnston, eds., *The Middling Sorts: Explorations in the History of the American Middle Class* (New York: Routledge, 2001).

63. "Order of Home Construction in Beaux Arts Village by Year," list with property maps, in correspondence to author by Mrs. Helen Lewis, 1991, Beaux Arts Village; Tax assessor records for Beaux Arts Village, Puget Sound Regional Archives; Vogel speech, 10, 19–20; U.S. Census of Population, *Fourteenth Census of the United States, 1920,* schedule 1924, Enumeration District 32, Enatai Precinct, King County, Washington, microfilm

in National Archives and Records Service (Washington: NARS, 1993), hereafter cited as 1920 manuscript census. As the 1920 census surveyed the entire Enatai Precinct without delineating Beaux Arts Village boundary lines and/or numbering houses, it is difficult to accurately say who lived within the village. To determine who in the 1920 census was associated with Beaux Arts, I cross-referenced names to a 1919 village list of families assessed for the cost of constructing a house on the wharf.

64. 1920 manuscript census. Many immigrants surrounded Beaux Arts Village, however. In the Newport Precinct, to the south, thirty-four of the forty-one families were Japanese farmers or coal miners. The Hazilwood Precinct contained largely Scandinavian and French Canadian immigrants.

65. For a fuller discussion of Clancey Lewis and his Beaux Arts Village house, see Janet Ore, "Pagoda in Paradise: Clancey Lewis's Craftsman Bungalow and the Contradictions of Modern Life," *Pacific Northwest Quarterly* 92 (Summer 2001): 115–26. See Rutherford, *Selling Mrs. Consumer,* for another biography of a prominent Progressive reformer that embodied a similar duality as did Lewis.

66. "Beaux Arts," *Bungalow Magazine* 2 (July 1913): 21–29. Biographical material on Clancey Lewis in *Pacific Builder and Engineer* 4 (20 October 1906): 4; *Pacific Builder and Engineer* 5 (23 February 1907): 3; *Pacific Builder and Engineer* 20 (31 July 1915): 39, 43, 56; *Pacific Builder and Engineer* 20 (11 September 1915): 98; Polk City directories, 1908–1951; *Seattle Daily Times,* 20 April 1941; *Seattle Times,* 25 July 1943; *Seattle Times,* 19 May 1950 (obituary).

67. "Beaux Arts," *Bungalow Magazine* 2 (July 1913): 26.

68. *Pacific Builder and Engineer* 4 (20 October 1906): 3; *Pacific Builder and Engineer* 5 (23 February 1907): 3; "Beaux Arts," *Bungalow Magazine* 2 (July 1913): 26.

69. *Pacific Builder and Engineer* 20 (11 September 1915): 98; *Pacific Builder and Engineer* 20 (31 July 1915): 39, 43; *Pacific Builder and Engineer* 20 (11 September 1915): 98; Vogel speech. For a fuller discussion of the labor turmoil and struggle over the open shop during the mid-1910s, see Richard C. Berner, *Seattle 1900–1920: From Boomtown, Urban Turbulence, to Restoration* (Seattle: Charles Press, 1991), 160–73.

70. For more discussion of the therapeutic nature of the Arts and Crafts movement, see Lears, *No Place of Grace;* Boris, *Art and Labor;* and Winter, "Arts and Crafts as Social Movement." Quote in Boris, *Art and Labor,* 156.

71. For Beaux Arts Village's early activities, I used Beaux Arts Village archival materials. See unidentified newspaper clippings, "Artist Commends the Beaux Arts Society" and "Watercolor Show Across the Lake," in Beaux Arts Village scrapbook #1; unidentified newspaper advertisements "The Village of Beaux Arts" (circa 1909), "Unique Plan for Home Building" (30 July 1909), "Beaux Arts Village" (30 October 1909), "Site is Bought for B.A. Village" (5 September 1909), "Artists Ready to Establish Colony" (*Seattle Post Intelligencer,* 28 May 1909), and "Beaux Arts Village" (1 June 1913), in Beaux Arts Village scrapbook #1; "Beaux Arts Village, Home of the Beaux Arts Society," 5; "Beaux Arts Village," promotional brochure, circa 1913–14, 8, copy provided by Mrs. Helen Lewis of Beaux Arts Village. The only artistic product of the Beaux Arts Society seems to have been the 1913 publication of a large book of photos, entitled *Homes and Gardens of the Pacific Coast.* The book ended with depictions of Beaux Arts Village and an explanation of the group's plans for an arts and crafts school.

72. "Beaux Arts," *Bungalow Magazine* 2 (July 1913): 14.

73. Unidentified newspaper advertisements "Learn to Live Near to Nature" (circa 1909) and "Beaux Arts Village: A Craftsmen Community of Nature Lovers" (1 June 1913), in Beaux Arts Village scrapbook #1; Renfro, "Beaux Arts Village," 7–8.

74. Margaret Ditty Martin, "Life in Beaux Arts as a Child," "Story Number One: Daddy's Wild Dream," unpublished documents in Beaux Arts Village Archives, n.d., 1–3. Both Dolores Hayden and Daphne Spain show that the isolation of women in single-family homes and especially in distant communities like Beaux Arts Village reinforced patriarchal control and curtailed women's participation in the public world. Ironically, as Arts and Crafts reformers attempted to gradually diminish gender segregation within the home, they reinforced a basic gender separation between the public/productive and private/consumptive realms when they advocated rustic living. See Dolores Hayden, *The Grand Domestic Revolution: A History of Feminist Designs for American Homes, Neighborhoods, and Cities* (Cambridge: MIT Press, 1981), and Daphne Spain, *Gendered Spaces* (Chapel Hill: University of North Carolina Press, 1992).

75. Unidentified newspaper advertisements "Beaux Arts Village" (1 June 1913) and "Learn to Live Near to Nature" (circa 1909), in Beaux Arts Village scrapbook #1; "Beaux Arts Village," promotional brochure, circa 1913–14, 8. The Building Committee still exists and reviews all construction and remodeling in the village.

76. Vogel speech, 5–6; Martin, "Life in Beaux Arts as a Child" and "Auntie Dunn," unpublished documents in Beaux Arts Village Archives, n.d.

77. De Bit quoted in *Seattle Star,* 29 July 1915. See "Learn to Live Near To Nature" clipping, note 75.

78. Davis quoted in *Seattle Star,* 4 August 1915.

79. Vogel speech, unnumbered first page. Ralph De Bit remained close to Beaux Arts Village; the 1920 manuscript census showed him in the same precinct and listed him as a manager for an auto freight company, married to Elizabeth (not Dorothy), and living with four children and a grandmother in the home.

80. Unidentified newspaper advertisement, "Beaux Arts Village," 1 June 1913, in Beaux Arts Village scrapbook #1; "Beaux Arts Village," promotional brochure, circa 1913–14.

81. "Learn to Live Near to Nature," clipping.

82. Renfro, "Beaux Arts Village," 8; Renfro, "We Built Our House," 13.

83. "Beaux Arts Village," 1 June 1913, in Beaux Arts Village scrapbook #1; "Beaux Arts Village," promotional brochure, circa 1913–14, 8; Renfro, "Beaux Arts Village," 14–16; "Articles of Incorporation of the Beaux Arts Society," 1913, #17612, Puget Sound Regional Archives; Vogel speech, 4–7.

84. Quote from Vogel speech, 15; Vogel speech, 3, 4, 15; Vogel noted that the north road of the village was an old skid road and early townspeople found "old saws, files, etc." on lot 2, block 11 of the plat.

3 BUILDING THE SEATTLE BUNGALOW

1. Since I had no information on the precise conditions for the Fred Berg Building Company, I pieced together material from the following sources. See U.S. Department of Labor, *Economics of the Construction Industry* (Washington, D.C.: Government Printing

Office, 1919), 201; William Haber, *Industrial Relations in the Building Industry* (Cambridge, MA: Harvard University Press, 1930), 318; and *Seasonal Operation in the Construction Industries: The Facts and Remedies,* Report and Recommendations of a Committee of the President's Conference on Unemployment (New York: McGraw-Hill Book Co., 1924), 21–46, for the wages, hours, and seasons carpenters worked. Bob Reckman, "Carpentry: The Craft and Trade," *Case Studies on the Labor Process,* ed. Andrew Zimbalist (New York: Monthly Review Press, 1979), 96, discusses the continuing artisanal traditions.

2. On the economics behind dwelling simplification, see Gwendolyn Wright, *Moralism and the Model Home: Domestic Architecture and Cultural Conflict in Chicago, 1873–1913* (Chicago: University of Chicago Press, 1980); Wright, "The Minimal House," chapter 8, 231–53; and Michael J. Doucet and John C. Weaver, *Housing the North American City* (Montreal: McGill-Queen's University Press, 1991), chapter 5, "Material Culture and the North American House: The Era of the Common Man, 1870s-1980s," 201–42.

3. *Seattle Post-Intelligencer,* 21 August 1910, Real Estate sec., 6; Ned Eichler, *The Merchant Builders* (Cambridge, MA: MIT Press, 1982).

4. For an excellent description of the rise of contracting and the influence of capitalism on the building field, see Catherine W. Bishir, "A Spirit of Improvement: Changes in Building Practice, 1830–1860," in *Architects and Builders in North Carolina: A History of the Practice of Building,* ed. Catherine W. Bishir, Charlotte V. Brown, Carl R. Lounsbury, and Ernest H. Wood III (Chapel Hill: University of North Carolina Press, 1990), 146–61; and Charlotte V. Brown, "The Advance in Industrial Enterprise," in *Architects and Builders in North Carolina,* 259–64. Robert A. Christie, *Empire in Wood: A History of the Carpenters' Union* (Ithaca: Cornell University Press, 1956), 19–28; and Mark Erlich, *With Our Hands: The Story of Carpenters in Massachusetts* (Philadelphia: Temple University Press, 1986) chronicle changes influencing unionized carpenters. Howard Davis, *The Culture of Building* (New York: Oxford University Press, 1999), chapter 2, "Four Building Cultures in History," 43–66, has a good overview of artisanal and contractual building. Doucet and Weaver, *Housing the North American City,* 207–15, give examples of how building contractors operated in Canada. Donna J. Rilling, *Making Houses, Crafting Capitalism: Builders in Philadelphia, 1790–1850* (Philadelphia: University of Pennsylvania Press, 2001), is a good case study of how entrepreneurial craftsman transformed building practices in the early nineteenth century.

5. On Seattle's building component industry, see Richard C. Berner, *Seattle 1900–1920: From Boomtown, Urban Turbulence, to Restoration* (Seattle: Charles Press, 1991), 29; and Calvin F. Schmid, *Social Trends in Seattle* (Seattle: University of Washington Press, 1944), 23–25. On the industrialization of components, see Fred W. Peterson, *Homes in the Heartland: Balloon Frame Farmhouses of the Upper Midwest, 1850–1920* (Lawrence: University Press of Kansas, 1992), 5–24; Doucet and Weaver, *Housing the North American City,* 206–9; Herbert Gottfried and Jan Jennings, *American Vernacular Design, 1870–1940* (New York: Van Nostrand Reinhold Co., 1985), viii; Carl R. Lounsbury, "The Wild Melody of Steam: The Mechanization of the Manufacture of Building Materials, 1850–1900," *Architects and Builders in North Carolina,* 193–239.

6. "Operations of Urban Home Builders," *Monthly Labor Review* 52 (May 1941): 1283–85. The Bureau of Labor statistics stated that two-thirds of builders erected only one house

per year, but these figures included a significant number of owner-builders and build-ing craftsmen who built their own homes. These sources mention small builders in the house construction business: Erlich, *With Our Hands,* 16–20; Christie, *Empire in Wood,* 13–18; Davis, *Culture of Building,* 77–78.

7. Sherman J. Maisel, *Housebuilding in Transition* (Berkeley: University of California Press, 1953), 54–55, 134; Bishir, "A Proper Good Nice and Workmanlike Manner," in *Architects and Builders in North Carolina,* 71.

8. Maisel, *Housebuilding in Transition,* 46; John and Marian Culbertson Wallace interview, 5 March 1991, Seattle, Washington; building permit #133684, for 4203 Woodlawn Avenue, June 24, 1914, King County Office of Construction and Land Use, Seattle, Washington.

9. "The Calder Report on the Building Situation," *Monthly Labor Review* 12 (June 1921): 1212–18, "Irregular Employment in the Building Industry," *Monthly Labor Review* 13 (July 1921): 165–68, "Causes of Seasonal Fluctuations in the Construction Industry," *Monthly Labor Review* 33 (September 1931): 492–519. By the 1920s, the federal government had recognized the inefficiencies of seasonal work and actively sought to change building practices. A good source for these efforts is *Seasonal Operation in the Construction Industries.*

10. Maisel, *Housebuilding in Transition,* 134.

11. Wright, *Moralism and the Model Home,* chapter 8, "The Minimal House," 231–53; Doucet and Weaver, *Housing the North American City,* chapter 5, "Material Culture and the North American House: The Era of the Common Man, 1870s–1980s," 201–42.

12. "The Calder Report on the Building Situation," *Monthly Labor Review* 12 (June 1921): 1212–18, "Irregular Employment in the Building Industry," *Monthly Labor Review* 13 (July 1921): 165–68, "Causes of Seasonal Fluctuations in the Construction Industry," *Monthly Labor Review* 33 (September 1931): 492–519.

13. Davis, *Culture of Building,* 66; Maisel, *Housebuilding in Transition,* 50, 58–60. Some con-tractors believed that subcontracting led to shoddy work due to lack of oversight. See Charles W. Carkeek, "Subcontracting," *Pacific Builder and Engineer* 22 (28 July 1916): 13; and *Pacific Builder and Engineer* 37 (17 January 1931): 22.

14. Doucet and Weaver, *Housing the North American City,* 231.

15. Quote from John M. Gries and James Ford, eds., *House Design, Construction and Equipment* (Washington, D.C.: The President's Conference on Home Building and Home Own-ership, 1932), 248, 251; U.S. Department of Commerce, Bureau of the Census, *United States Census of Housing: 1940,* vol. 2, *General Characteristics,* part 5, *Washington* (Washington, D.C.: Government Printing Office, 1943), 737, hereafter cited as 1940 Housing Census; *Bungalow Magazine* 4 (October 1915): 671–83.

16. George E. Walsh, "Economy in Bungalow Construction," *Bungalow Magazine* 6 (Novem-ber 1917): 663–64; "General Residential Costs" and "Actual Experience Costs Revised to Date," April 1935, Hainsworth Construction Company Papers, Manuscripts and University Archives Division, University of Washington Libraries, Seattle, Washington, hereafter cited as Hainsworth Papers; Gries and Ford, *House Design,* 260. In 1917, outlets cost from $1.50 to $2 each, so by limiting the numbers, builders kept down overall elec-trical costs. By the early 1930s, putting basic knob-and-tube wiring into a modest $3,500 house cost 2.3 percent of total construction, or $3.75 per outlet.

17. Quotes from "Seattle Electrical Week," *Pacific Builder and Engineer* 28 (29 September 1922): 14; Gries and Ford, *House Design,* 258; "The Electric Show," *Pacific Builder and Engineer* 29 (27 July 1923): 6; "The 1923 House Electric," *Pacific Builder and Engineer* 29 (24 August 1923): 2–3; "Crowds Flock to Seattle's Electric Appliance Show," *Pacific Builder and Engineer* 29 (31 August 1923): 6. For a further discussion of electrical modernization in general, see Ronald C. Tobey, *Technology as Freedom: The New Deal and the Electrical Modernization of the American Home* (Berkeley: University of California Press, 1996). The 1922 electrical houses were located at North Broadway and Allison Street and 3134 Lakewood Avenue in the Mount Baker Park neighborhood. The 1923 electric house, now demolished, was at the corner of Bothell Way and Twelfth Avenue Northeast.

18. Gries and Ford, *House Design,* 264–65: Hainsworth Papers.

19. Frederick West to B. O. Deitz, 6 July 1901 and 12 August 1901, box 2 book 7, West and Wheeler Associates records, 1888–1974, Manuscripts and University Archives Division, University of Washington Libraries, Seattle, Washington; Maureen Ogle, *All the Modern Conveniences: American Household Plumbing, 1840–1890* (Baltimore: Johns Hopkins University Press, 1996). See appendix, table 4, "Plumbing Features in 1937."

20. Seattle's 1905 ordinance required permits and inspections for plumbing installation and mandated that workplaces have one "lavatory" for every sixteen people, that hotels have one for each fifteen rooms, that apartments have one for each floor of ten persons, and that dwellings or residences have "at least one lavatory and one sink." "Seattle's Plumbing Ordinance," *Pacific Financial, Real Estate, Building Record* (becomes *Pacific Builder and Engineer*) 3 (26 August 1905): 3; 1940 Housing Census, 736; Ogle, *All the Modern Conveniences,* discusses plumbing innovations preceding bungalows.

21. Gries and Ford, *House Design,* 216–24.

22. Hugh Miracle interview, 28 September 1991, Seattle, Washington; Kathi and Ray Abendroth interview, 26 September 1991, Seattle, Washington; Gries and Ford, *House Design,* 216–24; 1940 Housing Census, 736; Ellen Lupton and J. Abbott Miller, *The Bathroom, The Kitchen, and the Aesthetics of Waste: A Process of Elimination* (Cambridge, MA: MIT List Visual Arts Center, 1992), is a good general overview of household plumbing that includes great illustrations.

23. Joseph G. Hildebrand, "A Cause for Divorce," *Pacific Builder and Engineer* 37 (17 January 1931): 6.

24. Ruth Hughbanks interview, 9 January 1991, Seattle, Washington; 1937 tax assessor form for 6214 Thirty-seventh Northwest, located in Puget Sound Regional Archives, Bellevue, Washington; Ruth Lange Fall interview, 23 September 1991, Seattle, Washington.

25. Walsh, "Economy in Bungalow Construction," 664; Gries and Ford, *House Design,* 235; Hainsworth Papers. Simple fixtures in a small 1915 bungalow cost approximately 50 dollars per item, or 75 dollars each in a larger house. In 1931 and 1932, 70 percent of Seattle plumbing costs went to material, 30 percent to labor. See "Employment in the Construction of an Apartment House," *Monthly Labor Review* 35 (October 1932): 782–87.

26. A. G. King, "Modern Methods of Heating and Ventilation," *Architects' and Builders' Magazine* 8 (April 1907): 325–28; Gries and Ford, *House Design,* 118–19; Hugh Miracle interview; Stan Stapp interview, 13 September 1991, Seattle, Washington; *North Seattle Press,* 29 July–11 August 1987. The simplest furnace was "pipeless," meaning that the

hot air passively passed through registers to upstairs rooms. In Seattle's north end, pipe-less furnaces were never widely used, possibly because they provided an uneven heat and required more coal to heat the air sufficiently to rise. A few home owners in the north end installed hot-water heating systems, in which gravity or a pump forced hot water from a coal or wood-fired boiler through a network of radiators. Although this system gave a comfortable, uniform heat, it was much more expensive to construct than the hot-air furnace. In 1915, hot water heat cost about 65 percent more to install than a hot-air furnace. Once in place, hot water systems were more efficient and 50 percent less expensive to operate. For the moderate-income family, the high initial cost of hot-water heating during house construction might have helped them decide on hot-air furnaces instead. Gries and Ford, *House Design,* 119; Charles Hart Nichols, "The Choice of a Heating System for your Home," *The Craftsman* 28 (April 1915): 132–34. See appendix, table 5, "Heating Systems in 1937."

27. "Three Bungalows Eloquent of Aesthetic Tendency in Fashioning the Modern Economic Home," *Bungalow Magazine* 4 (June 1915): 353; Hainsworth Papers; "Employment in the Construction of an Apartment House," *Monthly Labor Review* 35 (October 1932): 782–87; Gries and Ford, *House Design,* 121. The furnace's expense placed it beyond the range of homes worth $2,500 or less in 1932, so reformers had little choice but to continue to recommend stoves for this class of homes.

28. Advertisement for laundry trays, *Pacific Financial, Real Estate, Building Record* (becomes *Pacific Builder and Engineer*) 3 (5 August 1905): 4; Gries and Ford, *House Design,* 226–27. See appendix, table 3, "Houses without Basements."

29. "Three Bungalows Eloquent," *Bungalow Magazine* 4 (June 1915): 353; "Employment in the Construction of an Apartment House," *Monthly Labor Review* 35 (October 1932): 782–87. John Wallace remembered excavation of his basement in 1941 with a bulldozer that cost only 25 dollars. John and Marian Culbertson Wallace interviews, 5 March 1991, and 26 September 1991.

30. U.S. Department of Labor, *Economics of the Construction Industry* (Washington, D.C.: Government Printing Office, 1919), 15, 41, 44; Le Roy K. Sherman, "Comparative Costs of Building, 1913 and 1918," *Monthly Labor Review* 10 (February 1920): 553–55; *Pacific Builder and Engineer* 26 (29 October 1920): 14.

31. H. L. Cunliffe, "The Building Situation," *Pacific Builder and Engineer* 27 (27 May 1921): 6; U.S. Department of Labor, *Economics of the Construction Industry,* 183, 185, 201; Sherman, "Comparative Costs," *Monthly Labor Review* 10 (February 1920): 553–54. The cost of a kitchen sink east of the Mississippi River, for instance, was $13.98 in 1913, compared to a high of $27.56 in 1918, although the price fell to $25.44 later that year.

32. Walsh, "Economy in Bungalow Construction," *Bungalow Magazine* 6 (November 1917): 662.

33. The Bungalow Company, "Bungalows" plan book, circa 1912, n.p., Seattle Public Library, Seattle, Washington, hereafter cited as Bungalow Company plan book.

34. "FHA Chief Gives Seven Principles for Small Homes," *Pacific Builder and Engineer* 43 (15 May 1937): 3. See Greg Hise, *Magnetic Los Angeles: Planning the Twentieth-Century Metropolis* (Baltimore: Johns Hopkins University Press, 1997), for a good discussion of the evolution of minimalistic, low-cost housing between 1900 and 1950.

35. On the effect of the industrialization of building components, see Davis, *Culture of Building,* 79–81; Reckman, "Carpentry," 95–98; and Sherman, "Comparative Cost," *Monthly Labor Review* 10 (February 1920): 551–52.

36. "Practical Home Building," *Pacific Builder and Engineer* 17 (21 February 1914): 104; Marc A. Weiss, *The Rise of the Community Builders: The American Real Estate Industry and Urban Land Planning* (New York: Columbia University Press, 1987). *Seattle Post-Intelligencer,* 21 August 1910, Real Estate sec., 6, discusses Brice's activities in Wallingford.

37. "The Hoover Dwelling House Code," *Pacific Builder and Engineer* 29 (23 February 1923): 9.

38. Rexmond C. Cochrane, *Measures for Progress: A History of the National Bureau of Standards* (Washington, D.C.: U.S. Department of Commerce, National Bureau of Standards, 1966), 250–51, 253–62; "The Hoover Dwelling House Code," *Pacific Builder and Engineer* 29 (23 February 1923): 9; "Minimum Requirements for Small Dwelling Construction," *Pacific Builder and Engineer* 29 (30 March 1923): 13. Through a "crusade for standardization," Hoover believed contractors could erect small, affordable houses. In 1921, the new Division of Building Housing issued a report that claimed that $600 in construction and 20 percent of plumbing costs in the average small home could be saved through systematizing local codes and creating national standardized regulations. "Value of Standardization," *Pacific Builder and Engineer* 27 (29 July 1921): 5. Simultaneously, Hoover helped launch a campaign, Better Homes in America, to educate the public about the benefits of home ownership and household efficiency. See Hise, *Magnetic Los Angeles,* 38–41, and Janet Hutchison, "The Cure for Domestic Neglect: Better Homes in America, 1922–1935," in *Perspectives in Vernacular Architecture,* vol. 2, ed. Camille Wells (Columbia: University of Missouri Press, 1986), 168–78.

39. For examples of building component standardization, see "Standardizing Materials," *Pacific Builder and Engineer* 18 (26 December 1914): 35; "Simplification of Building Materials," *Pacific Builder and Engineer* 28 (31 March 1922): 12; "Brick Standardization," *Pacific Builder and Engineer* 29 (17 August 1923): 6; "Mills to Standardize Shingles," *Pacific Builder and Engineer* 30 (28 June 1924): 5–6; "Simplification Effective," *Pacific Builder and Engineer* 30 (6 September 1924): 25; "Hot Water Tanks Standardized," *Pacific Builder and Engineer* 30 (29 November 1924): 6. U.S. Department of Commerce, "Recommended Minimum Requirements for Small Dwelling Construction" (Washington, D.C.: Government Printing Office, 1923); Haber, *Industrial Relations,* 84–85; Hise, *Magnetic Los Angeles,* 56–85, and Cochrane, *Measures for Progress,* 256–57, provide an overview of standardization.

40. Cochrane, *Measures for Progress,* 254.

41. "Perfect Mechanical Brick Layer," *Pacific Builder and Engineer* 30 (16 February 1924): 5, "Plastering Machine Perfected," *Pacific Builder and Engineer* 30 (19 April 1924): 5; "Building Trades Lose Much Time," *Pacific Builder and Engineer* 30 (28 June 1924): 6; Haber, *Industrial Relations,* 83–85, 96–125; *Seasonal Operation in the Construction Industries,* 2, 21, 23, 76.

42. *Seasonal Operation in the Construction Industries,* 2.

43. These works discuss the lingering characteristics of artisanal labor: Maisel, *Housebuilding in Transition,* 50; Erlich, *With Our Hands,* 146; Reckman, "Carpentry," 96; Doucet and Weaver, *Building the North American City,* 219–20, 225, 240.

44. *Seattle Post-Intelligencer,* 21 August 1910, Real Estate Sec., 6; Polk City directories, 1900–1923; articles of incorporation papers for the Andrew Peterson Construction Company,

1908, Puget Sound Regional Archives. Berner mentions that in 1915 Brice constructed a "tent-colony" company town for Italian, Russian, Greek, and Austrian workers in which conditions were so "incredibly bad" that local Issaquah residents provided them with food. Officials arrested Brice for forcing his crews to work ten to sixteen hours a day, violating the eight-hour law on public projects. Clearly, Brice thought like an industrial entrepreneur, not a typical contractor. See Berner, *Seattle, 1900–1920*, 171–72. Most of Seattle's businesses/builders who operated from the 1910s into the 1940s were small compared to later building companies. They conform to what Maisel identified as medium-sized firms. He describes such enterprises as being in transition from small, mostly contractual companies into large, merchant builders. See Maisel, *Housebuilding in Transition*, 67–94.

45. *Seattle Post-Intelligencer,* 21 August 1910, Real Estate sec., 6.

46. Brice's troubles in 1915 with the law mentioned in note 44 also may have interfered with construction at 4203 Woodlawn. Maisel, *Housebuilding in Transition,* 83–84; Bungalow Company plan book, n.p.; building permits for 4203, 4207, 4211, 4215, and 4219 Woodlawn, King County Office of Construction and Land Use, Seattle, Washington; deed for 4203 Woodlawn, Henry and Kate Brice to the Scandinavian-American Bank, 13 September 1917, vol. 987, book D, p 620, King County Clerk and Recorder's Office, Seattle, Washington.

47. Articles of incorporation for the Birch Loan Company, 1908, #11482, and certificate of amended articles of incorporation of Birch Loan Company by which corporate name is changed to "The Bungalow Co., Inc.," 1909, #12659, Puget Sound Regional Archives; Polk City directories, 1909–1915; Clarence Bagley, *History of Seattle from the Earliest Settlement to the Present Time* (Chicago: S. J. Clarke Publishing Co., 1916), vol. 3, 246–47; Bungalow Company plan book, n.p.

48. Bungalow Company plan book, n.p.; see "Bungalow Showing Japanese Influence is Solution of Problem Met in Difficult Site," *Bungalow Magazine* 5 (April 1916): 209, for an example of Coles's work.

49. Bungalow Company plan book, n.p.; "Operations of Urban Home Builders," *Monthly Labor Review* 52 (May 1941): 1283–85; *Seattle Post Intelligencer,* 24 April 1910, State, Northwest and Alaska sec., 3.

50. Maisel, *Housebuilding in Transition,* 83–84, 188–90; Bungalow Company plan book, n.p.

51. Bungalow Company plan book, n.p.

52. Ilan D. Wallis, *Wheel Estate: The Rise and Decline of Mobile Homes* (New York: Oxford University Press, 1991).

53. David J. Vergobbi, *Seattle Master Builders Association* (Seattle: Seattle Master Builders Association, circa 1988), 43–44.

54. Ibid., 50; Maisel, *Housebuilding in Transition,* 107–12; Weiss, *Rise of the Community Builders.*

55. Articles of incorporation of New Housing, Inc., 1941, #57336 and #57337, Puget Sound Regional Archives. My sample area in Ballard included ten of the dwellings that Stringfellow built. Descriptions of these structures came from an architectural database of that sample area, which derived from the 1937 tax assessor forms.

56. Davis, *Culture of Building;* Maisel, *Housebuilding in Transition,* 44–45, 48, 69.

4 SELLING THE SEATTLE BUNGALOW

1. Polk City directory, 1918; Stan Stapp interview, 13 September 1991, Seattle, Washington.

2. The following works argue that professionals, reformers, developers, architects, and other members of the middle class were responsible for the twentieth-century urban environment: Gwendolyn Wright, *Moralism and The Model Home: Domestic Architecture and Cultural Conflict in Chicago, 1873–1913* (Chicago: University of Chicago Press, 1980); Marc A. Weiss, *The Rise of the Community Builders: The American Real Estate Industry and Urban Land Planning* (New York: Columbia University Press, 1987); Mary Corbin Sies, "Toward a Performance Theory of the Suburban Ideal, 1877–1917," in *Perspectives in Vernacular Architecture,* vol. 4, ed. Thomas Carter and Bernard L. Herman (Columbia: University of Missouri Press, 1991): 197–207. For an excellent recap and historiography of the debate over who shaped twentieth-century suburbs, see Mary Corbin Sies, "North American Suburbs, 1880–1950, *Journal of Urban History* 27 (March 2001): 313–46, and Andrew Wiese, "Stubborn Diversity: A Commentary on Middle-Class Influence in Working-Class Suburbs, 1900–1940," *Journal of Urban History* 27 (March 2001): 347–54.

3. Janet Ore, "Jud Yoho, 'The Bungalow Craftsman,' and the Development of Seattle Suburbs," in *Shaping Communities: Perspectives in Vernacular Architecture,* vol. 6, ed. Carter Hudgins and Elizabeth Cromley (Knoxville: University of Tennessee Press, 1997), 231–43. Particularly influential in my understanding of bungalows as artifacts of a burgeoning consumerism is the growing literature on the history of consumption. See T. J. Jackson Lears, *No Place of Grace: Antimodernism and The Transformation of American Culture, 1880–1920* (New York: Pantheon, 1981); William Leach, *Land of Desire: Merchants, Power, and the Rise of a New American Culture* (New York: Vintage Books, 1993); Daniel Horowitz, *The Morality of Spending: Attitudes Toward the Consumer Society in America, 1875–1940* (Baltimore: Johns Hopkins University Press, 1985); and Richard Bushman, *The Refinement of America: Persons, Houses, Cities* (New York: Vintage Books, 1992). Jim Cullen, *The Art of Democracy: A Concise History of Popular Culture in the United States* (New York: Monthly Review Press, 1996), helped me see houses as part of twentieth-century popular culture influenced from the bottom up.

4. Weiss, *Rise of Community Builders,* 20–21; Michael J. Doucet and John C. Weaver, *Housing the North American City* (Montreal: McGill-Queen's University Press, 1991), 20–126.

5. Roger Sale, *Seattle Past to Present* (Seattle: University of Washington Press, 1976), 51; Doucet and Weaver, *Housing the North American City,* 20–126.

6. Biographical material file, Edward C. Kilbourne Papers, Manuscripts and University Archives Division, University of Washington Libraries, Seattle, Washington (hereafter cited as Manuscripts Division, U.W. Libraries).

7. *Seattle Post-Intelligencer,* 20 December 1902; Doucet and Weaver, *Housing the North American City,* 20–126.

8. Weiss, *Rise of Community Builders,* 28. To understand the professionalization of the real estate field, see Jeffrey M. Hornstein, "The Rise of the Realtor: Professionalism, Gender, and Middle-Class Identity, 1908–1950," in *The Middling Sorts: Explorations in the History of the American Middle Class,* ed. Burton J. Bledstein and Robert D. Johnston (New York: Routledge, 2001), 217–33.

9. *Pacific Building, Real Estate and Financial Record* (becomes *Pacific Builder and Engineer*) 2 (13 August 1904): 11.

10. Charles Remsberg to Henry F. Lloyd, 8 July 1913, folder 5, acc. 4024, Charles E. Remsberg Papers, Manuscripts and University Archives Division, University of Washington Libraries, Seattle, Washington.

11. *Seattle Post-Intelligencer,* 4 February 1902 and 19 November 1905; articles of incorporation for the Home Building Company, 1908, #11969, Puget Sound Regional Archives, Bellevue, Washington; *Volume of Memoirs: A Genealogy of Representative Citizens of the City of Seattle and County of King* (New York: Lewis Publishing Company, 1903), 680–82, hereafter cited as *Volume of Memoirs; Fremont Colleague,* 2 January 1904, 4.

12. *Fremont Colleague,* 16 December 1905, 28 March 1908, and 2 January 1909.

13. For material on DeLong, see *Volume of Memoirs,* 348–51; articles of incorporation for the Ballard Home Building Company, 1902, #5017, Puget Sound Regional Archives; Polk City directories, 1901–1931; W. W. DeLong and Mrs. W. W. DeLong, *Seattle Home Builder and Home Keeper* (Seattle: Commercial Publishing Co., 1915), 10; Dennis A. Andersen and Katheryn H. Krafft, "Plan and Pattern Books: Shaping Early Seattle Architecture," *Pacific Northwest Quarterly* 85 (October 1994): 156–58. Andersen and Krafft's work also appears in Jeffrey Karl Ochsner, ed., *Shaping Seattle Architecture: A Historical Guide to the Architects* (Seattle: University of Washington Press, 1994), 64–71, 354. I did find W. W. DeLong noted in an undated membership book in the carpenters and joiners papers. See undated membership book, Carpenters and Joiners of America, Local 131, #1228, University of Washington Manuscripts, Seattle, Washington. World War I or the 1919 architect's licensing law seems to have ended DeLong's architectural career. In the 1920s, Wilson's Modern Business College employed him as an accountant and teacher. My gratitude to Kate Krafft for acquainting me with DeLong's work.

14. DeLong and DeLong, *Seattle Home Builder and Home Keeper,* 10.

15. *Volume of Memoirs,* 348–51.

16. Quote in Jud Yoho, "Craftsman Bungalow Co.," plan book (Seattle: Edition De Luxe, 1913), 3. *Pacific Builder and Engineer,* 11 (5 August 1911): 41. See Ore, "Jud Yoho" for further details of Yoho's career. Andersen and Krafft, "Plan and Pattern Books," 156. For the most comprehensive study of Yoho and his architecture, see Erin M. Doherty, "Jud Yoho and The Craftsman Bungalow Company: Assessing the Value of the Common House," (master's thesis, University of Washington, 1997).

17. The primary source material for Yoho came from *Seattle Post-Intelligencer,* 10 May 1908, sec. 2, and 17 May 1908, sec. 2; articles of incorporation for the Craftsman Bungalow Company, 1911, #15477 and #15525, Puget Sound Regional Archives; U.S. Census of Population, *Twelfth Census of the United States, 1900,* schedule 1745, King County, Washington, E.N. #118, sheet 30, line 8, microfilm in U.S. National Archives and Records Service (Washington: NARS, 1973; manuscript); U.S. Census of Population, *Thirteenth Census of the United States, 1910,* schedule 1658, King County, Washington, E.D. #68, 16 (Washington: NARS, 1983; manuscript); and Polk Seattle City directories, 1894–1942. Rob Anglin, "Briefing Paper on Bungalows in Seattle," report submitted to the Seattle Landmarks Preservation Board, 1982. Ore, "Jud Yoho," 232–33, and Doherty, "Jud Yoho," 36–40, delve further into Yoho's history. See Lisa Mighetto and Marcia Montgomery, *Hard Drive to the Klondike: Promoting Seattle During the Gold Rush* (Seattle: University of Washington Press, 2002), 56; and Leslie Blanchard, *The Street Railway Era in Seattle: A*

Chronicle of Six Decades (Forty Fort, PN; Harold E. Cox, 1968), 65, for material on Seattle's growth in this period.

18. James L. Garvin, "Mail-Order House Plans and American Victorian Architecture," *Winterthur Portfolio* 16 (Winter 1981): 309–34; Thomas Harvey, "Mail-Order Architecture in the Twenties," *Landscape* 25 (1981): 1–9. Kingston Heath makes the interesting point that some local architects leased their plans for use. See Kingston W. Heath, *The Patina of Place: The Cultural Weathering of a New England Industrial Landscape* (Knoxville: University of Tennessee Press, 2001), 125.

19. Hewitt-Lea-Funck Company usually placed a full-page advertisement for their "prize plan book" in the back of *Bungalow Magazine*. See *Bungalow Magazine* 3 (June 1914): back page.

20. "Plan Factories," *Pacific Builder and Engineer* 5 (14 September 1907): 11. See advertisement for plan books in *Pacific Financial, Real Estate, Building Record* 4 (24 February 1906): 14; *Seattle Post-Intelligencer,* 17 March 1907, Magazine sec.; *Seattle Post-Intelligencer,* 11 February 1912; *Seattle Post-Intelligencer,* 10 March 1912, opinion sec.; and *Bungalow Magazine* 2 (June 1913): 70, 72, 74, 76, 78.

21. Quote in Jud Yoho, "Craftsman Bungalow," n.p. *Pacific Builder and Engineer* 11 (9 December 1911): 424; Ore, "Jud Yoho," 233; Doherty, "Jud Yoho," 40–49.

22. Building permit #119746 for 4207 Corliss Avenue North, located in the microfilm library, Department of Building and Construction, Seattle, Washington; Ore, "Jud Yoho," 233–34; Doherty, "Jud Yoho," 41. For an example of Yoho's title of "architect," see "January Supplement Bungalow," *Bungalow Magazine* 3 (January 1914): 3. In most instances, Yoho was careful about using "architect" in the journal, noting instead "the Craftsman Bungalow Company, architects." I suspect that Yoho and the Craftsman Bungalow Company got their "ideas," if not outright designs, directly from southern California architecture. In 1912, the *Seattle Post-Intelligencer* reported that Virgil Hall, who was "connected with the Craftsman Bungalow Company" and associate of Edward L. Merritt, had "returned from a five weeks sojourn throughout California . . . travel[ing] a greater part of the distance from Southern Oregon throughout California by means of a motor car." My guess is that this was more than just a pleasure trip. See *Seattle Post-Intelligencer,* 24 March 1912, Real Estate Section. For material on the Heineman brothers, see Robert Winter, "Arthur S. and Alfred Heineman," in *Toward a Simpler Way of Life: The Arts and Crafts Architects of California* (Berkeley: University of California Press, 1997), 137–48.

23. For an example of architect's commission, see *Seattle Post-Intelligencer,* 28 August 1910, Real Estate and Auto sec. On commissions generally, see Clifford Clark, *The American Family Home, 1800–1960* (Chapel Hill: University of North Carolina Press, 1986), 87.

24. "Plan Factories," *Pacific Builder and Engineer* 5 (14 September 1907): 11.

25. *Western Life,* December 1907, clipping in Architects' reference files on Victor W. Voorhees, Special Collections, University of Washington Libraries, Seattle, Washington, hereafter cited as Special Collections, U.W. Libraries; *Bungalow Magazine* 3 (April 1914): back page.

26. *Seattle Post-Intelligencer,* 25 April 1909, Magazine sec. 2.

27. DeLong and DeLong, *Seattle Home Builder,* 11.

28. *Bungalow Magazine* 2 (May 1913): title page; Anglin, "Briefing Paper," 6; Doucet and Weaver, *Housing the North American City,* 234; Doherty, "Jud Yoho," 49–52. For example, *Bungalow Magazine* 7 (March 1918): 21, included an article by Charles Alma Byers entitled "Three Charming Little Colonial Bungalows," which *The Craftsman* had published in 28 (July 1915): 409–14, under the title "The 'Colonial Bungalow': A New and Charming Variation in Home Architecture." Doherty has clarified that Yoho's *Bungalow Magazine* was not a successor of or related to the earlier *Bungalow Magazine* out of Los Angeles. See Doherty, "Jud Yoho," 49–50.

29. *Bungalow Magazine* 4 (January 1915): title page; "Wicker Furniture, Ideal for Bungalows," *Bungalow Magazine* 4 (May 1915): 295; Polk City directories, 1898–1928; Anglin, "Briefing Paper"; Clarence Bagley, *History of Seattle From the Earliest Settlement to the Present Time,* vol. 3 (Chicago: S. J. Clarke Publishing Co., 1916), 843–44; Doherty, "Jud Yoho," 52, 56, 59, 61.

30. "Six Colonial Bungalows of Unusual Merit," *Bungalow Magazine* 7 (January 1918): 20. See *Bungalow Magazine* 4 (15 January 1915) for an example of the magazine's plan service.

31. Constitution and bylaws, folder 2 box 1, and Jones to Morrison, June 16, 1939, folder 11, both records in American Institute of Architects Collection, Manuscripts Division, University of Washington Libraries.

32. An English immigrant, Edwin Ivey's father, Edwin Ivey, Sr., was a builder and developer. For information on Ellsworth Storey, see Jeffrey Karl Ochsner, ed., *Shaping Seattle Architecture: A Historical Guide to the Architects* (Seattle: University of Washington Press, 1994), 102–7; *Seattle Times,* 1 June 1960 (obituary); "A Bungalow Worthwhile," *Bungalow Magazine* 3 (March 1914): 161; "March Supplement Bungalow," *Bungalow Magazine* 5 (March 1916): 137; "Bungalow Type Home in Near Colonial Style Built on Sloping Ground at a Cost of $4500," *Bungalow Magazine* 5 (June 1916): 347. For W. R. B. Willcox's contributions, see "A Fine Type of Four-Room House," *Bungalow Magazine* 6 (October 1917): 577, and Ochsner, *Shaping Seattle Architecture,* 138–43. On Edwin Ivey, see Ochsner, *Shaping Seattle Architecture,* 345–46; *Seattle Daily Times,* 26 February 1940 (Edwin Ivey Jr.'s obituary); and *Seattle Daily Times,* 20 March 1941. Ivey's architecture appears in *Bungalow Magazine* 4 (July 1915): 432; "Colonial Bungalow Designed for Hilly Site and to Secure Advantage of Exquisite Scenery," *Bungalow Magazine* 4 (September 1915): 557–62; Edwin J. Ivey, "Kitchen Coolers to Preserve All Kinds of Perishable Foods Necessary for the Modern Bungalow," *Bungalow Magazine* 5 (January 1916): 43; "Colonial Bungalow Type House Built to Fit Romantic Scenery by Man Who Longed For Home," *Bungalow Magazine* 5 (March 1916): 158–74; "Architect Solves Difficult Problems In Successful Design of $4200 Colonial Bungalow," *Bungalow Magazine* 5 (October 1916): 619; "Six Colonial Bungalows of Unusual Merit," *Bungalow Magazine* 7 (January 1918): 19–38. Another architect who sometimes published in *Bungalow Magazine* was Charles Haynes. See "September Supplement Bungalow," *Bungalow Magazine* 3 (September 1914): 539; "January Supplement Bungalow," *Bungalow Magazine* 6 (January 1917): 3.

33. Christopher P. Wilson, "The Rhetoric of Consumption: Mass-Market Magazines and the Demise of the Gentle Reader, 1880–1930," in *The Culture of Consumption: Critical Essays in American History, 1880–1980,* ed. Richard Wightman Fox and T. J. Jackson Lears (New York: Pantheon Books, 1983), 42–43.

34. Quote from Take Down Manufacturing Company, "Craftsman Master Built Homes," (Seattle: Take Down Mfg. Co., 1915), 1; Articles of incorporation of the Take Down Manufacturing Company, 1915, #18947 and #21432, Puget Sound Regional Archives; Doherty, "Jud Yoho," 52–55.

35. T. J. Jackson Lears explains this cooptation further in "From Salvation to Self-Realization: Advertising and the Therapeutic Roots of the Consumer Culture, 1880–1930," in *The Culture of Consumption: Critical Essays in American History, 1880–1980,* ed. Richard Wightman Fox and T. J. Jackson Lears (New York: Pantheon, 1983), 21.

36. Lendol Calder, *Financing the American Dream: A Cultural History of Consumer Credit* (Princeton: Princeton University Press, 1999), 111.

37. Quote from Calder, *Financing the American Dream,* 157, 180. On early financing in building associations, see W. A. Linn, "Co-operative Home-Winning: Some Practical Results of Building Associations," *Scribner's Magazine* 7 (May 1890): 571; and W. A. Linn, "Building and Loan Associations," *Scribner's Magazine* 5 (June 1889): 711; For the best explanation of savings and loans mortgages, see Calder, *Financing the American Dream,* 66. Clark, *American Family Home,* 95–97, and Doucet and Weaver, *Housing the North American City,* 243–304, also have good discussions of home financing.

38. Frederick West to Mrs. K. E. Schaffhausen, 10 January 1901, letterpress book 6, 703, box 1, West and Wheeler Associates records, Manuscripts Division, U.W. Libraries.

39. Weiss, *Rise of Community Builders,* 32; *Fremont Colleague,* 18 June 1910; Frederick West to T. J. West, 26 June 1900, letterpress book 6, box 1, West and Wheeler Associates records, Manuscripts Division, U.W. Libraries; G. A. Wright to James Wheeler, 18 November 1927, "Bellingham" file, box 146, West and Wheeler Associates records, Manuscripts Division, U.W. Libraries.

40. Calder, *Financing the American Dream,* has the best history of installment selling, 156–208. John M. Gries and Thomas M. Curran, "Present Home Financing Methods," Department of Commerce (Washington, D.C.: Government Printing Office, 1928), 7–9; and John M. Gries and James S. Taylor, "How to Own Your Home: A Handbook for Prospective Home Owners," Department of Commerce (Washington, D.C.: 1923), 4–9, show the expanding use of land contracts in the 1920s. Kenneth T. Jackson, *Crabgrass Frontier: The Suburbanization of the United States* (New York: Oxford University Press, 1985), 30; *Seattle Post-Intelligencer,* 17 April 1910, Real Estate sec., 10; Calvin Bradford, "Financing Home Ownership: The Federal Role in Neighborhood Decline," *Urban Affairs Quarterly* 14 (March 1979): 318–20. Upton Sinclair's *The Jungle* graphically tells the story of how unscrupulous real estate agents utilized contracts for deed to exploit immigrants. See Upton Sinclair, *The Jungle* (New York: Doubleday, Page & Co., 1906).

41. Seattle Chamber of Commerce, *Seattle Illustrated* (Seattle: Baldwin, Calcutt and Blakely Publishing Co., 1890), 41.

42. *Seattle Budget,* 3 May 1890; *Fremont Colleague,* 5 December 1908; 2 January 1909. Newspaper advertising of land was a recent innovation to Seattle in the early twentieth century. In 1890, the Seattle Chamber of Commerce gave credit for initiating the idea to F. J. Monroe, a real estate broker who came to the city in the late 1880s. "Heavy display advertising in popular newspapers," the Chamber remarked, "[was] a move by Mr. Monroe which was

widely copied and served to bring Seattle prominently before the people, . . . and many people of Seattle owe their present prosperity to this wholesome publicity of what they had to sell or wanted to buy." When Seattle's building boom hit, large realty firms continued using this medium to reach potential buyers. See Seattle Chamber of Commerce, *Seattle Illustrated,* 41.

43. *Seattle Post-Intelligencer,* 28 August 1910, classifieds; *Seattle Post-Intelligencer,* 27 August 1911, classifieds; *Fremont Colleague,* 2 January 1909; *Fremont Colleague,* 28 March 1908.

44. *Seattle Post-Intelligencer,* 14 January 1912, Real Estate sec.

45. *Seattle Post-Intelligencer,* 7 April 1907; *Seattle Post-Intelligencer,* 28 August 1910; *Seattle Post-Intelligencer,* classifieds; *Seattle Post-Intelligencer,* 27 August 1911, classifieds (example). For a discussion of some of consumption's contractions, see Leach, *Land of Desire.* Gwendolyn Wright, Marc Weiss, Mary Corbin Sies, and Margaret Marsh, who write about early twentieth-century domestic environments, make assumptions about the origin and meaning of twentieth-century domestic architecture based on planned communities. Most common neighborhoods of the period, however, arose in a piecemeal fashion as many individuals made decisions about its development and housing. See Wright, *Moralism and the Model Home;* Weiss, *Rise of the Community Builders;* Sies, "Toward a Performance Theory"; and Margaret Marsh, *Suburban Lives* (New Brunswick, NJ: Rutgers University Press, 1990).

46. On the discipline needed to make payments, see Calder, *Financing the American Dream,* 28–33. On the increasing dependency on technical systems, see Thomas J. Schlereth, "Conduits and Conduct: Home Utilities in Victorian America, 1876–1915," in *American Home Life, 1880–1930: A Social History of Spaces and Services,* ed. Jessica H. Foy and Thomas J. Schlereth (Knoxville: University of Tennessee Press, 1992), 238–39.

47. John F. Yoho and family arrived in Seattle around 1896. A 1908 advertisement for Jud Yoho and Co. stated "est. 1896," when Jud would have been only fourteen years old. The Polk City directories, however, first noted John in 1898. See *Seattle Post-Intelligencer,* 10 May 1908, sec. 2, 5, and Polk Seattle City directories, 1894–1925. Both John and his wife, Esther, were born in Ohio; they married in 1877, when John was twenty years old and Esther only thirteen. The next year, the Yohos had their first child in Texas. Two more children were born in Texas, including Jud, and another in Colorado between 1882 and 1885. *Twelfth Census; Thirteenth Census; Seattle Post-Intelligencer,* 17 May 1908, sec. 2, 5. Jud may have been compelled to open his own business by the fortunes of his father. In the 1905 city directory, John was listed as "inventor" rather than "real estate agent," and by the next year, Jud's occupation had changed from an employee (bookkeeper) to independent real estate and insurance agent. The directory listed no occupation for John in 1907, and he died in 1908 at the age of fifty-one. I speculate that ill health possibly sidelined John, forcing Jud to venture out on his own. John apparently had some limited success as an inventor. In 1904, *Pacific Builder and Engineer* reported that he had "invented a new style of instantaneous heater" to be manufactured in Vancouver "by the Yoho bath heater co., ltd." *Pacific Builder and Engineer* 2 (23 April 1904): 1; Doherty, "Jud Yoho," 37.

48. The *Thirteenth Census* shows Yoho renting his dwelling at 1639 King Street, Seattle. My conclusions about who lived in bungalows derive from a sampling of homes in four Seat-

tle neighborhoods—Ballard, Fremont, Green Lake, and Wallingford. Using detailed 1937 tax assessment descriptions and photographs and the 1920 manuscript census, I created an architectural and demographic data base of 20 percent (approximately 800) of the houses within the four sample areas. From this material, I generally grouped heads of households according to their occupation and associated these groups with the type of houses they lived in. In Wallingford, I sampled 20 percent of the houses between North Forty-fifth Street, Bagley, Woodlawn, and North Thirty-fourth Street. Among the salesmen, accountants, clerks, and agents, 73 percent selected bungalows. The rest picked four-squares, and there was a solitary Dutch Colonial chosen; Doherty, "Jud Yoho," 40, 61.

49. *Seattle Post-Intelligencer,* 14 August 1904; West to R.C. Whitman, 23 October 1897, letterpress book 2, box 1, West and Wheeler Associates records, Manuscripts Division, U.W. Libraries.

50. *Seattle Post-Intelligencer,* 14 August 1904.

51. Ibid.; "Plan Factories," *Pacific Builder and Engineer* 5 (14 September 1907): 11; "Small House Service," *Pacific Builder and Engineer* 33 (19 January 1924): 5.

52. *Seattle Post Intelligencer,* 6 April 1907; *Seattle Post Intelligencer,* 3 December 1910; *Seattle Post Intelligencer,* 7 April 1907; *Seattle Post Intelligencer,* 5 May 1907. For a good discussion of large-scale housing developments in the 1920s, with examples, see Carolyn S. Loeb, *Entrepreneurial Vernacular: Developers' Subdivision in the 1920s* (Baltimore: Johns Hopkins University Press, 2001). A good example of a large-scale Seattle development company was West and Wheeler. Fred W. West and his family had arrived in Seattle from Indiana during its 1880s expansion. By the early 1890s, he operated his own real estate office. He hung on during the difficult 1890s by managing various rentals, negotiating sales and loans, and investing in low-priced property, particularly in the northern suburbs. When Seattle's tremendous building surge hit after the 1897 Klondike strike, he was poised to flourish. His lots in the north end, especially in the Green Lake and Fremont neighborhoods, sold rapidly. By 1901, James W. Wheeler had joined West's office. Raised by a carpenter father in Fremont, Wheeler entered real estate while still in high school, making one of his first sales to West. In 1903, the two men, with Jacob Dierning, incorporated West and Wheeler. It proved to be a fruitful partnership. They established "elaborate offices" in the Marion Building in 1918, the same year West joined the Washington Mutual Savings Bank's board of trustees, which in 1923, elected him first vice president of the bank. By the late 1920s, the firm no longer just brokered other people's sales but began subdividing and marketing mainly its own properties. It owned thousands of acres throughout Washington and Oregon, including townsites and subdivisions. As the Great Depression ensued, West and Wheeler operated as a large, integrated, multifunctional organization with individual departments and managers to handle real estate, rentals, insurance, and mortgages. The two men had moved far from their roots as struggling individual brokers. Frederick West to Mrs. K. E. Schaffhausen, 10 January 1901, letterpress book 6, box 1, #2777, West and Wheeler Associates records, Manuscripts Division, U.W. Libraries; Seattle-King County Board of Realtors, "Sixty-Six Years of Progress and a Look to the Future, Seattle-King County Board of Realtors, 1903–1969," Special Collections, University of Washington Libraries, Seattle, Washington; articles of incorporation of West

and Wheeler, 1903, #7122, Puget Sound Regional Archives; "Bank Honors F. W. West," undated clipping, scrapbook, box 148, "Wheeler Personal Scrapbooks," West and Wheeler Associates records, Manuscripts Division, U.W. Libraries; undated, unnamed newspaper article, scrapbook, box 147, West and Wheeler Associates records, Manuscripts Division, U.W. Libraries; partial copy of *The Key* (official publication of West and Wheeler), vol. I, no. 2 (November 1936), scrapbook, box 148, West and Wheeler Associates records, Manuscripts Division, University of Washington Libraries.

53. *Seattle Post-Intelligencer,* 20 October 1912.

54. *The Pacific Financial, Real Estate, Building Record* (became the *Pacific Builder and Engineer*) noted 125 brokers in the association in June 1904. For stories on agents organizing, see *Pacific Financial, Real Estate, Building Record* 2 (4 June 1904): 6; *Pacific Financial, Real Estate, Building Record* 2 (9 April 1904): 9; Seattle-King County Board of Realtors, "Sixty-Six Years of Progress," 4; *Seattle Post-Intelligencer,* 17 April 1910, Real Estate and Auto sec.; *Seattle Post-Intelligencer,* 14 August 1904; *Seattle Post-Intelligencer,* 22 August 1909; undated, unnamed clipping, scrapbook, box 148, West and Wheeler Associates records, Manuscripts Division, U.W. Libraries; "Real Estate Broker Licensing Act" in *Session Laws of American States and Territories, Washington, Laws Extraordinary Session* (Olympia, WA: State of Washington, 1925), chapter 129, 218. James Wheeler was also active in the National Association of Real Estate Boards, which by the 1920s was a large and influential organization of individual boards nationwide.

55. S. C. Ericksen, "Proposal to License Contractors," *Pacific Builder and Engineer* 25 (25 April 1919): 16.

56. "Jerry Affects Home Building," *Pacific Builder and Engineer* 37 (18 April 1931): 9.

57. *Pacific Builder and Engineer* 9 (12 February 1910): 49. For more information about the 1906 strike between the Master Builders Association and the Building Traders Assembly, see *Pacific Financial, Real Estate, Building Record* 4 (24 November 1906): 13; *Pacific Financial, Real Estate, Building Record* 4 (29 December 1906): 3; *Pacific Builder and Engineer,* 5 (6 April 1907): 3; *Pacific Financial, Real Estate, Building Record* 5 (24 August 1907): 17. For more information about organized builders' positions on the open-shop, see *Pacific Builder and Engineer* 5 (21 December 1907): 11–12 and *Pacific Builder and Engineer* 6 (11 April 1908): 149. Vergobbi, *Seattle Master Builders Association,* 11, 21–22, 99; S. C. Ericksen, "Proposal to License Contractors," *Pacific Builder and Engineer* 25 (25 April 1919): 16; "Depression's Lessons," *Pacific Builder and Engineer* 37 (16 May 1931): 9; "Washington Contractors Law Passed," *Pacific Builder and Engineer* 43 (20 March 1937): 4; "Registration of Contractors Law," in *Session Laws of American States and Territories, Washington, Laws Extraordinary Session* (Olympia, WA: State of Washington, 1963), chapter 77, 476. Originally an organization formed to coordinate the separate associations within the building industry, not much is known about the Builders' Exchange. Although noted as a group separate from the Master Builders' Association, by 1911 it shared the same office. Around then, it faded from mention in *Pacific Builder and Engineer.* See, for example, "Builders Exchange Recently Organized," *Pacific Builder and Engineer* 5 (24 August 1907): 5, and *Pacific Builder and Engineer* 11 (4 February 1911): 47.

58. "Proposed Architect's Law," *Pacific Builder and Engineer* 22 (29 December 1916): 1; *Pacific Builder and Engineer* 25 (28 March 1919): 14. Quote in "Registration of Architects," in *Ses-*

sion Laws of American States and Territories, Washington, Laws Extraordinary Session, chapter 205, 719.

59. "Plan Factories," *Pacific Builder and Engineer* 5 (14 September 1907): 11. Quote in "Small House Service," *Pacific Builder and Engineer* 30 (19 January 1924): 5; Robert Gutman, *The Design of American Housing: A Reappraisal of the Architects' Role* (New York: Publishing Center for Cultural Resources, 1985), 15–18.

60. Carl F. Gould, "The House of Tomorrow," *Pacific Builder and Engineer* 25 (25 July 1919): 11; Harvey, "Mail-Order Architecture," 2.

61. Quote in Charles H. Alden, "Better Architecture for Small Homes," *Pacific Builder and Engineer* 30 (9 August 1924): 10, 21; *Pacific Builder and Engineer* 29 (29 June 1923): 17; "Small House Service," *Pacific Builder and Engineer* 30 (19 January 1924): 5; *Pacific Builder and Engineer* 27 (24 June 1921): 13; *Pacific Builder and Engineer* 38 (16 January 1932): 5; Harvey, "Mail-Order Architecture," 9.

62. *Pacific Builder and Engineer* 38 (16 January 1932): 5.

63. On community building, see Weiss, *Rise of the Community Builders,* passim. Quotes from *Seattle Post-Intelligencer,* 3 April 1907; and *Seattle Post-Intelligencer,* 7 April 1907; Folke Nyberg and Victor Steinbrueck, "Mount Baker Park: An Inventory of Buildings and Urban Design Resources" (Seattle: Historic Seattle Preservation and Development Authority, 1975); *Seattle Republican,* 12 November 1909.

64. See Doherty, "Jud Yoho," for a complete inventory of Yoho's houses, including those in Mount Baker Park.

5 LIVING IN THE SEATTLE BUNGALOW

1. Obituary for Orrill V. Stapp, *North Central Outlook* (Seattle), 12 September 1968 (written by Stan Stapp), hereafter cited as Stapp obituary; *The Triton,* vol. 1, no. 2, n.d., n.p., two copies in possession of the author, original in possession of Stan Stapp.

2. Polk Seattle City directory, 1918.

3. Stan Stapp interview, 13 September 1991, Seattle, Washington; *North Seattle Press,* 1–14 July 1987.

4. How much the middle class used their home for economic pursuits figures in the larger debate over who shaped the suburban landscape. See Mary Corbin Sies, "North American Suburbs, 1880–1950," *Journal of Urban History* 27 (March 2001): 325, 327; and Andrew Wiese, "Stubborn Diversity: A Commentary on Middle-Class Influence in Working-Class Suburbs, 1900–1940," *Journal of Urban History* 27 (March 2001): 349. A growing number of urban historians has explored working-class suburbs where home-based enterprises were common. See Richard Harris, *Unplanned Suburbs: Toronto's American Tragedy, 1900–1950* (Baltimore: Johns Hopkins University Press, 1996), 116–121; and Becky M. Nicolaides, *My Blue Heaven: Life and Politics in the Working-Class Suburbs of Los Angeles, 1920–1965* (Chicago: University of Chicago Press, 2002), 29, 33–35. For a provocative discussion of the importance of understanding the built environment through its uses and over time, see Kingston W. Heath, *The Patina of Place: The Cultural Weathering of a New England Industrial Landscape* (Knoxville: University of Tennessee Press, 2001), 182–186.

5. To evaluate how twentieth-century families lived in their houses, I have examined in depth portions of Seattle's northern neighborhoods. This chapter bases its conclusions

on an architectural and demographic database of over 800 houses in four sample areas extracted from north-end neighborhoods. All statistics, tables, and graphs come from this source.

6. Alan Gowans, *The Comfortable House: North American Suburban Architecture, 1890–1930* (Cambridge: MIT Press, 1986). Folke Nyberg and Victor Steinbrueck, "Inventory of Buildings and Urban Design Resources," Historic Seattle Preservation and Development Authority. These inventories of Seattle neighborhoods are great sources of information on local histories, significant buildings, and landscape features. See appendix, graph 1, "Total Houses Built Each Year in All Four North End Sample Areas."

7. Across the four sample areas, the average age of the head of household in 1920 was forty-five. The average number of children per household was two. Wallingford's 1920 sample included four working wives; Fremont, five; Green Lake, two; and Ballard, only one. Of the nearly five hundred 1920 households in all four sample areas, only two contained Italian families. Only one Russian immigrant in Green Lake represented any householder of the "new" immigration.

8. For an example of the conflation of middle class and home ownership, see Clifford Clark, The *American Family Home, 1800–1960* (Chapel Hill: University of North Carolina Press, 1986), xiii. Richard Harris, "Working-Class Home Ownership in the American Metropolis," *Journal of Urban History* 17 (November 1990): 46–69; and Michael J. Doucet and John C. Weaver, *Housing the North American City* (Montreal: McGill-Queen's University Press, 1991), 318–33, have the best discussions of class and home ownership. Doucet and Weaver thoroughly discuss the problems of connoting occupation with class. Class, of course, is a slippery concept, as it has both economic and cultural meanings. However, with few sources for ordinary people, researchers are forced to rely on listings of occupation for class categorization. I grouped heads of household in my sample areas similarly to Doucet and Weaver. Easiest were laborers, which the manuscript census usually noted as such. I lumped all tradespeople and those in occupations requiring a trained skill in another category. I placed foremen with them because, although technically management, these workers usually rose from the ranks of skilled workers and thus shared a culture with them. I divided white-collar occupations into two groups: those who participated directly in the new consumer economy as service workers and those who had professional or managerial expertise. Entrepreneurs made up a final group. These groupings obviously do not reflect the subtleties of class identity or the influence of other family members such as women. However, they do provide a rough categorization that recognizes the changing economy and cultural systems related to one's position within this economy. See appendix, table 11, "Occupational Groups in 1920 Compared to Style of Residences."

9. The scholarship overwhelmingly demonstrates that home ownership provided a crucial independence to working people and that they owned homes more commonly than the middle class. The following specifically discuss this aspect of workers' lives: Harris, "Working-Class Home Ownership," 47, 52, 64; Richard Harris, *Unplanned Suburbs: Toronto's American Tragedy, 1900–1950* (Baltimore: Johns Hopkins University Press, 1996), 130–40; Richard F. Hamilton, "The Behavior and Values of Skilled Workers," in *Blue-Collar World: Studies of the American Worker,* ed. Arthur B. Shostak and William Gomberg

(Englewood Cliffs: Prentice-Hall, 1964), 45; Gerald Handel and Lee Rainwater, "Persistence and Change in Working-Class Life Style," in *Blue-Collar World,* 39; Olivier Zunz, *The Changing Face of Inequality: Urbanization, Industrial Development, and Immigrants in Detroit, 1880–1920* (Chicago: University of Chicago Press, 1982); Becky M. Nicolaides, "'Where the Working Man Is Welcomed': Working-Class Suburbs in Los Angeles, 1900–1940," *Pacific Historical Review* 68 (November 1999): 517–59; Nicolaides, *My Blue Heaven,* 39–63; Matthew Edel, Elliott D. Sclar, and Daniel Luria, *Shaky Palaces: Homeownership and Social Mobility in Boston's Suburbanization* (New York: Columbia University Press, 1984). For an extensive discussion and historiography about working-class and middle-class suburbanization that includes the issue of home ownership, see Mary Corbin Sies, "North American Suburbs, 1880–1950," *Journal of Urban History* 27 (March 2001): 313–46; and Andrew Wiese, "Stubborn Diversity: A Commentary on Middle-Class Influence in Working-Class Suburbs, 1900–1940," *Journal of Urban History* 27 (March 2001): 347–54. See appendix, table 10, "Ownership and Household Head Occupational Group in 1920."

10. See appendix, table 13, "Ballard Sample Area 1920 Occupational Groups and Home-ownership." John Howard Owen, "The Evolution of The Popular House in Seattle" (master's thesis, University of Washington, 1975).

11. Zunz, *Changing Face of Inequality,* 77. For the best discussion of home ownership among the working class and immigrants, see Joseph C. Biggot, *From Cottage to Bungalow: Houses and the Working Class in Metropolitan Chicago, 1869–1929* (Chicago: University of Chicago Press, 2001); and Thomas C. Hubka and Judith T. Kenny, "The Workers' Cottage in Milwaukee's Polish Community: Housing and the Process of Americanization, 1870–1920," in *People, Power, Places: Perspectives in Vernacular Architecture,* vol. 8, ed. Sally McMurry and Annmarie Adams (Knoxville: University of Tennessee Press, 2000). Also very helpful are Jules Tygiel, "Housing in Late Nineteenth-Century American Cities: Suggestions for Research," *Historical Methods,* 12 (Spring 1979): 84–97; Robert G. Barrows, "Beyond the Tenement: Patterns of American Urban Housing, 1870–1930," *Journal of Urban History* 9 (August 1983): 395–420; and H. E. Riley, "Evolution in the Worker's Housing Since 1900," *Monthly Labor Review* 81 (August 1958): 854–61.

12. Anne Marie Frodeson Steiner interview, 10 January 1991, Seattle, Washington; 1937 tax assessor form for 6416 Thirty-sixth Avenue Northwest, Puget Sound Regional Archives, Bellevue, Washington. For more information on Ballard's immigrant community, see Marianne Forssblad, "Scandinavians in King County: Excerpts from Ballard's Oral History Project," in *More Voices, New Stories: King County, Washington's First 150 Years,* ed. Mary C. Wright (Seattle: Pacific Northwest Historians Guild, 2002), 133–154; and Lynn Moen, ed., *Voices of Ballard: Immigrant Stories from the Vanishing Generation* (Seattle: Nordic Heritage Museum, 2001), 150–55.

13. Harris, "Working-Class Home Ownership," 47. See appendix, table 10 "Ownership and Household Head Occupational Group in 1920."

14. Ibid.

15. See appendix, table 11, "Occupational Groups in 1920 Compared to Style of Residences."

16. Quote in Gustav Stickley, *Craftsman Homes: Architecture and Furnishings of the American Arts*

and Crafts Movement (New York: Craftsman Publishing Co., 1909; repr., New York: Dover Publications, 1979), 196. Citations are to the Dover edition. That ordinary people used their single-family houses as economic tools for a measure of economic independence helps explain why a feminist, cooperative domesticity, as advocated by turn-of-the-century reformers like Charlotte Perkins Gilman, may have had little appeal. The realms of work and family were never so separate for them as for the middle class such as those who lived in Beaux Arts Village. See Dolores Hayden, *The Grand Domestic Revolution: A History of Feminist Designs for American Homes, Neighborhoods, and Cities* (Cambridge: MIT Press, 1981).

17. Fourteen percent of all 1920 households in the four sample areas included a boarder (or lodger or roomer) and, in a few cases, a servant or housekeeper. In Wallingford, twenty-five bungalows included boarders, extended family, or servants. Eight had attic rooms mentioned in 1937. Of these eight, five had boarders, not family members. Other than bungalows, only one four-square and one house with Colonial elements included any extended family or boarders. See appendix, table 14, "Boarders, Extended Family, and Servants in Different Housing Types." Richard Harris, "The End Justified the Means: Boarding and Rooming in a City of Homes, 1890–1951," *Journal of Social History* 26 (Winter 1992): 331–58.

18. Harry Jacobsen interview, 28 September 1991, Seattle, Washington; 1937 tax assessor form for 4136 Baker Avenue, Puget Sound Regional Archives. Harry Jacobsen remembered the house number as 4138.

19. John and Jane Boitano interview, 6 March, 1991, Seattle, Washington; 1937 tax assessor form for 5018 Seventeenth Avenue Northwest, Puget Sound Regional Archives.

20. Hugh Miracle interview, 28 September 1991, Seattle, Washington.

21. Ibid.; 1937 tax assessor forms for 1101-5 East Forty-fifth Street and 4338 Eleventh Avenue Northeast show two corners of the Miracle's house at 4340 Eleventh Avenue Northeast, Puget Sound Regional Archives.

22. Miracle interview. Miracle's mother, Kathryn, defied conventional ideologies in other ways. Between 1922 and 1925, she served with Bertha Knight Landes, one of the first woman to sit on Seattle's city council. In 1928, she ran unsuccessfully for mayor. See Sandra Hoarsager, *Bertha Knight Landes of Seattle, Big City Mayor* (Norman, OK: University of Oklahoma Press, 1994), 70–71, 192.

23. Ray and Kathi Judkins Abendroth interview, 26 September 1991, Seattle, Washington; 1937 tax assessor form for 1538 West Sixtieth Street., Puget Sound Regional Archives. In 1920, a similar twelve-room four-square constructed at 2426 West Fifty-eighth Street in 1909 served as a sort of birthing clinic and hospital. By 1937, it also had been converted back to its original intent as a large, single-family home.

24. Miracle interview; Eileen McElhoe Wolgamott interview, 4 March 1991, Seattle, Washington.

25. *The Triton.*

26. Stapp interview, 1991. Quote in *North Seattle Press,* 29 July–11 August 1987.

27. Stapp obituary; Stapp interview, 1991; "The Little Paper with the Many Friends," circa 1928, pamphlet published by the *North Side Outlook,* original in possession of Stan Stapp, hereafter cited as 1928 pamphlet; *Washington Newspaper* 55 (September 1970): 9.

28. *The North Seattle Press,* 1–14 July 1987; *The North Seattle Press,* 15–28 July 1987; *The North Seattle Press,* 29 July–11 August 1987; Stapp obituary; Stapp interview, 1991; "The Little Paper with the Many Friends," 1928 pamphlet.

29. On the feminine Victorian parlor, see Katherine C. Grier, *Culture and Comfort: People, Parlors, and Upholstery, 1850–1930* (Rochester, NY: Strong Museum, 1988). On the attempt to masculinize living rooms and public spaces in bungalows, see Margaret Marsh, *Suburban Lives* (New Brunswick: Rutgers University Press, 1990); and Cheryl Robertson, "Male and Female Agendas for Domestic Reform," *Winterthur Portfolio* 26 (Summer/Autumn 1991): 123–41. Daphne Spain, *Gendered Spaces* (Chapel Hill: University of North Carolina Press, 1992), shows how homes remain gendered as female spaces.

30. Ruth Lange Fall interview, 23 September 1991, Seattle, Washington; 1937 tax assessor form for 1205 North Forty-sixth Street, Puget Sound Regional Archives. The 1937 tax assessor form showed Hattie E. Lange as the house's owner.

31. Fall interview; Steven Mintz and Susan Kellogg, *Domestic Revolutions: A Social History of American Family Life* (New York: The Free Press, 1988), 117.

32. John and Jane Boitano interview, 6 March 1991.

33. Charlotte Williams Lenz interview, 10 January 1991, Seattle, Washington.

34. Ibid.; Wolgamott and Fall interviews.

35. Both Marsh, *Suburban Lives,* 74–83; and Robertson, "Male and Female Agendas," 123–41, express the ideal of gender-blurring that reformers hoped to foster in bungalows.

36. *The North Seattle Press,* 1–14 July 1987; *The North Seattle Press,* 15–28 July 1987; Stapp interview, 1991.

37. John and Jane Boitano interview, 6 March 1991; Robert Blair St. George, "'Set Thine House in Order': The Domestication of the Yeomanry in Seventeenth-Century New England," in *Common Places: Readings in American Vernacular Architecture,* ed. Dell Upton and John Michael Vlach (Athens: University of Georgia Press, 1986), 336–64. St. George uses the idea of concentric circles emanating from the seventeenth-century "feminine" farm hearth to the outermost, "masculine" fields. I have borrowed his schematic, while realizing that my sources do not so clearly define feminine and masculine spaces.

38. Kingston William Heath, *The Patina of Place: The Cultural Weathering of a New England Industrial Landscape* (Knoxville: University of Tennessee Press, 2001), 148–49.

39. Steiner, Miracle, and Stapp (1991) interviews.

40. Fall, Jacobsen, Steiner, and Stapp (1991) interviews; *The North Seattle Press,* 29 July–11 August 1987.

41. Ruth Hughbanks interview, 9 January 1991, Seattle, Washington; 1937 tax assessor form for 6214 Thirty-seventh Avenue Northwest, Puget Sound Regional Archives.

42. Fall and Hughbanks interviews.

43. Wolgamott interview.

44. Stapp interview, 1991; *North Seattle Press,* 29 July–11 August 1987.

45. Fall and Stapp (1991) interviews; Karen Halttunen, "From Parlor to Living Room: Domestic Space, Interior Decoration, and the Culture of Personality," in *Consuming Visions: Accumulation and Display of Goods in America, 1880–1920,* ed. Simon J. Bronner (New York: Norton, 1989), 157–89. All interviewees remembered Christmas celebrations occurring in the living room.

46. Hughbanks and Stapp (1991) interviews; Betty Purves Bostrom interview, 27 September 1991, Seattle, Washington .

47. Bostrom, Lenz, Steiner, Boitano (6 March 1991), Stapp (1991), Jacobsen, Miracle, and Fall interviews.

48. Lenz and Wolgamott interviews.

49. Mintz and Kellogg, *Domestic Revolutions,* 109; Stickley, *Craftsman Homes,* 197; Robertson, "Male and Female Agendas," 123–41.

50. Mintz and Kellogg, *Domestic Revolutions,* 109; Miracle and Jacobsen interviews. Of the total 494 households from 1920, 10 (2 percent) included divorced people. Fifty-seven (12 percent) included widowed or widower heads of households. Of these 57, 49 were women, so 10 percent of all households included a widow. Sixty-two households (13 percent) were headed by a single-parent, either divorced or widowed, but 54 (11 percent) were women. In the total sample, only 8 male single-parent heads of households appeared. Bostrom interview. See appendix, table 16, "Divorced or Widowed People within 1920 Sample Households."

51. Bostrom and Jacobsen interviews.

52. Bostrom and Jacobsen interviews.

6 LEGACY OF THE SEATTLE BUNGALOW

1. John M. Faragher, "Bungalow and Ranch House: The Architectural Backwash of California," *Western Historical Quarterly* 32 (Summer 2001): 149–73.

2. Obituary for Orrill V. Stapp, *North Central Outlook* (Seattle), 12 September 1968 (written by Stan Stapp); Stan Stapp interview, 13 September 1991, Seattle, Washington.

3. Stapp obituary, *North Central Outlook;* Stapp interview, 1991; Polk City directories, 1929–1968; *The Triton* 1, no. 1 (no date): 34–35, 40, 41 (two copies in possession of the author; originals in possession of Stan Stapp); Stapp interview, 8 June 1998, Seattle, Washington.

4. *The North Seattle Press,* 1–14 July 1987, 3, and *The North Seattle Press,* 26 August–8 September 1987, 3; Polk City directories, 1933–44; *The Seattle Times,* 17 April 1991 (Milton Stapp obituary).

5. Greg Hise, *Magnetic Los Angeles: Planning the Twentieth-Century Metropolis* (Baltimore: Johns Hopkins University Press, 1997), 56–85; Stapp interview, 1991; tax assessor's form for 2122 North 117 Street, Puget Sound Regional Archives, Bellevue, Washington.

6. Stapp interview, 1991; tax assessor form for 16718 Thirty-seventh Avenue Northeast; Faragher, "Bungalow and Ranch House"; Gary G. Peterson, "Home Off the Range: The Origins and Evolution of Ranch Style Architecture in the United States," *Design Methods and Theories* 23 (n.d.): 1040–59; Thomas C. Hubka, "The American Ranch House: Traditional Design Method in Modern Popular Culture," *Traditional Dwellings and Settlements Review* 7 (1995): 33–39.

7. Tax assessor form for 16718 Thirty-seventh Avenue Northeast.

8. *Washington Newspaper* 55 (September 1970): 9; clipping, Special Collections, University of Washington, Seattle, WA; tax assessor's form for 4273–77 Woodland Park Avenue, Puget Sound Regional Archives.

BIBLIOGRAPHY

ARCHIVE AND MANUSCRIPT COLLECTIONS

American Institute of Architects, Seattle chapter records. Manuscripts and University Archives Division. University of Washington Libraries, Seattle, Washington.

Architects' reference files. Special Collections. University of Washington Libraries, Seattle, Washington.

Articles of Incorporation. Puget Sound Regional Archives, Bellevue, Washington.

Artists scrapbooks. Fine Arts Department. Seattle Public Library, Seattle, Washington.

Beaux Arts Village Archives, Beaux Arts Village, Washington.

"Beaux Arts Village, Home of the Beaux Arts Society." Pamphlet. Special Collections. University of Washington Libraries, Seattle, Washington.

Carpenters and Joiners of America Records, Local 131, #1228. Manuscripts and University Archives Division. University of Washington Libraries, Seattle, Washington.

Hainsworth Construction Company Papers. Manuscripts and University Archives Division. University of Washington Libraries, Seattle, Washington.

Kilbourne, Edward C., Papers. Manuscripts and University Archives Division. University of Washington Libraries, Seattle, Washington.

Plan book Collection. Fine Arts Department. Seattle Public Library, Seattle, Washington.

Remsberg, Charles E., Papers. Manuscripts and University Archives Division. University of Washington Libraries, Seattle, Washington.

Seattle City building permits. Department of Building and Construction, Seattle, Washington.

Seattle-King County Board of Realtors. "Sixty-Six Years of Progress and a Look to the Future, Seattle-King County Board of Realtors, 1903–1969." Special Collections. University of Washington Libraries, Seattle, Washington.

Stapp, Stan. Private Collection. Seattle, Washington.

Tax assessor records. Puget Sound Regional Archives, Bellevue, Washington.

West and Wheeler Associates records. Manuscripts and University Archives Division. University of Washington Libraries, Seattle, Washington.

NEWSPAPERS, PERIODICALS, AND CITY DIRECTORIES

Bungalow Magazine

The Craftsman

Fremont Colleague

Monthly Labor Review

North Seattle Press

Pacific Builder and Engineer

Seattle Polk City directories, 1894–1951

Seattle Post-Intelligencer

Seattle Republican

Seattle Times

The Triton

INTERVIEWS

All interviews were conducted by the author.

Abendroth, Ray, and Kathi Judkins Abendroth. 26 September 1991. Seattle, Washington.

Boitano, John, and Jane Boitano. 15 January 1991 and 6 March 1991. Seattle, Washington.

Bostrom, Betty Purves. 27 September 1991. Seattle, Washington.

Fall, Ruth Lange. 23 September 1991. Seattle, Washington.

Hughbanks, Ruth. 9 January 1991. Seattle, Washington.

Jacobsen, Harry. 28 September 1991. Seattle, Washington.

Lenz, Charlotte Williams. 10 January 1991. Seattle, Washington.

Miracle, Hugh. 28 September 1991. Seattle, Washington.

Stapp, Stan. 13 September 1991 and 8 June 1998. Seattle, Washington.

Steiner, Anne Marie Frodeson. 10 January 1991. Seattle, Washington.

Wallace, John, and Marian Culbertson Wallace. 5 March 1991 and 26 September 1991. Seattle, Washington.

Wolgamott, Eileen McElhoe. 4 March 1991. Seattle, Washington.

GOVERNMENT DOCUMENTS

Gries, John M., and Thomas M. Curran. "Present Home Financing Methods." U.S. Department of Commerce. Washington, D.C.: Government Printing Office, 1928.

Gries, John M., and James Ford, eds. *House Design, Construction and Equipment.* Washington, D.C.: President's Conference on Home Building and Home Ownership, 1932.

Gries, John M., and James S. Taylor. "How to Own Your Home: A Handbook for Prospective Home Owners." U.S. Department of Commerce. Washington, D.C.: Government Printing Office, 1923.

King County Clerk and Recorder's Office. Deeds. Seattle, Washington

King County Office of Construction and Land Use. Building permits. Seattle, Washington.

U.S. Census of Population, 1900 (manuscript). Schedule 1745: King County, Washington. Microfilm in U.S. National Archives and Records Service. *Twelfth Census of the United States, 1900.* Washington: NARS, 1973.

U.S. Census of Population, 1910 (manuscript). Schedules 1657 and 1658: King County, Washington. Microfilm in U.S. National Archives and Records Service. *Thirteenth Census of the United States, 1910.* Washington: NARS, 1983.

U.S. Census of Population, 1920 (manuscript). Schedules 1924, 1925, and 1926: King County, Washington. Microfilm in U.S. National Archives and Records Service. *Fourteenth Census of the United States, 1920.* Washington: NARS, 1993.

U.S. Department of Commerce: Bureau of the Census. *United States Census of Housing: 1940.* Vol. 2, part 5, *General Characteristics, Washington.* Washington, D.C.: Government Printing Office, 1943.

U.S. Department of Commerce. National Bureau of Standards. *Measures for Progress: A History of the National Bureau of Standards,* by Rexmond C. Cochrane. Washington, D.C.: National Bureau of Standards, 1966.

U.S. Department of Commerce. "Recommended Minimum Requirements for Small Dwelling Construction." Washington, D.C.: Government Printing Office, 1923.

U.S. Department of Commerce. "Recommended Minimum Requirements for Small Dwelling Construction." Washington, D.C.: Government Printing Office, 1932.

U.S. Department of Labor. *Economics of the Construction Industry.* Washington, D.C.: Government Printing Office, 1919.

Washington State. "Regulation of Architects." Chapter 205. In *Session Laws of American States and Territories.* Olympia, WA: State of Washington, 1919.

Washington State. "Real Estate Broker Licensing Act." Chapter 129. In *Session Laws of American States and Territories, Washington, Laws Extraordinary Session.* Olympia, WA: State of Washington, 1925.

Washington State. "Registration of Contractors Law." Chapter 77. In *Session Laws of American States and Territories.* Olympia, WA: State of Washington, 1963.

PRIMARY SOURCES

Alden, Charles H. "Better Architecture for Small Homes." *Pacific Builder and Engineer* 30 (9 August 1924): 10, 21.

Bagley, Clarence. *History of Seattle From the Earliest Settlement to the Present Time.* Vol. 3. Chicago: S. J. Clarke Publishing Company, 1916.

"Beaux Arts: The Community Problem Solved." *Bungalow Magazine* 2 (July 1913): 13–29.

"Beaux Arts: The Community Problem Solved." *Bungalow Magazine* 2 (August 1913): 32–48, 63.

Bellevue-Mercer Islander, 26 November 1953. Clancey M. Lewis obituary.

Bingham, Persis. "Buttressed Openings Between Rooms in Bungalow Made to Serve Many Useful Purposes." *Bungalow Magazine* 3 (October 1916): 439.

"Brick Standardization." *Pacific Builder and Engineer* 29 (17 August 1923): 6.

"Builders' Exchange Recently Organized." *Pacific Builder and Engineer* 5 (24 August 1907): 5.

"Building Trades Lose Much Time." *Pacific Builder and Engineer* 30 (28 June 1924): 6.

Bungalow Company. "Bungalows." Plan book. Seattle: n.p., circa 1912.

"Bungalow Equipped with Many Electric Devices Attracts Much Notice at Big Exposition." *Bungalow Magazine* 4 (August 1915): 505.

"Bungalow Showing Japanese Influence Is Solution of Problem Met in Difficult Site." *Bungalow Magazine* 5 (April 1916): 209.

Byers, Charles Alma. "The 'Colonial Bungalow': A New and Charming Variation in Home Architecture." *The Craftsman* 28 (July 1915): 409–14.

——. "The Message of the Western Pergola to American Home- and Garden Makers." *The Craftsman* 22 (August 1912): 474.

——. "Planning the Bungalow Den." *Bungalow Magazine* 5 (March 1916): 175.

——. "A Suggestion of Kitchen Planning." *Bungalow Magazine* 7 (January 1918): 41.

——. "Three Charming Little Colonial Bungalows." *Bungalow Magazine* 7 (March 1918): 21.

"The Calder Report on the Building Situation." *Monthly Labor Review* 12 (June 1921): 1212–18.

Calvert, Frank, ed. *The Cartoon: A Reference Book of Seattle's Successful Men.* N.p., 1911.

——. *Homes and Gardens of the Pacific Coast.* Vol. 1, Seattle. Beaux Arts Village, Lake Washington: Beaux Arts Society Publishers, 1913.

——. *Homes and Gardens of the Pacific Coast.* Vol. 1, Seattle. Beaux Arts Village, Lake Washington: Beaux Arts Society Publishers, 1913. Reprint edited by Christopher Laughlin, 1974.

Carkeek, Charles W. "Subcontracting." *Pacific Builder and Engineer* 22 (28 July 1916): 13.

Carman, Bliss. "The Use of Out of Doors." *The Craftsman* 10 (January 1907): 424.

"Causes of Seasonal Fluctuations in the Construction Industry." *Monthly Labor Review* 33 (September 1931): 492–519.

Claffey, W. L. "The Passing of the Carpet." *Bungalow Magazine* 6 (November 1917): 666–67.

"A Country Home for the Business Man: A Second Visit to Craftsman Farms." *The Craftsman* 19 (October 1910): 56.

"Crowds Flock to Seattle's Electric Appliance Show." *Pacific Builder and Engineer* 29 (31 August 1923): 6.

Cunliffe, H. L. "The Building Situation." *Pacific Builder and Engineer* 27 (27 May 1921): 6.

Delong, W. W. and, Mrs. W. W. Delong. *Seattle Home Builder and Home Keeper.* Seattle: Commercial Publishing Co., 1915.

"Depression's Lessons." *Pacific Builder and Engineer* 37 (16 May 1931): 9.

"The Dining Room as a Center of Hospitality and Good Cheer." *The Craftsman* 9 (November 1905): 229.

"Distinguishing Features of the Craftsman House." *The Craftsman* 23 (March 1913): 727–29.

Dunlea, Nancy C. "Don'ts for for [sic] the Home Builder." *Bungalow Magazine* 6 (April 1917): 213.

"An Education in Home-Building: The Need and the Opportunity of Studying This Art in America." *The Craftsman* 26 (April 1914): 78.

"The Electric Show." *Pacific Builder and Engineer* 29 (27 July 1923): 6.

"Employment in the Construction of an Apartment House." *Monthly Labor Review* 35 (October 1932): 782–87.

Ericksen, S. C., "Proposal to License Contractors." *Pacific Builder and Engineer* 25 (25 April 1919): 16.

"FHA Chief Gives Seven Principles for Small Homes." *Pacific Builder and Engineer* 43 (15 May 1937): 3.

Ford, James. "Fundamentals of Housing Reform." Annual Report of the Board of Regents of The Smithsonian Institution. Washington, D.C.: Government Printing Office, 1914.

Gould, Carl F. "The House of Tomorrow." *Pacific Builder and Engineer* 25 (25 July 1919): 11.

Hanford, C. H., ed. *Seattle and Environs, 1852–1924*. Vol. 2. Chicago: Pioneer Historical Publishing Company, 1924.

"The Heart of the Home: The Value of the Open Fireplace in Modern Housebuilding." *The Craftsman* 22 (July 1912): 444.

Hildebrand, Joseph G. "A Cause for Divorce." *Pacific Builder and Engineer* 37 (17 January 1931): 6.

"Home With a Personality." *Bungalow Magazine* 4 (January 1915): 3.

"The Hoover Dwelling Code." *Pacific Builder and Engineer* 29 (23 February 1923): 9.

"Hot Water Tanks Standardized." *Pacific Builder and Engineer* 30 (29 November 1924): 6.

"The Inglenook." *Bungalow Magazine* 6 (May 1917): 293.

"Irregular Employment in the Building Industry." *Monthly Labor Review* 13 (July 1921): 165–68.

Ivey, Edwin J. "Kitchen Coolers to Preserve All Kinds of Perishable Foods Necessary for the Modern Bungalow." *Bungalow Magazine* 5 (January 1916): 43.

"January Supplement Bungalow." *Bungalow Magazine* 3 (January 1914): 3.

"Jerry Affects Home Building." *Pacific Builder and Engineer* 37 (18 April 1931): 9.

King, A. G. "Modern Methods of Heating and Ventilation." *Architects' and Builders' Magazine* 8 (April 1907): 325–28.

Linn, W. A. "Building and Loan Associations." *Scribner's Magazine* 5 (June 1889): 700–712.

———. "Co-operative Home-Winning. Some Practical Results of Building Associations." *Scribner's Magazine* 7 (May 1890): 571–86.

"The Living Room, Its Many Uses and Its Possibilities for Comfort and Beauty." *The Craftsman* 9 (October 1905): 59.

Matson, Ester. "The Romance of the Window: How It Can Be Used Practically to Redeem Modern City Dwellings from Monotonous Ugliness." *The Craftsman* 12 (July 1907): 439.

"Mills to Standardize Shingles." *Pacific Builder and Engineer* 30 (28 June 1924): 5–6.

"Minimum Requirements for Small Dwelling Construction." *Pacific Builder and Engineer* 29 (30 March 1923): 13.

"The Modern Home and the Domestic Problem." *The Craftsman* 10 (January 1907): 453.

"Modern House Furnishing." *Pacific Builder and Engineer* 5 (14 September 1907): 10.

"Modern Kitchens More Convenient and Sanitary than Those of Olden Days." *Bungalow Magazine* 4 (April 1915): 236.

Moss, Herbert C. "Electric Cooking in the Bungalow." *Bungalow Magazine* 2 (December 1913): 48–55, 41.

"The New Built-In Sanitary Bathroom." *The Craftsman* 24 (April 1913): 109–11.

Nichols, Charles Hart. "The Choice of a Heating System for Your Home." *The Craftsman* 28 (April 1915): 132–35.

"The 1923 House Electric." *Pacific Builder and Engineer* 29 (24 August 1923): 2–3.

North Central Outlook (Seattle). 12 September 1968. Orrill Stapp obituary.

"Open-Air Rooms and Sleeping Porches: The Revolt Against the Shut-In Houses of Our Forefathers." *The Craftsman* 24 (July 1913): 434.

"Operations of Urban Home Builders." *Monthly Labor Review* 52 (May 1941): 1283–85.

"'The Order of the Bath': Comfort and Hygiene in the Modern Bathroom." *The Craftsman* 28 (April 1915): 126.

"Perfect Mechanical Brick Layer." *Pacific Builder and Engineer* 30 (16 February 1924): 5.

"Plan Factories." *Pacific Builder and Engineer* 5 (14 September 1907): 11.

"Plastering Machine Perfected." *Pacific Builder and Engineer* 30 (19 April 1924): 5.

"Porches, Pergolas and Balconies, and the Charm of Privacy Out of Doors." *The Craftsman* 9 (March 1906): 843–45.

"Practical Home Building." *Pacific Builder and Engineer* 17 (21 February 1914): 104.

"Proposed Architect's Law." *Pacific Builder and Engineer* 22 (29 December 1916): 1.

Renfro, Alfred. "We Built Our House on the Shore of Lake Washington." *Sunset Magazine* (September 1931): 13–15.

"Respect for the Kitchen." *The Craftsman* 28 (April 1915): 130.

Salmon, Lucy M. "Our Home Department; Philosophy, Art and Sense for the Kitchen." *The Craftsman* 10 (September 1906): 811.

Seasonal Operation in the Construction Industries: The Facts and Remedies. Report and Recommendations of a Committee of the President's Conference on Unemployment. New York: McGraw-Hill Book Co., 1924.

Seattle Budget. 3 May 1890.

Seattle Chamber of Commerce. *Seattle Illustrated.* Seattle: Baldwin, Calcutt and Blakely Publishing Co., 1890.

Seattle Daily Times. 20 April 1941.

"Seattle Electrical Week." *Pacific Builder and Engineer* 28 (29 September 1922): 14.

"Seattle's Plumbing Ordinance." *Pacific Financial, Real Estate, Building Record* (becomes *Pacific Builder and Engineer*) 3 (26 August 1905): 3.

Seattle Star. 29 July 1915.

Seattle Star. 4 August 1915.

"September Supplement Bungalow." *Bungalow Magazine* 4 (September 1915): 545.

Sherman, Le Roy. "Comparative Cost of Building, 1913 and 1918." *Monthly Labor Review* 10 (February 1920): 551–59.

"Simplification Effective." *Pacific Builder and Engineer* 30 (6 September 1924): 25.

"Simplification of Building Materials." *Pacific Builder and Engineer* 28 (31 March 1922): 25.

"Six Colonial Bungalows of Unusual Merit." *Bungalow Magazine* 7 (January 1918): 19–38.

"Small House Service." *Pacific Builder and Engineer* 30 (19 January 1924): 5.

"Some Craftsman Chimneypieces, Any One of Which Might Furnish the Key-note for an Entire Scheme of Decoration." *The Craftsman* 12 (April 1907): 39–50.

"Standardizing Materials." *Pacific Builder and Engineer* 18 (26 December 1914): 35.

Stickley, Gustav. "Als Ik Kan, The Craftsman Idea in Homebuilding." *The Craftsman* 24 (April 1913): 129.

———. "Als Ik Kan, Made in America." *The Craftsman* 27 (October 1914): 110.

———. "A Craftsman House Founded on the California Mission Style." In *Craftsman Homes:*

Architecture and Furnishings of the American Arts and Crafts Movement. New York: Craftsman
Publishing Co., 1909. Reprint, New York: Dover Publications, 1979.

———. "The Craftsman Idea of the Kind of Home Environment that Would Result from
More Natural Standards of Life and Work." In *Craftsman Homes: Architecture and Furnish-
ings of the American Arts and Crafts Movement.* New York: Craftsman Publishing, Co., 1909.
Reprint, New York: Dover Publications, 1979.

———. "The Value of Permanent Architecture as a Truthful Expression of National Character." *The Craftsman* 16 (April 1909): 80.

Thomas, Harlan. "Possibilities of the Bungalow as Permanent Dwelling." *The Craftsman* 9
(March 1909): 859–63.

"Three Bungalows Eloquent of Aesthetic Tendency in Fashioning the Modern Economic
Home." *Bungalow Magazine* 4 (June 1915): 353.

"Three Low-Cost Bungalows All in a Row." *Bungalow Magazine* 3 (September 1914): 562.

"Value of Standardization." *Pacific Builder and Engineer* 27 (29 July 1921): 5.

Vogel, Joshua H. "Model Your Home and See It Before You Start Work." *Popular Science
Monthly* (December 1930): 78–79, 143.

Volume of Memoirs: A Genealogy of Representative Citizens of the City of Seattle and County of King. New
York: Lewis Publishing Company, 1903.

Walsh, George E. "Economy in Bungalow Construction." *Bungalow Magazine* 6 (November
1917): 661–65.

"Washington Contractor's Law Passed." *Pacific Builder and Engineer* 43 (20 March 1937): 4.

Washington Newspaper 55 (September 1970): 9. Clipping. Special Collections, University of
Washington Libraries, Seattle, Washington.

"Wicker Furniture, Ideal for Bungalows." *Bungalow Magazine* 4 (May 1915): 295.

Yoho, Jud. "Built-In Conveniences for the Bungalow." *Bungalow Magazine* 4 (January 1915): 42.

———. "Craftsman Bungalow Co." Seattle: Edition De Luxe, 1913.

BOOKS, ARTICLES, AND THESES

Ames, Kenneth L. *Death in the Dining Room and Other Tales of Victorian Culture.* Philadelphia:
Temple University Press, 1992.

Andersen, Dennis A., and Katheryn H. Krafft. "Plan and Pattern Books: Shaping Early
Seattle Architecture." *Pacific Northwest Quarterly* 85 (October 1994): 156–58.

Anglin, Rob. "Briefing Paper on Bungalows in Seattle." Report submitted to the Seattle
Landmarks Preservation Board, 1982.

Barrows, Robert G. "Beyond the Tenement: Patterns of American Urban Housing, 1870–
1930." *Journal of Urban History* 9 (August 1983): 395–420.

Benson, Susan Porter. *Counter Cultures: Saleswomen, Managers, and Customers in American Department
Stores, 1890–1940.* Urbana: University of Illinois Press, 1986.

Berner, Richard C. *Seattle 1900–1920: From Boomtown, Urban Turbulence, to Restoration.* Seattle:
Charles Press, 1991.

Biggs, Lindy. *The Rational Factory: Architecture, Technology, and Work in America's Age of Mass Production.* Baltimore: Johns Hopkins University Press, 1996.

Bigott, Joseph C. *From Cottage to Bungalow: Houses and the Working Class in Metropolitan Chicago,
1869–1929.* Chicago: University of Chicago Press, 2001.

Bishir, Catherine W. "A Proper Good Nice and Workmanlike Manner." In *Architects and Builders in North Carolina: A History of the Practice of Building,* edited by Catherine W. Bishir, Charlotte V. Brown, Carl R. Lounsbury, and Ernest H. Wood III. Chapel Hill: University of North Carolina Press, 1990.

———. "A Spirit of Improvement: Changes in Building Practice, 1830–1860." In *Architects and Builders in North Carolina: A History of the Practice of Building,* edited by Catherine W. Bishir, Charlotte V. Brown, Carl R. Lounsbury, and Ernest H. Wood III. Chapel Hill: University of North Carolina Press, 1990.

Bishir, Catherine W., Charlotte V. Brown, Carl R. Lounsbury, and Ernest H. Wood III, eds. *Architects and Builders in North Carolina: A History of the Practice of Building.* Chapel Hill: University of North Carolina Press, 1990.

Blanchard, Leslie. *The Street Railway Era in Seattle: A Chronicle of Six Decades.* Forty Fort, PN: Harold E. Cox, 1968.

Bledstein, Burton J., and Robert D. Johnston, eds. *The Middling Sorts: Explorations in the History of the American Middle Class.* New York: Routledge, 2001.

Boris, Eileen. *Art and Labor: Ruskin, Morris, and the Craftsman Ideal in America.* Philadelphia: Temple University Press, 1986.

———. "Crossing Boundaries: The Gendered Meaning of the Arts and Crafts." In *The Ideal Home, 1900–1920: The History of the Twentieth-Century American Craft,* edited by Janet Kardon. New York: Harry N. Abrams Publishers in association with the American Craft Museum, 1993.

———. "'Dreams of Brotherhood and Beauty': The Social Ideas of the Arts and Crafts Movement." In *"The Art that is Life": The Arts and Crafts Movement in America, 1875–1920,* edited by Wendy Kaplan. Boston: Museum of Fine Arts, 1987.

Bradford, Calvin. "Financing Home Ownership: The Federal Role in Neighborhood Decline." *Urban Affairs Quarterly* 14 (March 1979): 313–35.

Braverman, Harry. *Labor and Monopoly Capital: The Degradation of Work in the Twentieth Century.* New York: Monthly Review Press, 1974.

Brody, David. *Workers in Industrial America: Essays on the Twentieth-Century Struggle.* New York: Oxford University Press, 1980.

Brooks, H. Allen. *Frank Lloyd Wright and the Prairie School.* New York: George Braziller, 1984.

———. *The Prairie School: Frank Lloyd Wright and his Midwest Contemporaries.* New York: Norton, 1972.

Brown, Charlotte V. "The Advance in Industrial Enterprise." In *Architects and Builders in North Carolina: A History of the Practice of Building,* edited by Catherine W. Bishir, Charlotte V. Brown, Carl R. Lounsbury, and Ernest H. Wood III. Chapel Hill: University of North Carolina Press, 1990.

Bushman, Richard. *The Refinement of America: Persons, Houses, Cities.* New York: Vintage Books, 1992.

Calder, Lendol. *Financing the American Dream: A Cultural History of Consumer Credit.* Princeton: Princeton University Press, 1999.

Chandler, Alfred D., Jr. *The Visible Hand: The Managerial Revolution in America.* Cambridge, MA: The Belknap Press of Harvard University Press, 1977.

Chase, Susan Mulchahey. "Rural Adaptations of Suburban Bungalows, Sussex County, Delaware." In *Gender, Class and Shelter: Perspectives in Vernacular Architecture,* vol. 5, edited by

Elizabeth Collins Cromley and Carter L. Hudgins, 179–92. Knoxville: University of Tennessee Press, 1995.

Christie, Robert A. *Empire in Wood: A History of the Carpenters' Union.* Ithaca: Cornell University Press, 1956.

Clark, Clifford. *The American Family Home, 1800–1960.* Chapel Hill: University of North Carolina Press, 1986.

Coben, Stanley. *Rebellion Against Victorianism: The Impetus for Cultural Change in 1920s America.* New York: Oxford University Press, 1991.

Cohen, Lizabeth. "Embellishing a Life of Labor: An Interpretation of the Material Culture of American Working-Class Homes, 1885–1915." In *Common Places: Readings in American Vernacular Architecture,* edited by Dell Upton and John Vlach, 261–78. Athens: University of Georgia Press, 1986.

———. *Making a New Deal: Industrial Workers in Chicago.* New York: Cambridge University Press, 1990.

Colquhoun, Alan. *Modern Architecture.* New York: Oxford University Press, 2002.

Conn, Peter. *The Divided Mind: Ideology and Imagination in America.* New York: Cambridge University Press, 1983.

Cullen, Jim. *The Art of Democracy: A Concise History of Popular Culture in the United States.* New York: Monthly Review Press, 1996.

Cumming, Elizabeth. "Sources and Early Ideals." In *The Arts and Crafts Movement,* edited by Elizabeth Cumming and Wendy Kaplan. London: Thames and Hudson, 1991.

Cumming, Elizabeth, and Wendy Kaplan. *The Arts and Crafts Movement.* London: Thames and Hudson, 1991.

Davis, Howard. *The Culture of Building.* New York: Oxford University Press, 1999.

———. "Four Building Cultures in History." In *The Culture of Building.* New York: Oxford University Press, 1999.

Denker, Bert, ed. *The Substance of Style: Perspectives on the American Arts and Crafts Movement.* Winterthur: Henry Francis du Pont Winterthur Museum, 1996.

Doherty, Erin M. "Jud Yoho and The Craftsman Bungalow Company: Assessing the Value of the Common House." Master's thesis, University of Washington, 1997.

Downey, Roger. "Tales of the Wild Eastside." *Seattle Weekly* 29 (May–4 June 1985): 33–39.

Doucet, Michael J., and John C. Weaver. *Housing the North American City.* Montreal: McGill-Queen's University Press, 1991.

———. "Material Culture and the North American House: The Era of the Common Man, 1870–1980." *Journal of American History* 72 (December 1985): 560–87.

———. "Material Culture and the North American House: The Era of the Common Man, 1870s–1980s." In *Housing the North American City.* Montreal: McGill-Queen's University Press, 1991.

Draper, Joan. "The École des Beaux-Arts and the Architectural Profession in the United States: The Case of John Galen Howard." In *The Architect: Chapters in the History of the Profession,* edited by Spiro Kostof. New York: Oxford University Press, 1977.

Duchscherer, Paul. *The Bungalow: America's Arts and Crafts Home.* New York: Penguin Studio, 1995.

Edel, Matthew, Elliot D. Sclar, and Daniel Luria. *Shaky Palaces: Homeownership and Social Mobility in Boston's Suburbanization.* New York: Columbia University Press, 1984.

Edsforth, Ronald. *Class Conflict and Cultural Consensus: The Making of a Mass Consumer Society in Flint, Michigan*. New Brunswick, NJ: Rutgers University Press, 1987.

Eggener, Keith L., ed. *American Architectural History: A Contemporary Reader*. London: Routledge, 2004.

Eichler, Ned. *The Merchant Builders*. Cambridge, MA: MIT Press, 1982.

Erenberg, Lewis A. *Steppin' Out: New York Nightlife and the Transformation Of American Culture, 1890–1930*. Westport, CT: Greenwood Press, 1981.

Erlich, Mark. *With Our Hands: The Story of the Carpenters in Massachusetts*. Philadelphia: Temple University Press, 1986.

Ewen, Stuart. *Captains of Consciousness: Advertising and The Social Roots of the Consumer Culture*. New York: McGraw-Hill Book Co., 1976.

Faragher, John M. "Bungalow and Ranch House: The Architectural Backwash of California." *Western Historical Quarterly* 32 (Summer 2001): 149–73.

Findlay, John. *Magic Lands: Western Cityscapes and American Culture After 1940*. Berkeley: University of California Press, 1992.

Fogelson, Robert M. *The Fragmented Metropolis: Los Angeles, 1850–1930*, 2nd ed. Berkeley: University of California Press, 1993.

Forssblad, Marianne. "Scandinavians in King County: Excerpts from Ballard's Oral History Project." In *More Voices, More Stories: King County, Washington's First 150 Years*, edited by Mary C. Wright. Seattle: Nordic Heritage Museum, 2001.

Foster, Mark S. "The Western Response to Urban Transportation: A Tale of Three Cities, 1900–1945." *Journal of the West* 18 (July 1979): 31–39.

Galambos, Louis. "The Emergent Organizational Synthesis in Modern American History." *Business History Review* 44 (Autumn 1970): 279–90.

Garvin, James L. "Mail-Order House Plans and American Victorian Architecture." *Winterthur Portfolio* 16 (Winter 1981): 309–34.

Gelernter, Mark. *A History of American Architecture: Buildings in their Cultural and Technological Context*. Hanover, NH: University Press of New England, 1999.

Glassie, Henry. *Folk Housing in Middle Virginia: A Structural Analysis of Historic Artifacts*. Knoxville: University of Tennessee Press, 1975.

———. *Pattern in the Material Folk Culture of the Eastern United States*. Philadelphia: University of Pennsylvania Press, 1968.

Glickman, Lawrence B., ed. *Consumer Society in American History: A Reader*. Ithaca: Cornell University Press, 1999.

Gottfried, Herbert, and Jan Jennings. *American Vernacular Design, 1870–1940*. New York: Van Nostrand Reinhold Co., 1985.

Gowans, Alan. *The Comfortable House: North American Suburban Architecture, 1890–1930*. Cambridge, MA: MIT Press, 1986.

Grier, Katherine C. *Culture and Comfort: People, Parlors, and Upholstery, 1850–1930*. Rochester, NY: Strong Museum, 1988.

Gutman, Robert. *The Design of American Housing: A Reappraisal of the Architect's Role*. New York: Publishing Center for Cultural Resources, 1985.

Haarsager, Sandra. *Bertha Knight Landes of Seattle, Big City Mayor*. Norman: University of Oklahoma Press, 1994.

Haber, William. *Industrial Relations in the Building Industry*. Cambridge: Harvard University Press, 1930.

Halttunen, Karen. "From Parlor to Living Room: Domestic Space, Interior Decoration, and the Culture of Personality." In *Consuming Visions: Accumulation and Display of Goods in America, 1880–1920,* edited by Simon J. Bronner, 157–89. New York: Norton, 1989.

Hamilton, Richard F. "The Behavior and Values of Skilled Workers." In *Blue-Collar World: Studies of the American Worker,* edited by Arthur B. Shostak and William Gomberg. Englewood Cliffs, NJ: Prentice-Hall, 1964.

Handel, Gerald, and Lee Rainwater. "Persistence and Change in Working-Class Life Style." In *Blue-Collar World: Studies of the American Worker,* edited by Arthur B. Shostak and William Gomberg. Englewood Cliffs, NJ: Prentice-Hall, 1964.

Handlin, David P. "Efficiency and the American Home." *Architectural Association Quarterly* 5 (October/December 1973): 50–54.

Hardwick, M. Jeff. "Homesteads and Bungalows: African-American Architecture in Langston, Oklahoma." In *Shaping Communities: Perspectives in Vernacular Architecture,* vol. 6, edited by Carter L. Hudgins and Elizabeth Collins Cromley, 21–32. Knoxville: University of Tennessee Press, 1997.

Harris, Richard. "The End Justified the Means: Boarding and Rooming in a City of Homes, 1890–1951." *Journal of Social History* 26 (Winter 1992): 331–58.

———. *Unplanned Suburbs: Toronto's American Tragedy, 1900–1950.* Baltimore: Johns Hopkins University Press, 1996.

———. "Working-Class Home Ownership in the American Metropolis." *Journal of Urban History* 17 (November 1990): 46–69.

Harvey, Thomas. "Mail-Order Architecture in the Twenties." *Landscape* 25 (Fall 1981): 1–9.

Hayden, Dolores. *The Grand Domestic Revolution: A History of Feminist Designs for American Homes, Neighborhoods, and Cities.* Cambridge, MA: MIT Press, 1981.

Hays, Samuel P. *The Response to Industrialism, 1885–1914.* Chicago: University of Chicago Press, 1957.

Heath, Kingston William. *The Patina of Place: The Cultural Weathering of a New England Industrial Landscape.* Knoxville: University of Tennessee Press, 2001.

Hewitt, Mark. *Gustav Stickley's Craftsman Farms: The Quest for an Arts and Crafts Utopia.* Syracuse: Syracuse University Press, 2001.

Hise, Greg. *Magnetic Los Angeles: Planning the Twentieth-Century Metropolis.* Baltimore: Johns Hopkins University Press, 1997.

Holdsworth, Deryck W. "Cottages and Castles for Vancouver Home-Seekers." *BC Studies* 69–70 (Spring–Summer 1986): 11–32.

———. "House and Home in Vancouver: Images of West Coast Urbanism, 1886–1929." In *The Canadian City: Essays in Urban and Social History,* edited by Gilbert A. Stelter and Alan F. J. Artibise, 187–209. Ottawa: Carleton University Press, 1984.

———. "Regional Distinctiveness in an Industrial Age: Some California Influences on British Columbia Housing." *American Review of Canadian Studies,* 12 (Summer 1982): 64–81.

———. "Vernacular Form in an Urban Context: A Preliminary Investigation of Facade Elements in Vancouver Housing." Master's thesis, University of British Columbia, 1971.

Hornstein, Jeffrey M. "The Rise of the Realtor: Professionalism, Gender, and Middle-Class

Identity, 1908–1950." In *The Middling Sorts: Explorations in the History of the American Middle Class,* edited by Burton J. Bledstein and Robert D. Johnston. New York: Routledge, 2001.

Horowitz, Daniel. *The Morality of Spending: Attitudes Toward the Consumer Society in America, 1875–1940.* Baltimore: Johns Hopkins University Press, 1985.

Howe, Daniel Walker. "Victorian Culture in America" In *Victorian America,* edited by Daniel Walker Howe. Philadelphia: University of Pennsylvania, 1976.

Hubka, Thomas C. "The American Ranch House: Traditional Design Method in Modern Popular Culture." *Traditional Dwellings and Settlements Review* 7 (1995): 33–39.

Hubka, Thomas, and Judith T. Kenny. "The Workers' Cottage in Milwaukee's Polish Community: Housing the Process of Americanization, 1870–1920." In *People, Power, Places: Perspectives in Vernacular Architecture,* vol. 8, edited by Sally McMurry and Annmarie Adams, 33–52. Knoxville: University of Tennessee Press, 2000.

Hutchinson, Janet. "The Cure for Domestic Neglect: Better Homes in America, 1922–1935." In *Perspectives in Vernacular Architecture,* vol. 2, edited by Camille Wells, 168–78. Columbia: University of Missouri Press, 1986.

Jackson, John Brinkerhoff. *Discovering the Vernacular Landscape.* New Haven, CT: Yale University Press, 1984.

Jackson, Kenneth T. *Crabgrass Frontier: The Suburbanization of the United States.* New York: Oxford University Press, 1985.

Kaplan, Wendy. *"The Art that Is Life": The Arts and Crafts Movement in America, 1875–1920.* Boston: Museum of Fine Arts, 1987.

———. "The Lamp of British Precedent: An Introduction to the Arts and Crafts Movement." In *"The Art that is Life": The Arts and Crafts Movement in America, 1875–1920.* Boston: Museum of Fine Arts, 1987.

———. "Regionalism in American Architecture." In *The Arts and Crafts Movement,* edited by Elizabeth Cumming and Wendy Kaplan. London: Thames and Hudson, 1991.

———. "Spreading the Crafts: The Role of the Schools." In *"The Art that is Life": The Arts and Crafts Movement in America, 1875–1920.* Boston: Museum of Fine Arts, 1987.

Kardon, Janet, ed. *The Ideal Home, 1900–1920: The History of the Twentieth-Century American Craft.* New York: Harry N. Abrams, Publishers, in association with the American Craft Museum, 1993.

King, Anthony. *The Bungalow: The Production of a Global Culture.* London: Routledge and Kegan Paul, 1984.

Klein, Maury. *The Flowering of Third America: The Making of an Organizational Society, 1850–1920.* Chicago: Ivan R. Dee, 1993.

Klingle, Matthew. "Urban by Nature: An Environmental History of Seattle, 1880–1970." Ph.D. diss, University of Washington, 2001.

Kreisman, Lawrence. *Made to Last: Historic Preservation in Seattle.* Seattle: Historic Seattle Preservation and Development Authority, 1985.

Lamar, Howard R., ed. *The New Encyclopedia of the American West.* New Haven, CT: Yale University Press, 1998.

Lancaster, Clay. *The American Bungalow, 1880–1930.* New York: Abbeville Press, 1985.

Lanier, Gabrielle M., and Bernard L. Herman. *Everyday Architecture of the Mid-Atlantic: Looking at Buildings and Landscapes.* Baltimore: Johns Hopkins University Press, 1997.

Leach, William. *Land of Desire: Merchants, Power, and the Rise of a New American Culture.* New York: Vintage Books, 1993.

Lears, T. J. Jackson. "From Salvation to Self-Realization: Advertising and the Therapeutic Roots of the Consumer Culture, 1880–1930." In *The Culture of Consumption: Critical Essays in American History, 1880–1980,* edited by Richard Wightman Fox and T. J. Jackson Lears. New York: Pantheon, 1983.

———. *No Place of Grace: Antimodernism and the Transformation of American Culture, 1880–1920.* New York: Pantheon, 1981.

Loeb, Carolyn S. *Entrepreneurial Vernacular: Developers' Subdivisions in the 1920s.* Baltimore: Johns Hopkins University Press, 2001.

Lounsbury, Carl R. "The Wild Melody of Steam: The Mechanization of the Manufacture of Building Materials, 1850–1900." In *Architects and Builders in North Carolina: A History of the Practice of Building,* edited by Catherine W. Bishir, Charlotte V. Brown, Carl R. Lounsbury, and Ernest H. Wood III. Chapel Hill: University of North Carolina Press, 1990.

Lupton, Ellen, and J. Abbott Miller. *The Bathroom, The Kitchen, and the Aesthetics of Waste: A Process of Elimination.* Cambridge, MA: MIT List Visual Arts Center, 1992.

McAlester, Virginia, and Lee McAlester. *A Field Guide to American Houses.* New York: Alfred A. Knopf, 1984.

Maddox, Diane. *Bungalow Nation.* New York: Harry N. Abrams, 2003.

Maisel, Sherman J. *Housebuilding in Transition.* Berkeley: University of California Press, 1953.

Marchand, Roland. *Advertising the American Dream: Making Way for Modernity, 1920–1940.* Berkeley: University of California Press, 1985.

Marsh, Margaret. *Suburban Lives.* New Brunswick, NJ: Rutgers University Press, 1990.

Martin, Ann Smart. "Makers, Buyers, and Users: Consumerism as a Material Culture Framework." *Winterthur Portfolio* 28 (Summer/Autumn 1993): 141–57.

Meyerowitz, Joanne J. *Women Adrift: Independent Wage Earners in Chicago.* Chicago: University of Chicago Press, 1988.

Mighetto, Lisa, and Marcia Montgomery. *Hard Drive to the Klondike: Promoting Seattle During the Gold Rush.* Seattle: University of Washington Press, 2002.

Mintz, Steven, and Susan Kellogg. *Domestic Revolutions: A Social History of American Family Life.* New York: The Free Press, 1988.

Moen, Lynn, ed. *Voices of Ballard: Immigrant Stories from the Vanishing Generation.* Seattle: Nordic Heritage Museum, 2001.

Montgomery, David. *The Fall of the House of Labor: The Workplace, The State, and American Labor Activism, 1865–1925.* New York: Cambridge University Press, 1987.

Morse, Kathryn. *The Nature of Gold: An Environmental History of the Klondike Gold Rush.* Seattle: University of Washington Press, 2003.

Moss, Roger. *Century of Color: Exterior Decoration for American Buildings, 1820–1920.* Watkins Glen, NY: American Life Foundation, 1981.

Nicolaides, Becky M. *My Blue Heaven: Life and Politics in the Working-Class Suburbs of Los Angeles, 1920–1965.* Chicago: University of Chicago Press, 2002.

———. "Where the Working Man Is Welcomed: Working-Class Suburbs in Los Angeles, 1900–1940." *Pacific Historical Review* 68 (November 1999): 517–59.

Nyberg, Folke, and Victor Steinbrueck. "An Inventory of Buildings and Urban Design Resources: Ballard, Wallingford, Fremont, University District, Mount Baker Park." Seattle: Historic Seattle Preservation and Development Authority, 1975.

Ochsner, Jeffrey, and Dennis Alan Andersen. *Distant Corner: Seattle Architects and the Legacy of H. H. Richardson.* Seattle: University of Washington Press, 2003.

Ochsner, Jeffrey Karl, ed. *Shaping Seattle Architecture: A Historical Guide to the Architects.* Seattle: University of Washington Press, 1994.

O'Connor, Carol A. "A Region of Cities." In *The Oxford History of the American West,* edited by Clyde Milner II, Carol O'Connor, and Martha Sandweiss. New York: Oxford University Press, 1994.

Ogle, Maureen. *All the Modern Conveniences: American Household Plumbing, 1840–1890.* Baltimore: Johns Hopkins University Press, 1996.

O'Gorman, James F. "The Prairie House." In *American Architectural History: A Contemporary Reader,* edited by Keith L. Eggener, 267–80. London: Routledge, 2004.

Ore, Janet. "Pagoda In Paradise: Clancey Lewis's Craftsman Bungalow and the Contradictions of Modern Life." *Pacific Northwest Quarterly* 92 (Summer 2001): 115–26.

———. "Ramsey, Montana and Company Towns of the American West." Paper presented at "Building the West: A Conference on Vernacular Architecture West of the Rockies." Reno, Nevada, September 1989.

———. "Jud Yoho, 'The Bungalow Craftsman,' and the Development of Seattle Suburbs." In *Shaping Communities: Perspectives in Vernacular Architecture,* vol. 6, edited by Carter Hudgins and Elizabeth Cromley, 231–43. Knoxville: University of Tennessee Press, 1997.

Orvell, Miles. *The Real Thing: Imitation and Authenticity in American Culture, 1880–1940.* Chapel Hill: University of North Carolina Press, 1989.

Owen, John. "The Evolution of the Popular House In Seattle." Master's thesis, University of Washington, 1975.

Peiss, Kathy. *Cheap Amusements: Working Women and Leisure in Turn-of-the-Century New York.* Philadelphia: Temple University Press, 1986.

———. *Hope in a Jar: The Making of America's Beauty Culture.* New York: Henry Holt and Co., 1998.

Peterson, Fred W. *Homes in the Heartland: Balloon Frame Farmhouses of the Upper Midwest, 1850–1920.* Lawrence: University Press of Kansas, 1992.

Peterson, Gary G. "Home Off the Range: The Origins and Evolution of Ranch Style Architecture in the United States." *Design Methods and Theories* 23 (n.d.): 1040–59.

Reckman, Bob. "Carpentry: The Craft and Trade." In *Case Studies on the Labor Process,* edited by Andrew Zimbalist. New York: Monthly Review Press, 1979.

Reiff, Janice. "Urbanization and the Social Structure: Seattle, Washington, 1852–1910." Ph.D. diss., University of Washington, 1981.

Riley, H. E. "Evolution in the Worker's Housing Since 1900." *Monthly Labor Review* 81 (August 1958): 854–61.

Rilling, Donna J. *Making Houses, Crafting Capitalism: Builders in Philadelphia, 1790–1850.* Philadelphia: University of Pennsylvania Press, 2001.

Robertson, Cheryl. "Male and Female Agendas for Domestic Reform." *Winterthur Portfolio* 26 (Summer/Autumn 1991): 123–41.

Rosenzweig, Roy. *Eight Hours for What We Will: Workers and Leisure in an Industrial City, 1870–1920.* New York: Cambridge University Press, 1983.

Ross, Steven J. *Working-Class Hollywood: Silent Film and the Shaping of Class in America.* Princeton: Princeton University Press, 1998.

Roth, Leland. *American Architecture: A History.* Boulder, CO: Westview Press, 2001.

Rubin, Barbara. "A Chronology of Architecture in Los Angeles." *Annals of the Association of American Geographers* 67 (December 1977): 521–37.

Rutherford, Janice Williams. *Selling Mrs. Consumer: Christine Frederick and the Rise of Household Efficiency.* Athens: University of Georgia Press, 2003.

St. George, Robert Blair. *Material Life in America, 1600–1860.* Boston: Northeastern University Press, 1988.

———. "'Set Thine House in Order': The Domestication of the Yeomanry in Seventeenth-Century New England." In *Common Places: Readings in American Vernacular Architecture,* edited by Dell Upton and John Michael Vlach. Athens: University of Georgia Press, 1986.

Sale, Roger. *Seattle, Past to Present.* Seattle: University of Washington Press, 1976.

Sanders, Barry. *A Complex Fate: Gustav Stickley and the Craftsman Movement.* New York: John Wiley and Sons, 1996.

Schlereth, Thomas J. "Conduits and Conduct: Home Utilities in Victorian America, 1876–1915." In *American Home Life, 1880–1930: A Social History of Spaces and Services,* edited by Jessica H. Foy and Thomas J. Schlereth, 225–41. Knoxville: University of Tennessee Press, 1992.

———. *Victorian America: Transformations in Everyday Life, 1876–1915.* New York: HarperCollins, Publishers, 1991.

Schmid, Calvin F. *Social Trends in Seattle.* Seattle: University of Washington Press, 1944.

Scully, Vincent J., Jr. *The Shingle Style: Architectural Theory and Design from Richardson to the Origins of Wright.* New Haven, CT: Yale University Press, 1955.

Shaw, Diane. *City Building on the Eastern Frontier: Sorting the New Nineteenth-Century City.* Baltimore: Johns Hopkins Press, 2004.

Shi, David. *The Simple Life: Plain Living and High Thinking in American Culture.* New York: Oxford University Press, 1985.

Sies, Mary Corbin. "The City Transformed: Nature, Technology, and the Suburban Ideal, 1877–1917." *Journal of Urban History* 14 (November 1987): 81–111.

———. "North American Suburbs, 1880–1950: Cultural and Social Reconsiderations." *Journal of Urban History* 27 (March 2001): 313–46.

———. "Toward a Performance Theory of the Suburban Ideal, 1877–1917." In *Perspectives in Vernacular Architecture,* vol. 4, edited by Thomas Carter and Bernard L. Herman, 197–207. Columbia: University of Missouri Press, 1991.

Sinclair, Upton. *The Jungle.* New York: Doubleday, Page & Co., 1906.

Singal, Daniel Joseph. "Towards a Definition of American Modernism." *American Quarterly* 39 (Spring 1987): 7–26.

———. *The War Within: From Victorian to Modernist Thought in the South.* Chapel Hill: University of North Carolina Press, 1982.

Spain, Daphne. *Gendered Spaces.* Chapel Hill: University of North Carolina Press, 1992.

Stickley, Gustav, ed. *Craftsman Bungalows: Fifty-Nine Homes from "The Craftsman."* New Introduction by Alan Weissman. New York: Dover Publications, 1988.

———. *Craftsman Homes: Architecture and Furnishings of the American Arts and Crafts Movement*. New York: Craftsman Publishing Co., 1909. Reprint, New York: Dover Publications, 1979.

———. *More Craftsman Homes: Floor Plans and Illustrations for Seventy-Eight Mission Style Dwellings*. New York: The Craftsman Publishing Co., 1912. Reprint, New York: Dover Publications, 1982.

Stilgoe, John R. *Borderland: Origins of the American Suburb, 1820–1939*. New Haven: Yale University Press, 1988.

Stone, May N. "The Plumbing Paradox: American Attitudes Toward Late Nineteenth-Century Domestic Sanitary Arrangements." *Winterthur Portfolio* 14 (Autumn 1979): 283–309.

Strasser, Susan. *Never Done: A History of American Housework*. New York: Pantheon Books, 1982.

Susman, Warren. *Culture as History: The Transformation of American Society in the Twentieth Century*. New York: Pantheon, 1984.

Thomas, George E. "William Price's Arts and Crafts Colony at Rose Valley, Pennsylvania." In *The Ideal Home, 1900–1920: The History of Twentieth-Century American Craft*, edited by Janet Kardon. New York: Harry N. Abrams Publishers, in association with the American Craft Museum, 1993.

Tobey, Ronald C. *Technology as Freedom: The New Deal and the Electrical Modernization of the American Home*. Berkeley: University of California Press, 1996.

Tygiel, Jules. "Housing in Late Nineteenth-Century American Cities: Suggestions for Research." *Historical Methods* 12 (Spring 1979): 84–97.

Upton, Dell. *Holy Things and Profane: Anglican Parish Churches in Colonial Virginia*. New York: Architectural History Foundation. Cambridge, MA: MIT Press, 1986.

Upton, Dell, and John Vlach, eds. *Common Places: Readings in American Vernacular Architecture*. Athens: University of Georgia Press, 1986.

Vergobbi, David J. *Seattle Master Builders Association*. Seattle: Seattle Master Builders Association, [circa 1988].

Via, Marie, and Marjorie Searl, eds. *Head, Heart and Hand: Elbert Hubbard and the Roycrafters*. Rochester, NY: University of Rochester Press, 1994.

Wallis, Allan D. *Wheel Estate: The Rise and Decline of Mobile Homes*. New York: Oxford University Press, 1991.

Warner, Sam Bass, Jr. *Streetcar Suburbs: The Process of Growth in Boston (1870–1900)*. Cambridge, MA: Harvard University Press, 1962.

Weisiger, Marsha. *Boosters, Streetcars, and Bungalows*. Phoenix: Roosevelt Action Association, 1984.

Weiss, Marc A. *The Rise of the Community Builders: The American Real Estate Industry and Urban Land Planning*. New York: Columbia University Press, 1987.

Whiffen, Marcus, and Frederick Koeper. *American Architecture*. Vol. 2, *1860–1976*. Cambridge, MA: MIT Press, 1995.

Wiebe, Robert. *The Search for Order, 1877–1920*. New York: Hill and Wang, 1967.

Wiese, Andrew. "Stubborn Diversity: A Commentary on Middle-Class Influence in Working-Class Suburbs, 1900–1940." *Journal of Urban History* 27 (March 2001): 347–54.

Wilson, Christopher P. "The Rhetoric of Consumption: Mass-Market Magazines and the Demise of the Gentle Reader, 1880–1930." In *The Culture of Consumption: Critical Essays in American History, 1880–1980*, edited by Richard Wightman Fox and T. J. Jackson Lears. New York: Pantheon, 1983.

Winter, Robert. "Arthur S. and Alfred Heineman." In *Toward a Simpler Way of Life: The Arts and Crafts Architects of California.* Berkeley: University of California, 1997.

———. "The Arts and Crafts as a Social Movement." In *Aspects of the Arts and Crafts Movement in America,* edited by Robert Judson Clark, special issue, *Record of the Art Museum, Princeton University* 34 (1975): 36–40.

———. *The California Bungalow.* Los Angeles: Hennessey and Ingalls, 1980.

Winter, Robert, ed. *Toward A Simpler Way of Life: The Arts and Crafts Architects of California.* Berkeley: University of California Press, 1997.

Wright, Gwendolyn. "The Minimal House." Chapter 8 of *Moralism and the Modern Home: Domestic Architecture and Cultural Conflict in Chicago, 1873–1913.* Chicago: University of Chicago Press, 1980.

———. *Moralism and the Model Home: Domestic Architecture and Cultural Conflict in Chicago, 1873–1913.* Chicago: University of Chicago Press, 1980.

———. "The Progressive Housewife and the Bungalow." In *Building the Dream: A Social History of Housing in America.* Cambridge, MA: MIT Press, 1981.

Wright, Mary C., ed. *More Voices, New Stories: King County, Washington's First 150 Years.* Seattle: Pacific Northwest Historians Guild, 2002.

Zunz, Olivier. *The Changing Face of Inequality: Urbanization, Industrial Development, and Immigrants in Detroit, 1880–1920.* Chicago: University of Chicago Press, 1982.

———. *Making America Corporate, 1870–1920.* Chicago: University of Chicago Press, 1990.

INDEX

References in italics refer to illustrations

Alaska-Yukon-Pacific Exposition, 79; and north Seattle growth, 10, 105

American Institute of Architects (AIA): and advertising, 84–85; Seattle members in *Bungalow Magazine*, 85; and Small House Service Bureau, 94; Washington State chapter, 93

Anglin, Rob, 82

architects: and architects licensing law, 93; and *Bungalow Magazine*, 84–85;competition with salespeople, 91–92, 93–94; as diversified salespeople, 77; emulating housing salespeople, 94; inability to curb nonprofessionals, 93; as originators of modern houses, 3; and stock plans, 80, 94

Architects' Small House Service Bureau, 94

architectural change, reciprocal nature of, 5

architectural styles: colonial bungalow, 118; Colonial Revival, 11; modern, definition of, 140–41n2; period revival, 7, 59, *101;* as "trickling down," 141n4; Victorian, defined, 139–41n2. *See also* Craftsman architecture; ranch style; Tudor Revival style; Victorian architecture

artisanal system, 54; and desire for independence, 56; labor relations of, 53–54, 55; and new technologies, 57

Andrew Peterson Construction Company, 67

Arts and Crafts communities: Beaux Arts Village as example of, 24–27; as critique and accommodation to capitalism, 26–27; Roycroft, 18; tensions within, 25–26; as therapeutic retreats, 46. *See also* Beaux Arts Village

Arts and Crafts movement: as accommo-dation to modernity, 46; architectural design principles of, 21; chapters in United States, 22; commodification of, 74, 79, 86; communitarian vision of, 24–25; and

Arts and Crafts movement *(continued)*
cooperative communities, 21; as critique
of Victorianism, 18; design schools, 24;
divergent purposes of, 147n11; emphasis on aesthetics, 22; English critique
of industrial capitalism, 21; growth in
United States, 21–23; influence on
ordinary architecture, 98, 99; revival
of handicraft, 21; reversal of movement,
73; in Seattle, 23–24
Ashbee, C. R., 24–25
Atelier Square (Beaux Arts Village), 25–26
Auntie Dunn (Beaux Arts Village), 48

Ballard: Boitano family in, 104; bungalows
in, 98–99; class and home ownership in,
100; DeLong's role in, 77; ethnicity and
home ownership in, 100; Hughbanks
house in, 59, 118; McElhoe house in, 107;
medical clinic in, 106–7; New Housing,
Incorporated, houses in, 70; settlement
of, 10
Ballard Home Building Company, 77
basements: costs of, 62; daylight, 19; heating
in, 37, 61; in ranch house, 128; requirements for modern houses, 62; as sites of
production, 97, 106, 107, 109; in Stapp
house, 53. *See also* heating systems
bathrooms, *60, 61;* competition for use of,
108; in Craftsman architecture, 39–
40; in Miracle rooming house, 106; in
Pierrott house, 107; as requirement for
modern house, 59; as women's domain,
40, 116. *See also* plumbing systems
Beaux Arts Society (also Society of Beaux
Arts), 23, 24
Beaux Arts Village: ambivalence to modernity, 20; anti-industrial symbolism in,
27–34; architectural conformity in, 49;
architecture compared to Seattle's north
end, 98–99; Arts and Crafts idealism
of, 20; bathrooms in houses of, 39–40;
Craftsman architecture in, 26–41; and
De Bit, 48–49; description of, 25–26;
domestic ideal compared to ordinary

people's, 123; domestic technologies of,
37; ethnicity of residents, 42; as exclusive
community, 47–48; industrial values in
and features of houses in, 35–41; kitchens in houses of, 38–39; Lewis house
described, 41–46; logo of, 27; map of, 25;
masculine domesticity of, 116; minorities in, 48; origins of, 24–27; Park Board
of, 50; as representative of professional
middle class, 41–46, 98, 99; residents
compared to Seattle's north end, 99;
shift to business orientation, 49; shift
from artists' colony, 46–47; similarity
to Mount Baker Park, 95; as therapeutic
retreat, 49; as therapy for professional
men, 47; women's attitudes toward, 47
Beaux Arts Workshop, 46; as business arm
of Western Academy of Beaux Arts, 24;
origins of design school, 23
bedrooms: in Boitano house, 104; children's,
117–18, 120; crowding and, 118; in Miracle rooming house, 105–6; in Renfro
house, 32; and separation from children,
118; as women's space, 116
Better Homes in America campaign, 158n38
Birch Loan Company, 68
boarding, 103–6
Boeing Airplane Company, 14
Boitano, John: boarders in household of,
103–4; children in kitchen of, 120; house
of, *105;* as patriarchal household, 115, 117
Boris, Eileen, 21, 22, 46
Bostrom, Betty Purves, 122
Brace and Herbert Mill Company, 69
breakfast nooks. *See* kitchens
Brice, Henry, 53; as entrepreneur, 67; labor
abuses of, 159n44; as owner of 4203
Woodlawn, 55; and rationalization of
home building, 65, 66–67; speculative
houses on Woodlawn Avenue, 74
Brooks, Allen, 33
building and loan associations, 86–87
building components industry, 54, 64; and
standardization, 65
building industry professionals, 16. *See also*

architects; community builders; merchant builders; real estate agents

Bungalow Company: and definition of bungalow, 63–64; history of, 67–68; and stock plans, 82

Bungalow Magazine: advertising Seattle builders, 84; and Beaux Arts Village, 38, 45, 47; and electricity, 57; and houses by Coles, 68; and selling houses, 84–86; as shaping ordinary people's choices, 85; and simplification of structures, 63; and Yoho, 78

Bungalow Publishing Company, 84

bungalows: and accommodation to modernity, 41; basements in, 62; bathrooms of, *61*; and blended families, 121–22; and blurring of spaces, 112; boarders in, 102–4; business and domestic functions in, 107–12; California bungalows, 6; children's spaces of, 117–18; as commodities, 74; and consumer economy, 97; continuity of patriarchal authority in, 115; continuity of women's spaces, 117–18; definition of, 3, 5–6, 57, 63–64; design principles of, 64; diversity of styles, 7, 71, 85; and electricity, 57–58; exterior styles of, 6; factory design principles of, 35; and family ideals, 121; female authority in, 113–17; as first modern popular house type, 124; flexible use of spaces, 16, 97; form as product of efficiency, 65; at 4203 Woodlawn, *1, 2*; gendered spaces of, 40–41, 113–18, 120–21; heating systems in, 60–62; as house type, 5–6; income producing in, 103–12; influence of plumbing costs on, 60; informality with children in, 120; kitchens in, 38–39; masculine domesticity in, 116; modern characteristics of, 124; in Mount Baker Park, 95; open floor plans, 6, 118; origins of, 6; plan of, *3, 7*; plumbing systems, 58–60; pragmatic adjustments to, 97, 102; problems of blended spaces, 119; as product of new technologies and building simplification, 57; as progressive houses, 15; as

prototypes for modern houses, 17; and ranch houses, 70–71, 128; and rationalization of house building, 64–69; as salespeople's choice, 102; screening of strangers in, 119; in Seattle's north end, 98–99; similarities of living rooms and parlors, 119; simplification of form, 63; and single-parent families, 121; transition to modernity, 125; in western cities, 7; workers in, 119–20; World War I's effect on costs of, 62–63; and Yoho, 78–79, 81–82, 83–84, 86, 89–91; Yoho's bungalow, 90–91, *90*

Byers, Charles Alma, 84

Calvert, Frank: bathroom in house of, 39, 40; as Beaux Arts trustee, 50; and development of Beaux Arts Village, 25–26; as founding member of Beaux Arts Society, 24–25; Swiss chalet house of, 29, *30*; and Western Academy of Beaux Arts, 24

Campbell, Thomas L., 49

carpenters: as crew of small contractors, 54–55; at 4203 Woodlawn Avenue, 52; relationship to new tradesmen, 56; and seasonal building cycle, 55; and skepticism of prefabricated houses, 69

Carr, H. R., 77

Casey, Lorraine, 86

Casey, Ralph, 86

cities, 5, 7

class: definitions of, 169n8; and home ownership, 99–100

Coles, Norman E., 67–69. *See also* Bungalow Company

Coles Construction Company, 68

Committee on Fundamental Equipment, 57

the Commons (Beaux Arts Village), 25

community builders: and control of building industry, 92; and dwindling design diversity, 71–72; in Seattle, 70

companionate marriage, and open plan, 117

construction materials, 63

consumer credit system, 86. *See also* installment purchasing consumer economy, 4, 102

contract for deed, 87–89. *See also* installment purchasing

contractors: and *Bungalow Magazine*, 84; and choice of simpler houses, 56; and creation of bungalow form, 53, 71; and desire for independence, 56; as dominating bungalow construction, 16; dwindling importance of, 69–70; and industrialization of components, 64; inherent conservatism of, 69; and labor relations, 53–55; in nineteenth century, 53; and rationalization of home building, 64–69; as real estate agents, 77; and relationship to building tradesmen, 55; and seasonal cycle of building, 55; small company size of, 54; and stock plans, 80; and subcontractors, 56–57; and unions, 55

Contractors Registration Act, 93

contract system, 53–54

Craftsman architecture: as accommodation to modernity, 46; anti-industrial symbolism in, 27–34; bathrooms in, 39–40; and building industry changes, 53; built-in features of, 34; and bungalow house type, 22; and closeness to nature, 28; commercial activities in, 107–12; commodification of, 79; as a commodity, 74; as common suburban dwelling, 98; as a democratic house, 30–31; described in Beaux Arts Village, 26–41; domestic technologies of, 37–40; as expression of individualism, 34; fireplaces in, 34; as first modern style, 35; gendered spaces in, 40–41, 116; heating systems of, 37; and home economics movement, 35–36; and industrialization of components, 64; industrial values and features of, 35–41; informality in, 31–32; kitchens in, 38–39; males spaces as public spaces, 116; and middle-class ambivalence to modernity, 50–51; and middle-class exclusivity, 48; Northern European premodern symbolism of, 29–30; open plan and family ideal, 31–34; ordinary people's mean-

ings of, 98; porches and nature, 28–29; pragmatic uses vs. ideological intent, 97; preindustrial symbolism and technological systems of, 37; public and private spaces in, 32–34; as reflective of professional middle-class mind-set, 41–42; as refuge, 28–29; relationship to Second Industrial Revolution, 42; Renfro house as example of, 27–35, 36, 38, 39, 40; and scientific management, 35; Stapp house as example of, 15; tension between preindustrial symbolism and industrial values, 27; as therapy, 46, 49; windows in, 36

Craftsman Bungalow Company: and cost of bungalows, 82; origins of, 79; plan book, *81*

Craftsman bungalow paradox, 41. *See also* Craftsman architecture

Craftsman Magazine: as disseminator of Craftsman architecture, 23; similarity to *Bungalow Magazine*, 83–84

"Craftsman Master Built Homes," 86

craftsmen-contractors. *See* contractors

Cruse, Frank, 80

Daughters of Norway, 100

Davis, C. A., 48

daylight factory, 3

De Bit, Ralph, 48–49, 153n79

DeLong, Belle, 83

DeLong, Willard W.: his book as advertising, 83; end of architectural career, 161n13; as housing salesperson, 77–78; plan book of, 80

Denny and Hoyt addition, 75

Dierning, Jacob, 166n52

dining rooms, 40, 112; in Miracle rooming house, 105; in Pierrott house, 107; overlapping uses of in Stapp house, 110, *113*; as transitional space, 120

Distinctive Homes Company, 80

Ditty, James, 47; electricity to house of, 37; and Beaux Arts Village house of, 29, *31*

Dixon, S. P., 76, 89

domestic engineer, 40
domestic factories, 35–41

École des Beaux-Arts, 23, 24
Electrical Club of Seattle, 58
electricians, 56
electricity: in Beaux Arts Village, 37; cost
    of, 57; increasing complexity of in bun-
    galows, 58; as requirement for a modern
    house, 56, 57; in Seattle houses, 57

Fall, Ruth Lange, 114, 119
Federal Housing Act of 1934, 70
Federal Housing Administration, 64
financing houses. *See* building and loan
    associations; installment purchasing;
    mortgages
four-square house type, 7; boarders in, 103–
    4; as choice of salespeople, 102; example
    of, *105;* as lodging house, 105–6; medical
    facilities in, 106–7; of Pierrott, *106*
Fred Berg Building Company, 52, 55, 67
Fremont: builders and real estate agents in,
    76, 77; bungalows in, 98–99; bungalows
    as salespeople's choice, 102; development
    of, 10, 75
Fremont State Bank, 87
Frodeson, Frode, 100, *101*
Frodeson, Inga, 100
Frolich, Finn Haakon: as commissioner
    of Alaska-Yukon-Pacific Exposition,
    147n14; and creation of Western Acad-
    emy of Beaux Arts, 24; as founder of
    Seattle Arts and Crafts chapter, 23

Gaudens, Augustus, 23
gendered spaces, 40–41, 113–18, 120–21;
    bathrooms as, 40; and female authority,
    113–17; and masculine domesticity, 116;
    patriarchal households, 115, 117; in Stapp
    house, 116–17; women's attitudes to Beaux
    Arts Village, 47; women's spaces, 117–18
Gerber, Dorothy, 48
Gould, Carl F., 94
Great Depression, 106, 107

Great Northern Railroad, 7
Green, Elmer E., 80
Greene, Charles S., 3, 22
Greene, Henry M., 3, 22
Green Lake: bungalows in, 98–99; bun-
    galows as salespeople's choice, 102;
    settlement of, 10
Gwinn, Gardner J., 69

Hall, Virgil, 162n22
Harold, E. E., 85
Harris, O. W., 68
Harvey, Thomas, 94
Haynes, Charles, 163n32
Heath, Kingston, 97
heating systems: cost of in Seattle, 62; hot
    air furnaces, 61–62; hot water, 157n26;
    and influence on house design, 62; in
    Lewis house, 37; pipeless, 156–57n26;
    as requirement for modern home, 60–
    61; in Seattle houses, 61–62; stoves, 61
Heineman, Alfred, 82
Heineman, Arthur S., 82
Herrick Improvement Company, 81
Hewitt-Lea Lumber Company, 69, 80
Hildebrand, Joseph G., 59
hipped box house type, 11, *12*
home economics movement, 35–36
Hooker, Dolph E., 84
Hoover, Herbert, 65, 158n38
household technologies, 56–63; influence
    on house construction, 56–64; influence
    on house form, 15; and labor relations,
    52. *See also* electricity; heating systems;
    plumbing systems
housewives, 38
housing professionals, 91–95
housing publications, 83–85
housing salespeople: and innovative sales
    techniques, 74; and moderate-income buy-
    ers, 74; role in creating suburban landscape,
    74; as shapers of bungalow landscape, 77,
    91, 95; and stock plans, 80. *See also* archi-
    tects; contractors; real estate agents
Hower, P. J., 67

Hubbard, Elbert, 18, 25, 26. *See also* Arts and Crafts communities
Hughbanks, C. F., 59, 118, 119–20
Hughbanks, Ruth, 59, 118, 119–20

Installment purchasing: as financing for houses by ordinary people, 86–89; as new sales technique, 87–89; and nineteenth-century working class, 86–87
Ivey, Edwin J., 85

Jacobsen, Harry: blended family of, 121–22; boarders in household of, 103; and children's gendered spaces, 118; house of, *104*; tensions in blended families, 122

Kellogg, W. W., 69
Kilbourne, E. C., 75, 88
King, Anthony, 6
kitchens: in bungalows, 38–39, 112; as central-use room, 117; children in, 120; service people in, 120; as women's domain, 40, 116–17
Klondike Gold Rush, 10, 14

Labor relations, 66
Lake Union Brick Company, 69
Lancaster, Clay, 6
land contract, 87–89. *See also* installment purchasing
Lange, Hattie, 113–14, 116, 118
Lears, Jackson, 46
Leithead, N. S., 49
Lenz, Charlotte Williams, 115–16, 120–21
Lewis, Clancey, *43*; description of house, 42–46; division of work and home life, 98; education and training of, 42, 44, 45–46; floor plan of house, *44*; heating in house of, 37; house of, *43*; kitchen in house of, 38, 39; living room in house of, *45*; as representative of tensions in Craftsman architecture, 42–46
living rooms, 112; as ceremonial sites, 119; commercial uses in, 106, 107, 108; electrical outlets in, 57; in Lewis house, *45*;

and masculine aesthetic, 40; in Miracle rooming house, 105, 106; in Renfro house, 31, 40; renters in Jacobsen house, 103; in Stapp house, 74, 97, 107–8, *109*, 116, 119; in Stapp Rainier Beach house, 19; uses like parlors, 117; youths in, 120–21.
lodging houses, 104–5
Los Angeles, 6, 15
Lundquist Lilly Hour, 100

Madison Park, 8
Madison Street Cable Railway, 8
Magnolia, 70
mail-order plan books. *See* stock architectural plans
Maisel, Sherman, 56
Manufacturer's Association of Washington, 46
Martin, Margaret Ditty, 47
Massar, C. H., 70
medical clinics, 106–7
men's spaces as organic, 40–41
merchant builders, 53, 127; Gardner Gwinn as example of, 69; during and after World War II, 70
Merritt, Edward L., 162n22
Miracle, Hugh: and division of spaces in home of, 105–6; home as lodging house, 105–6; income-producing activities in house of, 107; single-parent family of, 121
Miracle, Kathryn, 105; income-producing activities in Great Depression, 106, 107; as Seattle city council member, 171n22
Mitchell, Donald V., 50, 147n14
modern houses, 3, 4, 140n2
modular homes, 69
Monroe, F. J., 88, 164n42
Montlake, 8
Morris, William: communitarianism of, 24, 26; as founder of English Arts and Crafts movement, 21; and Guild of Handicraft, 24; influence of on American design, 22; influence of socialism on Beaux Arts Society, 23. *See also* Arts and Crafts movement

mortgages, 86–87

Mount Baker Park, 8, 94–95

Mount Baker Park Improvement Club, 95

National Board of Fire Underwriters, 58

neighborhoods, map of, 9. *See names of individual neighborhoods*

Nelson, Guy, 79

New Housing, Incorporated, 14, 70, 71

North Side Outlook (Outlook) 109–11, 112, 114

Norwegian Hospital Association, 100

Norwegian immigrants, 100–101

Olmsted, Frederick Law, 94

Olmsted, John Charles, 94

ordinary people: as customers of housing salespeople, 79; domesticity of compared to Arts and Crafts ideal, 123; and flexible uses and meanings of home, 17, 111–12; influence on built environment, 4, 15, 17; reshaping homes through flexible use, 98; resistance to blurring of spaces, 117–21

Owen, John, 10

Pacific Builder and Engineer: and "jerry-built" houses, 93; Lewis as editor of, 46; and Seattle Electrical Week, 58; and speculative building, 76; and stock plans for ordinary people, 82

Parker, Joseph, 65

parlors, 33, 112; codes of conduct in, 121; as women's space, 40

pedestal basins, 59

Pembroke bathtubs, 59

Phinney, Guy, 10

Phinney Ridge, 103

Pierrott, Dr. Aloyce, 107

Pioneer period houses, 10

plan books. *See* stock architectural plans

Planned communities, 94–95

Plumbers, 55, 56

Plumbing and Heating Industries Association, 59

plumbing systems, 58–60

Porches: and closeness to nature, 28; in Miracle rooming house, 106; in Pierrott house, 107; in Renfro house, *22, 28*; in Stapp house, 110, *111, 114*; as transitional space, 119

Portland, 5, 6

Prairie style. *See* Wright, Frank Lloyd

President's Conference on Home Building and Home Ownership, 57

Price, Will, 25. *See also* Arts and Crafts communities

professional middle class: in Beaux Arts Village, 20; origins in Second Industrial Revolution, 41; and tensions between craftsmanship and unionism, 46

professional organizations, 92–95

Puget Land Company, 68

Puget Sound Shingle Manufacturers Association, 65

Purves, D. S., 122, *122*

Queen Anne cottage. *See* Victorian architecture

Queen Anne Hill, 8

Rainier Beach, 19, 96

ranch style, 10; bungalows as a precursor to, 70–71, 124; Stapp house, 127–28

rational factories, 35

rationalization, 64–69. *See also* contractors

real estate agents: and *Bungalow Magazine*, 84; diversified activities of, 76–77; growth of profession, 74–75; and home financing, 87; and licensing of agents, 92; origins of in Seattle, 75; and professional organizations, 92; and Seattle neighborhood development, 75–77; and stock plans, 80

"Recommended Minimum Requirements for Small Dwelling Construction," 65

reformers, 4

Remsberg, Charles E., 76

Remsberg and Dixon Bank (Fremont State Bank), 76

Renfro, Alfred: anti-industrial symbolism in house of, 27–34; bathroom of, 39; as Beaux Arts Village trustee, 50; built-in

Renfro, Alfred (*continued*)
features in house of, 34; and Craftsman
houses as personal therapy, 49; division
of work and home life of, 98; fireplace of,
33, 34; floor plan of house, *32*; as founding
member of Beaux Arts Society, 24–25;
gendered spaces in house of, 40; house
of as democratic architecture, 30–31;
house of as expression of individualism,
34; house of as refuge, 28–29; house
of as representative of Arts and Crafts
ideology, 27–34; house of as symbol of
Northern European premodernism, 29;
informality in house of, 31–32; kitchen
of, 38, 39; open plan and family ideal
of, 31–34; porch of, *28*; public/private
spaces in house of, 32–33; as representative of Arts and Crafts tensions, 50; and
Western Academy of Beaux Arts, 24;
windows in house of, 36. *See also* Craftsman architecture
Rich, Charles C., 92
Rininger, Eleanor, 48
rooming houses, 104–5
Ruskin, John, 21

Salespeople, 16
San Francisco Guild of Arts and Crafts, 22
sanitation, 37–38, 39–40
Sayward, William J., 44
Scandinavian immigrants, 100
Schmid, Calvin, 8
Scientific management, 35
Seattle: architectural styles in, 7; building
component industry in, 54; bungalow
in, *12*; bungalow as dominant type, 11;
class and home ownership in north end
of, 99–100; Colonial Revival style in,
11, 13; Craftsman style in, 11; entrepreneurs and home ownership in north end,
101; ethnic background of north-end
residents, 99; expansion of neighborhoods of, 8; growth and annexation of
north end, 8–10; hipped boxed houses
in, 11, *12*; income-producing activities in

north-end homes of, 103; influence of
transportation on, 8; modern economy
of, 14; nineteenth-century growth of,
7–8; north-end neighborhoods of, 10;
pioneer period houses in, 10; Queen
Anne cottages in, 10; ranch houses in,
11; residential growth, 1920s–1940, 11;
Second Industrial Revolution in, 14;
single-family homes in, 10; social differentiation of landscape in, 11; Tudor
revival style in, 11, *13*; twentieth-century
growth of, 8; as typical of western urban
expansion, 8. *See also* architectural styles;
names of individual neighborhoods
Seattle Electrical Week, 58
Seattle Home Builder and Home Keeper, 77, 83
Seattle Master Builders' Association, 92–93
Seattle Post-Intelligencer, 89
Seattle Real Estate Association, 92
Second Industrial Revolution, 20, 50, 123;
Craftsman houses as representative of,
35; and creation of professional middle
class, 41
Sharpless, H. F., 88
Sies, Mary Corbin, 4, 97
Simmonds, George, 76
single-parent families, 121
skilled tradesmen, 55–57
Small Home Planning Conference, 64
small houses, as commodities, 4. *See also*
bungalows; contractors
Smith, Howard Leland, 64
speculative building: by architects in *Bungalow Magazine*, 85; architects' concern over,
94; of Brice, 65, 66–67; Coles as example
of, 68; and homogeneity in neighborhood appearance, 71; in nineteenth
century, 66; by real estate agents, 76;
and Remsberg, 76–77; Stapp house as
example of, 53
Stapp, Arthur, 73, 109, 125
Stapp, Elbert, 73, 97
Stapp, Frances, 73; domestic spaces associated with, 116–17; and estrangement
from Orrill, 125; move to Seattle's north

end, 96; and blurred spaces in bungalow, 110

Stapp, Milton, 73, *110*; and living room as public space, 119; and newspaper, 97, 109, 125

Stapp, Orrill, *3*; arrival in Seattle, 1–2; as Arts and Crafts adherent, 18; construction of 4203 Woodlawn, 52; as critic of Victorian culture, 18; and decline of patriarchal authority, 125; description of Rainier Beach house, 19; dining room of, *113*; domestic spaces associated with, 116; as embodying ordinary people's definition of domesticity, 123; enclosed porch of, *114*; guest room and newspaper in home of, *112*; heating system in home of, 61–62; house as site of newspaper publishing, 16, 97; household technologies in home of, 52–53; inability to adapt to modernity, 125; income producing activities in home of, 107–12; labor in building home of, 67; living room of, *109*; and move to north end Seattle, 73, 96; music lessons in bungalow of, 108; newspaper in basement of, *110*, 111; overlapping domestic and business functions in home of, 108–12; problems in blended spaces of, 119; purchases 4203 Woodlawn, 74; Rainier Beach house of, *19*; Rainier Beach house as representative of Arts and Crafts, 19; and rationalization of home building, 64–69; as representative of Arts and Crafts tensions, 50; as representative of Seattle's ordinary families, 15; and School of Music, 73; tensions in household of, 116–17; as typical bungalow buyer, 74

Stapp, Stan: and blending of spaces in home of, 119; and children's gendered spaces, 118; and division of domestic and income-producing spaces in bungalow of, 110; and gendered spaces in home of, 116, 117; handicrafts of, 129; minimum house of, *127*; newspaper career of, 125, 126, 129; ranch house of, *127–28*; as representative of modern person, 126–29

State of Washington Society of Architects, 93

Steiner, Anne Marie Frodeson, 100; and gendered spaces, 117, 118

Stickley, Gustav: and blurring of spaces, 117; and Craftsman Farms, 27; as disseminator of Arts and Crafts ideals and Craftsman style, 3, 22; and home as a refuge, 102–3

stock architectural plans: and architects' disdain, 93; as benefiting ordinary people, 82; costs of, 82; as creating desire for houses, 83; as popular architecture, 80; as sales technique, 79–83; trickle up to professional architects, 94

Storey, Ellsworth, 85

Stringfellow, V. O. ("Bud"), 70. *See also* New Housing, Incorporated

subcontractors, 56–57

suburban ideal, 4, 89

suburbs, 142n7

Take Down Manufacturing Company, 86

Tolman, L. P., 36, 39

The Triton, 18, 20, 108

Tudor Revival style, 11, 118; and Ditty house, 30, *31*

U.S. Bureau of Standards, 65

U.S. Housing Corporation, 63

Vancouver, B.C., 6

Victorian architecture: closed plan of, 33; definitions of, 139–41n2; description of, 2; division of public and private spaces, 119

Victorianism, 2, 18, 140n2

Vogel, Helen, 48, 50

Voorhees, Victor W., 80

Wallace, John, 157n29

Wallingford, 1, 2; boarders in bungalows of, 103; building by Brice in, 67; bungalows in, 99; bungalows as salespeople's choice in, 102; as expressing ordinary people's

Wallingford (*continued*)
  values, 95; Lange family house in, 114;
  rent compared to installment purchasing
  in, 88–89; residents of, 91; settlement of,
  10; Yoho activities in, 79
Walsh, George E., 57, 63
Washington State chapter of American
  Institute of Architects, 93
West, Frederick: and mortgages, 87; plumb-
  ing in house of, 58; real estate career of,
  166n52
West and Wheeler, 91, 166–67n52
Western Academy of Beaux Arts (WABA):
  creation of, 24; as home owners asso-
  ciation, 50; and suit against Ralph De
  Bit, 48
West Seattle, 70
Wheeler, James W., 92, 166n52
Whittier Heights, 9
Wiese, Andrew, 97
Willcox, W. R. B., 85
Williams, Lewis, 115, 118
Wilson, Christopher P., 85
windows, 36–37
Wolgamott, Eileen McElhoe: blending of
  public/private spaces in house of, 118;
  gendered spaces for youths in house of,

121; house of, *108;* income-producing
  activities in home of, 107; role of mother,
  116
women and domestic authority, 113–16
women's spaces as technological, 40–41
World War I: downturn after, 96; effect on
  housing costs, 62–63; labor costs during,
  63; suburban building after, 93–94
Wright, Frank Lloyd: and Arts and Crafts
  influence on Prairie style, 22; open plan
  in Prairie style, 33; and Prairie style, 3, 7

Yoho, Elsie, 86, 91
Yoho, J. F. and Company, 79
Yoho, John: career of, 89–90; family and
  career of, 165n47; father of Jud, 79
Yoho, Jud, *78;* and *Bungalow Magazine,* 83–84;
  and Bungalow Publishing Company, 84;
  early life of, 79; as example of aspiring
  lower middle class, 89–91; as example of
  diversified housing salesman, 78–79, 101;
  house of, *90;* and land contracts, 88; plan
  books of, 81–82; and suburban ideal, 89
Young, C. E., 77
Youngs and Youngs, 77

Zunz, Olivier, 100